Culture Wise
NEW
ZEALAND

The Essential Guide to Culture, Customs & Business Etiquette

by
Graeme Chesters
&
John Irvine

SURVIVAL BOOKS • LONDON • ENGLAND
OCM 85692148

First published 2007

Copyright © Survival Books 2007
Cover photo © Peter Farmer (pmf290851@aol.com)
Other photographs – see page 230
Maps and cartoons © Jim Watson

Survival Books Limited
26 York Street, London W1U 6PZ, United Kingdom
☎ +44 (0)20-7788 7644, ▤ +44 (0)870-762 3212
✉ info@survivalbooks.net
🖥 www.survivalbooks.net

British Library Cataloguing in Publication Data.
A CIP record for this book is available
from the British Library.
ISBN 10: 1-905303-23-8
ISBN 13: 1-978-1-905303-23-6

Printed and bound in India by Ajanta Offset

ACKNOWLEDGEMENTS

The authors would like to thank their many friends, family members and colleagues – regretfully too many to mention here – who provided information for this book. The authors would also like to thank Sally Jennings for additional checking and research, David Hampshire for providing invaluable information and editing, Joe Laredo for additional editing, Lilac Johnston for proof-reading, Grania Rogers for photo selection and editing, Di Tolland for the DTP, Peter Farmer for the great cover photograph, and Jim Watson for the book and cover design, maps and cartoons. Finally, a special thank you to all the photographers – the unsung heroes – who provided the superb photos, without which this book would be dull indeed.

THE AUTHORS

Graeme Chesters (g.chesters@virgin.net) lives in London (England) and is an experienced journalist, copywriter, non-fiction and travel writer. He has travelled and written extensively on regions as diverse as Europe, the Middle and Far East, and Australasia. He is the editor of *Living and Working in New Zealand* and the author of *Buying a Home in Australia & New Zealand*. Graeme is also an enthusiastic wine drinker and writer and is the author of two wine books, including *Shopping for Wine in Spain* (Santana).

John Irvine (🖳 www.cooldragon.co.nz) was born in Lower Hutt, New Zealand in 1940. He travelled and worked in Australia for 28 years, and after a period in Papua New Guinea returned to New Zealand in 1996, and now lives with his writer/poet wife in Colville on New Zealand's picturesque Coromandel Peninsula. John is retired but still writes poetry; his first collection, *Man of Stone*, was published in 2005.

'If you need to find out how France works, then this book is indispensable. Native French people probably have a less thorough understanding of how their country functions.'

Living France

'It's everything you always wanted to ask, but didn't for fear of the contemptuous put down. The best English-language guide. Its pages are stuffed with practical information on everyday subjects and are designed to compliment the traditional guidebook.'

Swiss News

'Rarely has a 'survival guide' contained such useful advice. This book dispels doubts for first-time travellers, yet is also useful for seasoned globetrotters. In a word, if you're planning to move to the US or go there for a long-term stay, then buy this book both for general reading and as a ready-reference.'

American Citizens Abroad

'Let's say it at once. David Hampshire's *Living and Working in France* is the best handbook ever produced for visitors and foreign residents in this country; indeed, my discussion with locals showed that it has much to teach even those born and bred in l'Hexagone. It is Hampshire's meticulous detail which lifts his work way beyond the range of other books with similar titles. Often you think of a supplementary question and search for the answer in vain. With Hampshire this is rarely the case. He writes with great clarity (and gives French equivalents of all key terms), a touch of humour and a ready eye for the odd (and often illuminating) fact. This book is absolutely indispensable.'

The Riviera Reporter

'A must for all future expats. I invested in several books but this is the only one you need. Every issue and concern is covered, every daft question you have but are frightened to ask is answered honestly without pulling any punches. Highly recommended.'

Reader

'In answer to the desert island question about the one how-to book on France, this book would be it.'

The Recorder

'The ultimate reference book. Every subject imaginable is exhaustively explained in simple terms. An excellent introduction to fully enjoy all that this fine country has to offer, and save time and money in the process.'

American Club of Zurich

SAID ABOUT SURVIVAL BOOKS

'The amount of information covered is not short of incredible. I thought I knew enough about my birth country. This book has proved me wrong. Don't go to France without it. Big mistake if you do. Absolutely priceless!'

Reader

'When you buy a model plane for your child, a video recorder, or some new computer gizmo, you get with it a leaflet or booklet pleading 'Read Me First', or bearing large friendly letters or bold type saying 'IMPORTANT – follow the instructions carefully'. This book should be similarly supplied to all those entering France with anything more durable than a 5-day return ticket. It is worth reading even if you are just visiting briefly, or if you have lived here for years and feel totally knowledgeable and secure. But if you need to find out how France works then it is indispensable. Native French people probably have a less thorough understanding of how their country functions. Where it is most essential, the book is most up to the minute.

Living France

A comprehensive guide to all things French, written in a highly readable and amusing style, for anyone planning to live, work or retire in France.

The Times

Covers every conceivable question that might be asked concerning everyday life. I know of no other book that could take the place of this one.

France in Print

A concise, thorough account of the do's and don'ts for a foreigner in Switzerland. Crammed with useful information and lightened with humorous quips which make the facts more readable.

American Citizens Abroad

'I found this a wonderful book crammed with facts and figures, with a straightforward approach to the problems and pitfalls you are likely to encounter. The whole book is laced with humour and a thorough understanding of what's involved. Gets my vote!'

Reader

'A vital tool in the war against real estate sharks; don't even think of buying without reading this book first!'

Everything Spain

'We would like to congratulate you on this work: it is really super! We hand it out to our expatriates and they read it with great interest and pleasure.'

ICI (Switzerland) AG

NORTH ISLAND

NORTHLAND

Whangarei

Auckland

AUCKLAND

BAY OF PLENTY

GISBORNE

Hamilton

WAIKATO

Tauranga

Rotorua

New Plymouth

Gisborne

TARANAKI

Palmerston North

Napier

HAWKES BAY

Wanganui City

MANAWATU-WANGANUI

NELSON

TASMAN

Nelson

WELLINGTON

Tasman Sea

Wellington

Cook Strait

Pacific Ocean

WEST COAST

Southern Alps

MARLBOROUGH

CANTERBURY

Christchurch

SOUTH ISLAND

TAGO

SOUTHLAND

Dunedin

Invercargill

STEWART ISLAND

CONTENTS

1. A CHANGE OF CULTURE 13

New Zealand is Different 13
Culture Shock 14
Families 20
Multiculturalism 22
A New Life 22

2. WHO ARE THE NEW ZEALANDERS? 25

Timeline 26
The People 29
Maori 37
The Class System 43
Attitudes to Foreigners 43
Friends & Neighbours 44
Icons 48

3. GETTING STARTED 59

Immigration 59
Bureaucracy 60
Accommodation 61
Buying or Hiring a Car 64
Emergency Services 66
Health Services 66
Insurance 69
Education 72
Utilities 74
Staying Informed 76
Banking 81
Taxes 83
Cost of Living 83

4. BREAKING THE ICE 85

Neighbours 85
Sexual Attitudes 86
Meeting People 90

Invitations   92
Taboos   95
Topics of Conversation   96
Meeting Maori & Pacific Islanders   97
Confrontation   98
Dealing with the Police   98

5. THE LANGUAGE BARRIER   101

New Zealand English   101
English is Essential   104
Manners & Greetings   105
Maori   105
Body Language   109
Foreign Languages   109

6. THE NEW ZEALANDERS AT WORK   113

Work Ethic   113
Working Women   114
Work Visas & Permits   115
Finding a Job   116
Starting a Business   119
Self Employment   120
Black Economy   121
Business Etiquette   122
When to Avoid Doing Business   124

7. ON THE MOVE   127

Driving   127
Public Transport   134

8. THE NEW ZEALANDERS AT PLAY   143

Appearance & Dress   143
Eating   143
Cafes, Pubs & Restaurants   150
Drinking   156
Popular Culture   159
The Arts   169

9. RETAIL THERAPY   175

Opening Hours   176
Types of Shop   176
Food   179
Alcohol   181
Clothes   182
Buying Second Hand   184
Home Shopping   185
Receipts & Guarantees   185

10. ODDS & ENDS   189

Climate   189
Crime   190
Flag & National Anthem   191
Geography   193
Government   194
Military Service   196
Pets   197
Nuclear-Free Policy   198
Religion   199
Time Difference   199
Tipping   200
Toilets   200

APPENDICES   203

INDEX   221

Land of the long white cloud

INTRODUCTION

I f you're planning a trip to New Zealand or just want to learn more about the country, you'll find the information contained in *Culture Wise New Zealand* invaluable. Whether you're travelling on business or pleasure, visiting for a few days or planning to stay for a lifetime, Culture Wise guides enable you to quickly find your feet by removing the anxiety factor when dealing with a foreign culture.

Culture Wise New Zealand is essential reading for anyone planning to visit New Zealand, including tourists (particularly travellers planning to stay a number of weeks or months), business people, migrants, retirees, holiday homeowners and transferees. It's designed to help newcomers avoid cultural and social gaffes; make friends and influence people; improve communications (both verbal and non-verbal); and enhance their understanding of New Zealand and New Zealanders. It explains what to expect, how to behave in most situations, and how to get along with the locals and feel at home – rather than feeling like a fish out of water.

Adjusting to a different environment and culture in any foreign country can be a traumatic and stressful experience, and New Zealand is no exception. You need to adapt to new customs and traditions, and discover the New Zealand way of doing things; whether it's sculling a few stubbies with your bros after a day's hard yakka, feasting on greasies or savs and pavs after tramping to Erewhon and back, or enjoying a few sickies at your bach or crib.

A period spent in New Zealand is a wonderful way to enrich your life, broaden your horizons, and hopefully expand your circle of friends. We trust this book will help you avoid the pitfalls of visiting or living in New Zealand and smooth your way to a happy and rewarding stay.

Good luck!

Graeme Chesters & John Irvine
July 2007

1.

A CHANGE OF CULTURE

With almost daily advances in technology, ever-cheaper flights and knowledge about almost anywhere in the world at our fingertips, travelling, living, working and retiring abroad has never been more accessible, and current migration patterns suggest that it has never been more popular. However, although globalisation means the world has in effect 'shrunk', each country is still a world of its own with a unique culture.

> 'There are no foreign lands. It is the traveller only who is foreign.'
>
> Robert Louis Stevenson
> (Scottish writer)

Some people find it impossible to adapt to a new life in a different culture – for reasons that are many and varied. According to statistics, partner dissatisfaction is the most common cause because non-working spouses frequently find themselves without a role in the new country and sometimes with little to do other than think about what they would be doing if they were at home. Family concerns – which may include the children's education and worries about loved ones at home – can also deeply affect those living abroad.

Many factors contribute to how well you adapt to a new culture – for example, your personality, education, foreign language skills, mental health, maturity, socio-economic conditions, travel experience, and family and social support systems. How you handle the stress of change and bring balance and meaning to your life is the principal indicator of how well you'll adjust to a different country, culture and business environment.

NEW ZEALAND IS DIFFERENT

Many people underestimate the cultural isolation that can be experienced in a foreign country, particularly one with a different language. Even in a country where you speak the language fluently, you'll find that many aspects of the culture are surprisingly foreign despite the cosy familiarity engendered by cinema, television and books. New Zealand is perceived by many foreigners – particularly the British – as an easy option because of the English language, its traditional links with the UK, multicultural society and well-established foreign communities in the major cities.

However, when you move to New Zealand you'll need to adapt to a totally new environment and new challenges, which may include a new job, a new home and a new physical environment, which can be overwhelming – and all this before you even encounter the local culture. In your home country, you may have left a job where you were the boss, were extremely competent and knew everyone. In New Zealand, you may be virtually a trainee (especially if your English isn't fluent) and won't know any of your colleagues. The sensation that you're starting from scratch can be demoralising.

Even if you move to a major city, many things that you're used to and take for granted in your home country may be unavailable in New Zealand; for example, certain kinds of food, opportunities to practise your favourite hobby or sport, and books and television programmes in your mother tongue. This lack of home comforts can wear you down, and you will also have to contend with the lack of a local support network. At home you had a circle of friends, acquaintances, colleagues and possibly relatives who you could rely on for help and support. In New Zealand there's no such network, which can leave you feeling lost.

The degree of isolation you feel usually depends on how long you plan to spend in New Zealand and what you will be doing there. If you're simply going on a short holiday you may not even be aware of many of the cultural differences, although if you are it will enhance your enjoyment and may save you from a few embarrassing or confusing moments. However, if you're planning a business trip or intend to spend an extended period in New Zealand, perhaps working, studying or even living there permanently, **it's essential to understand the culture, customs and etiquette at the earliest opportunity.**

> 'If you reject the food, ignore the customs, fear the religion and avoid the people, you might better stay at home.'
>
> James A. Michener (American writer)

CULTURE SHOCK

Culture shock is the term used to describe the psychological and physical state felt by people when arriving in a foreign country, or even when moving to a new environment in their home country (where the culture and in some cases language

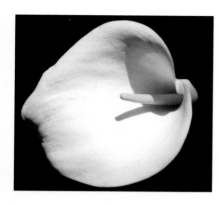

may vary considerably by region or social class). Culture shock can be experienced when travelling, living, working or studying abroad, when in addition to adapting to new social rules and values, you may need to adjust to a different climate, food and dress. It manifests itself in a lack of direction and the feeling of not knowing what to do or how to do things, not knowing what's appropriate or inappropriate. You literally feel like a fish out of water.

Culture shock is precipitated by the anxiety that results from losing all familiar rules of behaviour and cues to social intercourse. It involves the thousand and one clues to behaviour in everyday situations, such as when to shake hands and what to say when you meet people; how to buy goods and services; when and how much to tip; how to use a cash machine or the telephone; when to accept or refuse invitations; and whether to take statements seriously. These cues, which may be words, gestures or facial expressions, are acquired over a lifetime and are as much a part

of our culture and customs as the language we speak and our beliefs.

Our peace of mind and social efficiency depend on these cues, most of which are unconsciously recognised.

The symptoms of culture shock are essentially psychological and are caused by the sense of alienation you feel when you're bombarded by cultural differences in an environment where there are few, if any, familiar references.

You may also have physical symptoms, including an increased incidence of minor illnesses (colds and headaches) and more serious psychosomatic illnesses brought on by depression. You shouldn't underestimate the consequences of culture shock, although the effects can be lessened if you accept the condition rather than deny it.

> 'When you travel, remember that a foreign country is not designed to make you comfortable. It is designed to make its own people comfortable.'
>
> Clifton Fadiman (American writer)

Stages of Culture Shock

Severe culture shock – often experienced when moving to a country with a different language – usually follows a number of stages. The stages vary, as do the symptoms and effects, but a typical progression is as follows:

1. The first stage is commonly known as the 'honeymoon' stage and usually lasts from a few days to a few weeks after arrival

(although it can last longer, particularly if you're insulated from the usual pressures of life). This stage is essentially a positive (even euphoric) one, when a newcomer finds everything an exciting and interesting novelty.

The feeling is similar to being on holiday or a short trip abroad, when you generally experience only the positive effects of culture shock (although this depends very much on where you're from and the country you're visiting – see box).

Paris Syndrome

Every year, a dozen or so Japanese tourists have to be repatriated from the French capital after falling prey to what has become known as 'Paris Syndrome'. This is what some polite Japanese tourists suffer when they discover that Parisians can be rude or that the city doesn't meet their expectations. The experience can be so stressful that they suffer a nervous breakdown and need to be hospitalised or repatriated under medical

---

of time zone, extremes of hot or cold, and the strain of having hundreds of settling-in tasks to accomplish is an important symptom of this stage. You may also experience regression, where you spend much of your time speaking your own language, watching television and reading newspapers from your home country, eating food from home and socialising with expatriates who speak your language. You may also spend a lot of time complaining about the host country and its culture. Your home environment suddenly assumes a tremendous importance and is irrationally glorified. All difficulties and problems are forgotten and only the good things back home are remembered.

2. The second (rejection or distress) stage is often completely opposite to the first and is essentially negative and a period of crisis, as the initial excitement and holiday feeling wears off and you start to cope with the real conditions of daily life – except, of course, that life is nothing like anything you've previously experienced.

This can happen after only a few weeks and is characterised by a general feeling of disorientation, confusion and loneliness. Physical exhaustion brough on by a change

3. The third stage is often known as the 'flight' stage (because of the overwhelming desire to escape) and is usually the one that lasts the longest and is the most

difficult to cope with. During this period, you may feel depressed and angry, as well as resentful towards the new country and its people.

You may experience difficulties such as not being understood or feelings of discontent, impatience, frustration, sadness and incompetence. These feelings are inevitable when you're trying to adapt to a new culture that's very different from that of your home country, and they're exacerbated by the fact that you can see nothing positive or good about the new country. You focus exclusively on the negative aspects, refusing to acknowledge any positive points. You may become hostile and develop an aggressive attitude towards the country. Other people will sense this and may respond in a confrontational manner or try to avoid you.

There may be problems with the language, your house, job or children's school, transportation ... even simple tasks like shopping may be fraught with problems,

and the fact that the local people are largely indifferent to these problems only makes matter worse. They try to help but they just don't understand your concerns, and you conclude that they must be insensitive and unsympathetic.

4. The fourth stage (recovery or autonomy) is when you begin to integrate and adjust to the new culture and accept the customs of the country as simply another way of living. **The environment doesn't change – what changes is your attitude towards it.** You become more competent with the language and you feel more comfortable with the customs of the host country and can function without feeling anxiety. However, you still have problems with some of the social cues and you won't understand everything people say, particularly colloquialisms and idioms. Nevertheless, you have largely adjusted to the new culture and start to feel more at home. You're now familiar with the country and your place in it, and begin to realise that it has its good as well as bad points.

> The transition between your old culture and customs and those of your new country is a difficult one and takes time to complete. During this process, strong feelings of dissatisfaction may emerge. The period of readjustment can last six months, although there are expatriates who adjust earlier and (although rare) those who never get over the 'flight' stage and are forced to return home.

5. The fifth stage is termed 'reverse culture shock' and occurs when you return to your home country. You may find that many things have changed (you will also have changed) and that you feel like a foreigner in your own country. If you've been away for a long time and have become comfortable with the habits and customs of a new lifestyle, you may find that you no longer feel at ease in your homeland. Reverse culture shock can be difficult to deal with and some people find it impossible to re-adapt to their home country after living abroad for a number of years.

'The whole object of travel is not to set foot on foreign land; it is at last to set foot on one's own country as a foreign land.'
G. K. Chesterton (English writer)

The above stages occur at different times depending on the individual and the circumstances, and everyone reacts differently to them. Some stages last longer and are more difficult to cope with than others.

Reducing the Effects

Experts agree that almost everyone suffers from culture shock and there's no escaping the phenomenon; however, its negative effects can be reduced considerably and there are a number of things you can do before leaving home:

● **Positive attitude** – The key to reducing the negative effects of culture shock is to have a positive attitude towards New Zealand, whether you're visiting or planning to live there. If you aren't looking forward to a trip or relocation, you should question why you're going. There's no surer guarantee of unhappiness in a foreign environment than taking your prejudices with you. It's important when trying to adapt to a new culture to be sensitive to the locals' feelings and try to put yourself in their shoes wherever possible. This will help you understand why they react as they do. Bear in mind that they

Auckland at dus

have a strong, in-bred cultural code, just as you do, and react in certain ways because they're culturally 'trained' to do so. If you find yourself frustrated by an aspect of the local culture or behaviour, the chances are that they will be equally puzzled by your behaviour.

> **'Travellers never think that THEY are the foreigners.'**
>
> Mason Cooley (American aphorist)

- **Research** – Discover as much as possible about New Zealand before you go, so that your arrival and settling-in period doesn't spring as many surprises as it might otherwise. Reading up on New Zealand and its culture before you leave home will help you become familiar with the local customs and make the country and its people seem less strange on arrival. You will be aware of many of the differences in New Zealand and be better prepared to deal with them.

  This will help you avoid being upset by real or imaginary cultural slights and will reduce the chances of you offending the locals due to cultural misunderstandings. Being prepared for a certain amount of disorientation and confusion (or worse) makes it easier to cope.

  There are literally hundreds of publications about New Zealand as well as dozens of websites for expatriates (see the **Appendices**). Many sites provide access to expatriates already living in New Zealand who can answer questions and provide useful advice. There are also virtual notice boards on many websites where you can post messages or ask questions.

- **Visit New Zealand first** – If you're planning to live or work in New Zealand for a number of years or even permanently, it's important to visit first to see whether you would enjoy living there and could cope with the culture before making the leap. Before you go, try to find someone in your area who has visited New Zealand and talk about it. Some companies organise briefings for families before departure. Rent a property before buying a home and don't burn your bridges until you're certain that you've made the right decision.

- **Learn English** – As well as a positive attitude, overcoming the language barrier will be the most decisive factor in combating culture shock and enjoying your time in New Zealand. The ability to speak English and understand the local vernacular (see **Chapter**

5) isn't just a practical and useful tool (one that will allow you to buy what you need, find your way around, etc.) but the key to understanding New Zealand and its culture. If you can speak English, even at a basic level, your scope for making friends is immediately widened. Obviously not everyone is a linguist and learning English can take time and requires motivation. However, with sufficient perseverance virtually anyone can learn enough English to participate in the local culture.

> Look upon a period spent in New Zealand as an opportunity to redefine your life objectives and learn and acquire new perspectives. Culture shock can help you develop a better understanding of yourself and stimulate your creativity.

● **Be proactive** – Join in the activities of the local people, which could be a carnival, a religious festival or a sporting activity. There are often plenty of

local clubs where you can play sport or keep fit, join an arts club, learn to cook local dishes, taste wine, etc. Not only will this fill some of your spare time, giving you less time to miss home, but you'll meet new people and make friends. If you feel you cannot join a local club, perhaps because your English isn't good enough, you can participate in activities for expatriates, of which there are many in the major cities.

● **Talk to other expatriates** – Although they may deny it, many expatriates have been through exactly what you're experiencing and faced the same feelings of disorientation. Even if they cannot give you any advice, it helps to know that you aren't alone and that it gets better over time. However, don't make the mistake of mixing only with expatriates as this will alienate you from the local culture and make it much harder to integrate. Don't rely on social contact with your compatriots to carry you through, because it won't.

● **Keep in touch with home** – Keeping in touch with your family and friends at home and around the world by telephone, email and letters will help reduce and overcome the effects of culture shock.

● **Be happy** – Don't rely on others to make you happy or you won't find true and lasting happiness. There are things in life that you can change and if you need them to change, you must do it yourself. You have little or no

> 'And that's the wonderful thing about family travel: it provides you with experiences that will remain locked forever in the scar tissue of your mind.'
>
> Dave Barry (American writer & humorist)

control over most daily events and moaning about them will only make you unhappy. So be your own best friend and nurture your capacity for happiness.

FAMILIES

Family life may be completely different in New Zealand from what you're used to, and relationships can become strained under the stress of culture shock. Your family may find itself in a completely new and possibly alien environment, your new home may scarcely resemble your previous one (it may be much more luxurious or significantly smaller) and the climate may differ dramatically from that of your home country. If possible, you should prepare yourself for as many aspects of the new situation as you can and explain to your children the changes they're likely to encounter, while at the same time dispelling their fears.

Culture shock can affect non-working spouses and children more than working spouses. The husband (it's usually the husband) has his work to occupy him and his activities may not differ much from what he had been accustomed to at home. On the other hand, the wife has to operate in an environment that differs considerably from what she's used to. She will find herself alone more often, a solitude intensified by the fact that there are no relatives or friends nearby.

However, if you're aware that this may arise beforehand, you can act on it and reduce its effects. Working spouses should pay special attention to the needs and feelings of their non-working partners and children, because the success of a family relocation depends on the ability of the wife and children to adapt to the new culture.

Good communication between family members is vital, so make time to discuss your experiences and feelings, both as a couple and as a family. Questions should be raised and, if possible, answered, particularly when asked by children.

However difficult the situation may appear at the beginning, it helps to bear in mind that it's by no means unique, and that most expatriate families experience exactly the same problems and manage to triumph over them and thoroughly enjoy their stay abroad.

MULTICULTURALISM

New Zealand isn't a multicultural society in the same way that Australia, Canada and the UK are, and has never seen itself as one. However, with the influx of foreigners in recent years, particularly Asians, New Zealand has become more multicultural (to the horror of some and the delight of others) and foreigners have enriched its way of life, adding to its range of foods and restaurants, religions, businesses and ideas.

Multiculturalism

Coined in Canada in the '70s, multiculturalism is the term used for an ideology advocating that immigrants integrate into society while retaining and valuing the most important elements of their own culture, including speaking their own language and teaching it to their children.

Although newcomers to New Zealand are expected to embrace New Zealand's culture and values, they are also encouraged to maintain ties with their homeland and its culture, rather than abandon them. Most ethnic groups in New Zealand have clubs and societies to which newcomers are warmly welcomed, and marriage between ethnic groups – indigenous and non-indigenous – is common, and the country has a low level of inter-ethnic conflict and high levels of cooperation.

A NEW LIFE

Although you may find some of the information in this chapter a bit daunting, don't be discouraged by the foregoing catalogue of depression and despair; the negative aspects of travelling and living abroad have been highlighted only in order to help you prepare and adjust to a new life. The vast majority of people who travel and live abroad naturally experience occasional feelings of discomfort and disorientation, **but most never suffer the most debilitating effects of culture shock.**

As with settling in and making friends anywhere (even in your home country) the most important thing is to be considerate, kind,

open, humble and genuine – qualities that are valued the world over. Selfishness, brashness and arrogance will get you nowhere in New Zealand – or any other country. Treat New Zealand and its people with respect and they will reciprocate.

The majority of people who have emigrated to New Zealand would agree that, all things considered, they love living there – and are in no hurry to return home. A period spent in New Zealand is a wonderful way to enrich your life, broaden your horizons, make new friends and maybe even please your bank manager.

> 'Twenty years from now you will be more disappointed by the things you didn't do than by the ones you did do. So throw off the bowlines. Sail away from the safe harbour. Catch the trade winds in your sails. Explore. Dream. Discover.'
>
> Mark Twain (American writer)

2.

WHO ARE THE NEW ZEALANDERS?

N ew Zealand was the last country in the world to be settled when the Maori arrived from Polynesia around 800 years ago (and Europeans in the 18th century). However, it has come a long way in a relatively short time and today is one of the most civilised countries in the world with an enviable lifestyle.

Migrants have been drawn to New Zealand for over 200 years – mostly from the UK, and many New Zealanders still identify culturally with their British heritage. In recent decades, there has been an influx of migrants from other regions, mainly Asia and the Pacific Islands, with the result that the country has become increasingly multicultural.

Although New Zealand is far from perfect in regard to its race relations, it has done far better than any other country that has been colonised, including Australia, Canada, South Africa and the USA. The various nationalities generally manage to live, work and play together in harmony, and have enriched the country with their culture, customs and etiquette.

It's an egalitarian country and a land of equal opportunity for all, whatever, your colour, race or gender – the top three posts in the land are held by women – but it's also a masculine country, where men needed to be tough to survive in the rugged and unforgiving landscape.

New Zealand has a strong liberal, puritan tradition that aspired to

> 'If it would not look too much like showing off, I would tell the reader where New Zealand is.'
>
> Mark Twain (American writer)

fairness, where the greater good prevails over individual ambition. It remains a beacon of social progress, and was the first country to give both men (1867) and women (1893) the vote, and the first with old-age pensions (1898), labour arbitration (1894) and a widow's pension (1911).

The country attracts an increasing number of visitors each year who come to experience the bush, the wildlife and the high country sheep stations; the geysers, mudpools, mountains and lakes; the Maori heritage, rugby and bungee jumping; the vineyards, wine and seafood; the film-sets and spectacular unspoilt scenery; the trout fishing, tramping and the whales; the vast spaces and the easygoing friendly hospitality of the people.

It's fair to say that people aren't attracted to New Zealand for its culture, although it certainly isn't a cultural desert. Lifestyle has always taken priority over culture, and it's rated as one of the top countries in the world for its quality of life – Auckland is consistently ranked among the best cities in the world in which to live.

To help you become more familiar with New Zealand and New Zealanders, this chapter provides information about New Zealand's

history, its people and the country's icons.

TIMELINE

New Zealand has a relatively brief history of human settlement which is shorter than just about any other country, having been the last significant landmass settled by humans. This probably accounts for its natural beauty – we've had less time to inflict mindless havoc on the place. The date of the first human arrival on New Zealand is disputed, but is thought to have been between the 9th and 13th centuries.

Between 9th and 13th centuries – The first humans arrive in New Zealand, probably Maori and other peoples from East Polynesia.

1642 – The Dutch navigator Abel Janszoon Tasman becomes the first European to sight New Zealand. He named it (rather parochially) after the Dutch province of Zeeland; the locals prove unfriendly, however, and the place doesn't appear to have any gold, so Europeans are discouraged from having much to do with it over the next century or so.

1769 – Captain James Cook arrives on the first of his three voyages,

---

Demographics

Capital city: Wellington
Area: 268,680km² (103,738mi²)
Population: 4.18m
Population density: 14 people per km² (5.41 per mi²)
Largest cities: Auckland (1.2m), Wellington (380,000), Christchurch (372,500), Hamilton (190,000), Napier/Hastings (125,000), Dunedin (120,000)
Race: European 70%, Maori 8%, Asian 6%, Pacific Islander 4.5%, mixed 8%, others 3.5%
Languages: English 98%; Maori 4.2%, Chinese languages 3.5%, Samoan 2.3% and Hindi 1.2%.
Largest expatriate groups (overseas born): British (15 per cent), Chinese (13 per cent), Indian (12 per cent), South African (9 per cent), Fijian (6 per cent) and Samoan (5 per cent).
Religion: Christian (53%), Buddhist (1.2%), Hindu (1.2%), Muslim (1%); 40 per cent of people claim no religion.

returning in 1773 and 1777; he charts the north and the south islands accurately, particularly given the technology available at the time.

1840 – The Treaty of Waitangi (see box) is signed by Maori chiefs and the British government, ceding sovereignty of New Zealand to the British crown, who grant the Maori the status of British subjects.

> It's estimated that New Zealand's population will reach 5m by 2050. New Zealand's Maori population is currently around 565,000 – one in seven of its inhabitants.

1845-1872 – Maori Wars – despite the *Treaty of Waitangi* (see box) the British and Maori fought a number of battles (over land rights and other issues) in the decades after 1840, called the land or Maori wars.

1850 – New Zealand starts to become an important base for the world's whaling fleet.

1854 – New Zealand's settlers gain their own parliament, having previously been administered from New South Wales.

1892 – The New Zealand Rugby Football Union is established, thereby formalising what has become the nation's obsession (some say religion).

1893 – Women are given the vote – the first country in the world to do so.

1899 – Troops are sent to fight for Britain in the Boer War.

1901 – New Zealand decides not to join the Australian federation.

1905 – The New Zealand rugby union team tours England and becomes known as the All Blacks.

1907 – The country gains dominion status in the British Empire.

1914-18 – Thousands of Kiwis die in the First World War, most notably at the disastrous landing at Gallipoli (Turkey) in 1915 by the joint Australian and New Zealand Army Corps (ANZACs).

1938 – The Social Security Act extends the Welfare State, which was initiated in the late 19th century.

1939-45 – New Zealand participates in the Second World War.

1947 – The country gains full independence from Britain.

1950s – New Zealand sends troops to fight in Korea.

1951 – ANZUS Pacific security treaty signed between New Zealand, Australia and USA.

Mural in Katikati, North Island

1960s – New Zealand sends a small combat force to support US troops in Vietnam, which sparks a lively debate.

1973 – Britain joins the European Economic Community, which

Treaty of Waitangi

Known as Te Tiriti o Waitangi in Maori (or Te Reo, the official term for the Maori language), the Treaty of Waitangi was signed on 6th February 1840, at Waitangi in the Bay of Islands, by Captain William Hobson for the British Crown and some 45 Maori chiefs from the North Island. It was drawn up by the British with the purpose of gaining sovereignty over the country in return for a guarantee of the authority of the chiefs, the protection of Maori land and resource rights, and the granting to the Maori of the same rights and privileges as British citizens.

The treaty is short and of limited scope, and although people often refer to its principles and spirit, there's no consensus on what these actually are – partly because of discrepancies between the Maori and English-language versions. Therefore, although it's a crucial document in the 'founding' of New Zealand – it's generally considered to be the inception of New Zealand as a nation – it's the subject of heated debate. Many Maori think that the Crown hasn't kept its side of the bargain, while some non-Maori New Zealanders think the Maori use the treaty to push claims for more and more privileges.

has a significant economic and psychological effect on New Zealand – akin to being rejected by a parent.

1984 – Labour government elected, Prime Minister David Lange begins radical economic reforms.

1985 – The Greenpeace vessel Rainbow Warrior is blown up by the French secret service while anchored in New Zealand; New Zealand goes nuclear-free soon afterwards, partly as a reaction against French nuclear tests in the Pacific.

1986 – The Constitution Act ends Britain's few remaining legislative powers in New Zealand. US suspends it ANZUS obligations towards New Zealand after its nuclear ships are banned from visiting New Zealand.

1989 – Prime Minister Lange resigns and is replaced by Geoffrey Palmer.

1990 – Palmer resigns just before the general election, which is won by the opposition National Party. James Bolger becomes prime minister.

1993 – National Party narrowly wins election. Referendum introduces proportional representation.

1996 – Proportional representation is introduced, making coalition governments common. Under the new electoral system the number of Maori MPs rises from 6 to 15.

1997 – After a leadership challenge, Bolger resigns and Jenny Shipley becomes the country's first woman prime minister.

1998 – Waitangi Tribunal orders the government to return confiscated land in Turangi Township to its Maori owners.

1999 – Labour Party wins election

and Helen Clark becomes prime minister.

2002 – Helen Clark wins a second term in a general election, and the rival conservative National Party records its worst result in 70 years.
2004 – A bill is passed recognising civil unions between gay couples.
2005 – Incumbent PM Helen Clark secures a narrow third election victory over the resurgent National Party.

THE PEOPLE

This section attempts to capture the essence of the Kiwi character, which isn't as easy as it would appear on the surface. New Zealanders are far from being a homogenous mass of sheep-worrying, poorly-dressed folk, obsessed with rugby and other strange sports. Some do fit the popular stereotype, of course, but the same can be said of Australians, Americans and the British.

The Battle of Gallipoli, from April to December 1915 – during which New Zealand casualties were over 7,500 (2,721 dead) – was considered to mark the birth of the national identity of New Zealand (and Australia), replacing that of the collective identity of the British Empire.

Self-image

Most Kiwis like people to see their country as a creative, friendly, inventive place, punching above its weight in terms of achievement.

They realise, however, that they probably know a lot more about the rest of the world than it knows about

New Zealand: a small country, stuck somewhere near the much more interesting Australia and Antarctica.

As a result, many Kiwis grab any chance that presents itself to educate foreigners about their country and its achievements. When abroad, Kiwis are happy to hear any reference to their country in the local media, even if it's just a reference to (yet another) Kiwi sporting success. A mention means acknowledgement – they've actually heard of us!

New Zealanders have tended to regard themselves as one people, with two main groups: *Pâkehâ* and Maori themselves. This view is becoming blurred as the two groups intermarry and more Pacific Islanders arrive: there are now more Cook Islanders, Samoans and Niueans in Auckland than are left in the Cook Islands, Samoa and Niue, and the same will no doubt happen with other islands. Immigrants from elsewhere, notably Asia and Eastern Europe, are further 'muddying the waters'. The 'one people' idea has been challenged by a recent resurgence in Maori identity and calls for their 'problems' and land ownership to be resolved once

and for all.

New Zealanders still see themselves as outdoor people and, to a lesser extent, as rural sons of the soil. This self-image is belied by the fact that nearly three-quarters of the population live in the five main cities. The largest city, Auckland, has a strong sense of self-worth and sees itself as superior to the rest of New Zealand – which creates something of a gulf between Aucklanders and other Kiwis, who regard them as arrogant, loud and self-centred. Not surprisingly, Aucklanders disagree, seeing themselves as creative, lively and outward-looking, fortunate to live in New Zealand's most beautiful, most climatically-favoured city. The inhabitants of Wellington, New Zealand's capital city, not surprisingly, dispute Auckland's claim to be the country's seat of power.

The Kiwi Character

In spite of the pluralism of their society and their many differences, most Kiwis share some characteristics – principally the following:

Hubris & Humility

The first thing that strikes many new arrivals in New Zealand is the hospitality of Kiwis and their pleasure in showing off their country. They're used to foreigners and generally accept them without question, which stems partly from the fact that they live in a beautiful country which they want to share with others, but also from a sense of insecurity. New Zealanders sometimes feel ignored by the rest of the world; the population numbers just 4m and their geographical isolation means it's difficult to make their presence felt on the world stage, while they also tend to be overshadowed by their larger neighbour, Australia. They feel much better about themselves and their position in the world when they hear their country praised. As a result of their insecurity and a lack confidence about their achievements and place in the world, Kiwis sometimes display behaviour known as 'cultural cringe' (see box).

> **'If only I had a little humility, I'd be perfect.'**
> Ted Turner (American media mogul)

Whatever the reason, Kiwis have an entrenched sense of national pride, evidenced by the fact that they sometimes call their country 'Godzone' (short for 'God's own country'), a nickname coined by Dick Seddon, a late 19th-century prime minister. This pride can sometimes seem a little overdone – for example, the triumphant team in the 2000 America's Cup was treated to a massive tickertape parade. And personalised number

plates are popular in New Zealand, particularly if they include N and Z together. Pandering to a Kiwi's sense of national pride is a quick route to his or her heart, and you'll gain a lot of brownie points by complimenting the country or its achievements.

That said, Kiwis are also self-

> ### Cultural Cringe
>
> The term 'cultural cringe' was coined in 1950 to describe the ingrained feelings of inferiority that local intellectuals and artists struggled against, and which were most clearly pronounced in the theatre, music, art and letters. The term was widely accepted as a fact of New Zealand cultural life, although it has long been consigned to the dustbin of history (except, perhaps among some older New Zealanders) and today the country boasts an active and diverse cultural scene (at least in the major cities).

deprecating and understated, which makes them wary of praise (or too much) and wonder whether you're humouring or mocking them.

Therefore they tend to respond to praise by listing some of New Zealand's drawbacks. Don't agree too enthusiastically with any of these, as it's generally not a good idea to criticise New Zealand or to be seen to agree with criticisms of it. This is especially true if you hail from the UK or Ireland, the countries of origin of most New Zealanders, as you're expected to know better (unlike Australians, the Kiwis' 'overbearing' neighbours – or so they seem to Kiwis). Kiwi self-deprecation means that they

don't crow about their achievements and successes but will rib anybody who shows off. As a consequence, New Zealand has a 'tall poppy syndrome' (see box), whereby those who are considered to be getting too big for their boots (especially as a result of success achieved abroad) are cut down to size. This stems partly from the early pioneer days, when people had to cooperate, treat each other as equals and not get above themselves. Unfortunately, the tall poppy syndrome tends to discourage success, and those who prosper tend to hide or underplay their achievements. Sports stars are an exception and are allowed to flaunt the trappings of success.

Auckland harbour bridge

Kiwis don't like pretentiousness, 'fancy' behaviour or airs and graces, preferring informality and lack of ceremony. This again dates back to the pioneer days, when life was tough and there wasn't time for elaboration. Nevertheless, politeness is respected and expected. As in the UK, anyone you bump into in the street is likely to apologise to you before you get a chance to say 'sorry'. Most people who know each other in New Zealand are on first name terms, which isn't regarded as being over-familiar, but just another example of not being too formal or 'stuck up'.

Tall Poppy Syndrome

The term 'tall poppy syndrome' refers to the New Zealand trait (which they share with Australians) of cutting down to size those who are arrogant, presumptuous or attention-seeking. New Zealanders love an underdog – people who are humble, down to earth, almost embarrassed by their own talent or achievement. The tall poppy syndrome isn't, as is often thought, an expression of envy or resentment at a person's fame or success (although this trait has been inherited somewhat from the British).

Pioneering Spirit

Another common characteristic of New Zealanders is their versatility, which is understandable in a country without a large enough population to compete in many industries; among the fields in which they excel are dentistry, surgery and beer- and wine-making. Kiwis are also independent, inventive and rugged, partly because their forebears had to adapt to a demanding, isolated life in a rugged country. This pioneering spirit remains a defining characteristic of Kiwis, although many more regard themselves as 'bushmen' types than actually are.

In fact, the pioneering spirit is probably most evident today in the Kiwi obsession with sport (notably rugby) and the country's suspicion of anything that smacks of being overly intellectual. Physical strength and dexterity are still seen by many Kiwis as more admirable than a string of letters after your name.

Sense of Equality

Kiwis have a strong sense of equality and rail against all types of injustice, often with the typical expression 'fair go, mate' (a popular television programme called *Fair Go* exposes rip-offs and scams). Their sense of egalitarianism is regarded by some commentators as a reaction against the British class system, as many of the first settlers came to New Zealand to escape poverty in Britain. The country's pre-occupation with equality is illustrated by the fact that New Zealand was the first country to grant women the vote (in 1893), and the government's recent decision to do away with the titles 'Sir' and 'Dame' (the honours system remains but the titles have been consigned to history).

New Zealand was also one of the first countries to have a Race Relations Conciliator, although there's now a sense that the position has become alarmingly politically correct. Kiwis are individuals and don't like being told what to say and how to think. On the other hand, New Zealand is quite a politically correct society – probably because it's a land of immigrants, where people go out of their way to avoid offending each other.

> 'I believe we were all glad to leave New Zealand. It is not a pleasant place. Amongst the natives there is absent that charming simplicity ... and the greater part of the English are the very refuse of society.'
>
> Charles Darwin (British naturalist, writing in 1860)

Love of Animals

Animals have long been central to New Zealand's economy, and an interest in them and their welfare is ingrained in many Kiwis. It isn't, however, the sheep or the kiwi that can claim to be the nation's favourite animal. That honour falls to the horse. Children are particularly enamoured of horses but adults also love them, as was demonstrated by the uproar which greeted a government order to cull wild horses to prevent them eating endangered native flora. The government was forced to abandon the plan and have the horses rounded up and offered for 'adoption'. The Kiwi interest in horses is also reflected in their success in international horse events and their love of racing – the Totalisator Agency Board (i.e. betting shop), known as the tote, is a feature of all towns and suburbs.

Adventurousness

New Zealanders tend to be outward-looking people and know a fair amount about the outside world.

Their small population and isolated geographical position mean that they cannot afford to be parochial or navel-gazers. As a result, Kiwis are inveterate travellers, both for business and pleasure, and a higher percentage of the population have passports than in any other country (and they're well stamped).

The Kiwis' adventurous spirit means that they like to explore new places, although as a counterbalance to these adventurous types, some of the inhabitants of New Zealand's smaller towns and villages are homebound and conservative. In rural areas, people are expected to conform and stick to convention and tradition, and individuality and innovation may be viewed with suspicion.

The 'Big Overseas Experience' (Big OE) or working holiday is a national obsession, whereby young

Kiwis flee the nest to see the world.

It used to result in a brain drain as many didn't return, causing the anthropologist Margaret Mead to comment that it was New Zealand's function 'to send forth its bright young men and women to run the rest of the world.' The Big OE is still popular with young Kiwis, but they tend to return home nowadays after enjoying their time abroad, having realised there are few places better to live than New Zealand. They're also encouraged to return by the fact that cheap, easy global travel and the internet revolution mean that New Zealand is no longer the isolated backwater it once was.

> 'I've never been to New Zealand. But one of my role models – Xena, the warrior princess – comes from there.'
>
> Madeline Albright (American stateswoman)

Recklessness

The average New Zealander's sense of himself as an outdoor, sporting type has spawned a devil-may-care attitude – it isn't done to seem to be too concerned about your safety and wellbeing. This is reflected in

the accident and search-and-rescue statistics, most weekends seeing a crop of mishaps, broken limbs and rescues. As an extension of this macho image, men don't whinge about feeling ill, or 'a bit crook' as it's usually described, unless it's fairly serious.

New Zealand is trying to encourage individuals to take responsibility for their health, and Kiwis have taken notice, recently becoming more health-conscious.

For example, in response to the country's high rate of skin cancer, there's now a strong anti-sunbathing culture, and the bronzed look is less popular (unless it comes out of a jar or tube, in which case it's more of an 'oranged' look).

Climate Denial

A quirk of Kiwi behaviour is their strange insistence that they live in a balmy, sub-tropical climate and don't need to heat their houses (an insistence shared by the inhabitants of Mediterranean countries). Much of New Zealand has warm or mild weather for most of the year, but it can also be distinctly chilly at times and definitely cold in southern parts of the South Island, especially when the wind blows from the Antarctic. Despite this, many Kiwis don't have central heating, but open fireplaces, which is another throwback to the pioneer days. These look attractive but are notably inefficient at heating air more than three feet from the fireplace. As a result, many Kiwis spend their winters indoors bundled up in sweaters and cardigans, and on sunny winter days, it isn't uncommon for it to be warmer outdoors than indoors.

Number-eight-wire Mentality

Some argue that if you want to behave like a typical (or stereotypical) Kiwi man, you must play rugby and own a shed.

The latter is a reflection of the Kiwi tendency to be practical and proficient at DIY – once again, a throwback to the pioneer days, when people often had little option but to do things for themselves. It's also a reflection of the Kiwi 'give it a go' attitude, whereby having a go at something is highly regarded.

A shed is somewhere to keep your tools and a place to build and repair things – it's also a refuge from wives, children and other forms of responsibility. The Kiwi attitude to DIY is referred to as the 'number-eight-wire mentality,' after a type of thick wire commonly used in bygone days for livestock paddock fences and many other things. Not all Kiwis excel at practical tasks and home improvement, however, and there's a popular television programme called *Do-it-Yourself Rescue* about professionals trying to sort out DIY botch-ups.

It's a widely held belief that people in the new world, including Kiwis, spend a lot of time agonising over their national identity and 'who they are'. However, this certainly isn't true of most Kiwis, who are happy just to get on with life and leave the philosophising to others.

Sense of Humour

As in the UK and Australia, a sense of humour is a huge asset in New Zealand. Kiwis are self-deprecating and their humour often focuses on people who take themselves too seriously and who appoint themselves as authorities over others, for example politicians. Another common source of humour used to be good-humoured banter between *Pâkehâ* and Maori, but political correctness seems to have put paid to that.

New Zealanders are usually the butt of Aussie jokes, particularly those featuring sheep – which are sometimes known as 'ewe-phemisms'. However, Aussies are also the favourite target of Kiwi humour. ('What do you call an Aussie with half a brain? Gifted.' and 'What do you call a field full of Aussies? A vacant lot.') Differences of accent between Australia and New Zealand are another common source of humour, as is New Zealand's physical remoteness and the fact that Kiwis are seen by others as isolated and behind the times (although nowadays you don't need to put your watch back 20 years if you're visiting the cities). Kiwis are also good at mocking themselves, and you'll fit in if you can do the same. More specialised humour (which you'll only begin to understand when you know the country better) involves jokes about differences of accent and idiom found in different parts of New Zealand; for example the use of 'eh' at the end of sentences by Maori and North Islanders, and the rolled 'r' from the south of the South Island.

Family Life

The family group is important in New Zealand, particularly in Maori and Pacific Island communities, which have large extended families, where caring for older members of the family is central to Maori and Pacific Islander life. In contrast, in the rest of New Zealand society, there has been a growth in the rest-home industry, as is happening in Western Europe and the US. Whereas *Pâkehâ* communities tend to discard or ignore their senior citizens, their opinions are valued in Maori and Polynesian communities. It's common for children to be looked after mainly or even wholly by a grandparent or other older relative or person. This is less common than it was, however, as families fragment and live in different towns and cities, rather than remaining in one tribal area.

Kiwi society is following the

pattern of other developed societies, where an increasing percentage of over 65s will make up the population – by 2050 it's estimated that they will comprise up to a quarter of the population. Those who aren't consigned to care homes by their families often choose to live on the coast, where they're referred to as 'silver surfers' (they surf the waves in the morning and the internet in the afternoon).

New Zealand's experience of marriage reflects the pattern in many other parts of the developed world: the age for first marriages is rising (30 for women and 33 for men) and the marriage rate is declining, while the divorce rate is also increasing. The rising divorce rate is causing alarm, as those marrying later in life – when they're more mature and established financially and professionally – are expected to have a better chance of making successful marriages. New Zealand is also seeing higher rates of cohabitation and single parenthood.

Rural Life

New Zealand has a long agricultural tradition, and farming is still hugely

> 'There are 40m sheep in New Zealand and 4m of them think they're people.'
>
> Barry Humphries, aka Dame Edna Everage

important to the country's economy, although it no longer dominates it. As a result, farmers (especially sheep farmers) and sheep are central figures in Kiwi culture, despite sheep numbers having dropped from their high of the '80s as cattle grow in importance (butter and cheese are key products). Sheep shearers are highly valued in New Zealand and there's a long tradition of their being well looked after by farmers' wives – food-wise, that is.

> New Zealand Farmers are renowned for their grumbling – notably about the weather and the government – which has grown in volume since farming subsidies were abolished. More recently, farmers have been up in arms about proposed legislation concerning public access to land along the coastline and waterways, which they regard as a violation of their property rights, and fear will result in damage and theft to their property and livestock.

As well as the usual three meals, they're fed at 10am and 3pm (it's a wonder they find time to shear any sheep) – a tradition dating back to the time when most people smoked, and would break mid-morning and mid-afternoon for a smoke break. Breaks now revolve around the consumption of tea, cakes and scones.

MAORI

The Maori (*Mâori*) are the indigenous people of New Zealand, and are thought to have arrived between the 9th and 13th centuries. Maori legend says that they originated in 'Hawaiki', and came to *Aotearoa* (land of the long white cloud – New Zealand) around 1,000 years ago in *waka hourua* (large ocean-going canoes). There are several theories about Maori origins. Maori themselves think that Hawaiki might have been near Hawaii, but the theory currently in favour is that they originated in China and travelled via Taiwan, the Philippines and Indonesia to Melanesia and Fiji. From there, they spread to Samoa, the Marquesas, Tahiti, the Cook Islands and, finally, to New Zealand.

When the white man arrived in the 18th century, the Maori were the last major human community on earth untouched and unaffected by the wider world. Today some 400,000 Maori live in New Zealand, mostly in North Auckland (the Waikato region), comprising around 10 per cent of the country's 4m population.

European settlers in the 19th century referred to the indigenous people as aborigines, indians, natives or New Zealanders. However, *Mâori* was the term used by Maori to

describe themselves in a pan-tribal sense, and in 1947 the New Zealand government renamed the 'Department of Native Affairs' the 'Department of Maori Affairs' in recognition of this.

New Zealand doesn't have a separate category for people of mixed Maori and *Pâkehâ* (white or non-Maori) blood, neither does it insist that all people of Maori descent be classified as Maori. There are a number of ways of determining who is or isn't Maori, but anyone with a claim (however tenuous) to Maori ancestry can declare that he's Maori; however, where money (such as scholarships) is involved, the authorities generally require some demonstration of ancestry and/or cultural connection, but no minimum 'blood' requirement exists. Although there are few pure blood Maori left, Maori argue that their identity has more to do with culture than with genetic lineage.

A notable feature of Maori society is *mana*, which means 'prestige' or 'respect'. In many societies, prestige and status derive from a person's job and/or wealth, but in Maori society lineage (family background) is much more important. As a result, the most important people in a group of Maori might have humble jobs and little or no money, which wouldn't accord them much social status in other societies. It's important to be aware of this when dealing with Maori.

The name Maori originates from the term Ma-Uri (children of heaven).

During the 19th century the Maori lost most of their land to the *Pâkehâ* and went into a period of decline; by the late 19th century most people believed that the Maori would eventually cease to exist as a separate race and be assimilated into the European population. However, the predicted decline didn't happen and their numbers recovered, and – despite much intermarriage between Maori and Europeans – many Maori retained their cultural identity. The urbanisation of Maori proceeded apace in the latter half of the 20th century and most now live in cities and towns, with many having become estranged from their tribal roots and customs. The traditional Maori way of life has all but disappeared and today it isn't very different from that of *Pâkehâ*, although there's been a revival of Maori culture in the last few decades (see below)

Maori meeting house

Nevertheless, Maori have strong family ties (and large extended families) and retain membership in their particular tribes (*iwi*), even though they may be widely scattered throughout the country. They return periodically to their tribal *marae* (meeting place) for ceremonial gathering and take part in Maori action songs and *haka* groups. Above all, they feel that they are Maori and not *Pâkehâ*.

> The Maori population isn't large, but there isn't a single political or tribal authority that can speak on behalf of all Maori.

Politics

In the decades following the signing of the Waitangi Treaty (see above), few Maori qualified to vote under the property requirements as they 'owned' their lands communally and not under individual freehold or leasehold title like Europeans. To get around this requirement, in 1867, parliament agreed to create four electorates specifically for Maori and all Maori over 21 were eligible to vote (whereby Maori men achieved universal suffrage 12 years before European men). In 1996, the number of Maori seats was increased for the first time in 129 years to five, and again in 2002, to seven.

Maori are also free to stand and win 'general' (as 'European' seats are now known) seats, which means that their representation in parliament (pro rata) can exceed their actual share of the population.

Maori electors can also choose whether they are enrolled in general or Maori seats. The appropriateness and effectiveness of Maori seats has been the subject of debate ever since they were established, but despite opposition they have survived to become one of the most distinctive features of New Zealand's electoral system. Today, the Maori have their own political parties and the largest, the Maori Party, won four of the seven Maori seats in 2005 (previously held by the Labour Party).

In the changing face of New Zealand's politics, consultation with Maori has become a routine requirement for many New Zealand councils and government organisations.

Social Justice

Despite significant social, political and economic advances during the 20th century, Maori (and Pacific Islanders) still have a much lower standard of living than *Pâkehâ*, with inferior health services, educational success, job prospects, income and life expectancy. Maori also feature disproportionately highly in criminal and imprisonment statistics – although they make up just 10 per cent of the population, they comprise almost half the prison population.

However, their situation has never been as bad as that of Australia's Aborigines, and issues of inequality are being addressed. Like Australia's

Aboriginals, Maori have a much higher level of alcohol and drug-related problems than *Pâkehâ,* and suffer both institutional and direct racism.

Maori delegates travel the world to confer with Australian Aborigines, North American Natives and other peoples who have been overwhelmed by European invasion, in order to develop strategies to improve their peoples' prosperity and standing.

> Nearly 40 per cent of Maori aged 15 or over have no formal educational qualifications.

Land Rights

Since the '60s, growing Maori political activism and protest has led to limited redress for the confiscation of land and the violation of their property rights during the 19th century. The Treaty of Waitangi (see above) has occupied centre stage in the struggle by Maori for social justice, equality and a measure of self determination. However, because the treaty is of limited scope and there are discrepancies between the Maori and English-language versions, it's interpreted differently by the two sides.

In 1977, the government established the Waitangi Tribunal to investigate and make non-binding recommendations regarding land rights and other issues. The *hapu* (sub tribe) or *iwi* (tribe) must prove their traditional rights to land on the basis of occupation, conquest, or ancestry (the gifting of land is also taken into account). As a result of the redress already paid to many tribes, Maori now have substantial interests in the fishing and forestry industries.

Tensions remain, however, with complaints from Maori that settlements occur at just 1 to 2.5 cents on the dollar of the value of the confiscated lands. On the other hand, many *Pâkehâ* would like to see an end to the land rights issue (some 800 claims are currently under consideration), which they feel is now a gravy train, and there needs to be a deadline for the resolution of all outstanding issues. Some *Pâkehâ* are also resentful of the state handouts given to the Maori.

Culture

Maori culture (*Mâoritanga*) was traditionally transmitted orally, through the telling of stories, song (*waiata*) and the reciting of *whakapapa* (genealogies). It was

Maori newspapers and radio have also helped publicise the resurgence of self-expression and self-determination to the Maori people aided by myriad Maori organisations, including the New Zealand Maori Council, the Maori Women's Welfare League and the Maori Education Foundation. Nearly all New Zealand cities stage Maori cultural festivals and a National Polynesian Festival is held biennially.

also represented in stylised form in carvings and woven panels that adorned *whare* (meeting houses).

Tattoos were also a prominent feature, most obviously *moko* or full-face tattoos, which were traditionally limited to men (female facial tattoos being restricted to the chin). Maori music was suppressed in the 19th century by the early missionaries and now primarily lives on through *waiata*.

Since the '60s there has been a revival in Maori culture and language and an explosion of artistic expression within Maoridom (Maori society). Underlying the resurgence of Maori expression is a re-discovery of ancient Maori forms and values. Maori artists and writers have flourished in recent decades and concert (*kapa haka*) and dance groups, theatre, painters, sculptors, poets, story tellers, carvers and weavers have all prospered. There has also been a recent upsurge of *moko* as a reflection of the reassertion of Maori culture and identity.

Maori Legends

Maori culture is rich in legends and stories. Its creation story maintains that the world was formed by the violent separation of Ranginui, the Sky Father, and Papatuanuku, the Earth Mother, by their children (many Maori artworks and carvings depict this struggle). New Zealand's creation is described in the legend of Maui, a cheeky deity who fished up the North Island, which is called Te Ika a Maui (the fish of Maui). Some people think that an aerial map of the North Island does indeed resemble a fish, the far north being the tail of the fish and Wellington harbour the mouth. Maori call the South Island Maui's waka (canoe) and Stewart Island his punga (anchor).

Mâoritanga is also instructed in the urban *Maraes* for young city Maori separated from their tribal roots, where they can meet and learn the history of their people.

Maori symbols and treasures are now considered a source of pride and identity, rather than memories of a past world, Maori radio and television stations ensure the continuation of the Maori language, and Maori schools have grown and are increasing in number.

The Haka

One expression of Maori culture is the *haka*, a 'dance' performed by Kiwi sports teams before matches – most famously by the All Blacks rugby team – which was traditionally a challenge to an opposing tribe, who may have responded in a similar way. A *haka* is a Maori posture dance accompanied by chanted vocals, which may include facial gesticulation such as showing the whites of the eyes and poking out the tongue, and a variety of movements such as stamping the feet and slapping the hands against the body. The whole of the body is used to express whatever feelings are relevant to the purpose – for example, annoyance, courage or joy.

Haka are sometimes thought to be solely war dances but this isn't so. War *haka* were performed before battle, as a demonstration of strength and courage, designed to intimidate the enemy. Nowadays *haka* form part of welcoming ceremonies for distinguished visitors, adding to the importance of the occasion,

although it still has an element of challenge. Many types of *haka* are performed exclusively by men, but a small number are also performed by women.

The All Black rugby team and subsequently other touring sports teams have adopted the *Ka Mate* haka (see box). It was composed in the 1820s by Te Rauparaha, a notorious chief of the Ngati Toa tribe. Whilst being pursued by his enemies in war, Te Rauparaha took shelter with an ally, Te Wharerangi. Te Rauparaha was hidden, sheltered from the light and his enemy. He used the words of the *Ka Mate* haka to express his fear, courage, gratitude, strength and determination to live.

Ka Mate Haka	
Maori	**English Translation**
Ka mate! Ka mate!	I die! I die!
Ka ora! Ka ora!	I live! I live!
Tenei te tangata puhuruhuru	This is the hairy person
Nana i tiki maiwhakawhiti te ra!	Who fetched the sun and caused it to shine again
Hupane! Kaupane!	One upward step! Another upward step!
Whiti te ra!	And the sun shines!

> 'The huge effect Lord of the Rings had on me was discovering New Zealand. And even more precious were the people – not at all like Australians.'
>
> Sir Ian McKellen (British actor, filming in New Zealand)

THE CLASS SYSTEM

Kiwis sometimes denigrate the British as being class-conscious and snooty, and pride themselves on their lack of class-consciousness – and it's true that they don't have the same prejudices and pretensions common in the old world – yet New Zealand isn't the classless society that's sometimes portrayed. Status is a fact of New Zealand life, although it's defined not so much by your birthright, the school you went to, your accent, what work you do or how much you earn, as by your character and educational attainments. (Although accent is a strong indicator of social class; generally the lower the class the broader the accent and vice versa – the higher classes tend to speak with BBC English accents.) That said, New Zealanders don't always set much store by educational achievement and can be suspicious of anyone or anything that seems over-intellectual. New Zealand has no 'old school tie' barriers to success, and almost anyone, however humble his origins, can fight to the top of the heap.

New Zealanders expect to be treated as equals irrespective of their social, racial or financial background, and will treat you the same way. This is affirmed in the informal nature of Kiwi English, which uses first names instead of titles and the term 'mate', even when talking to strangers. Titles are respected, provided they've been earned, but are seldom used, by the holders or others. New Zealanders are hard to pin down, and it's often difficult to ascertain a New Zealander's wealth by the clothes he wears or the car he drives – indeed, successful people tend to hide their success, wanting to avoid becoming victims of 'tall-poppy syndrome' (see box in this chapter). New Zealand has fewer inequalities and a smaller gap between rich and poor than in many other countries, including the UK and US.

ATTITUDES TO FOREIGNERS

Although New Zealand has its share of racists, bigots, xenophobes and white supremacists, it certainly isn't a racist or xenophobic country (which would be hypocritical considering they're mostly immigrants themselves), although immigration can be a controversial

subject. Some people are uneasy about the fact that economic necessity has meant closer ties with Asian and Pacific countries, resulting in increased Asian immigration.

> 'New Zealanders who emigrate to Australia raise the IQ of both countries.'
>
> Robert Muldoon (New Zealand politician)

However, newcomers – wherever they are from – are usually warmly welcomed, and most Kiwis realise only too well that their country needs new people and skills and that its future lies in trading with its Asian neighbours rather than maintaining its traditional ties with the UK. Australians come in for a lot of stick and are the butt of many Kiwi jokes, but hundreds of thousands of New Zealanders live and work in Australia and there's a lot of mutual respect (and similarity) between them.

Kiwis generally live harmoniously with newcomers whatever their race, colour or creed, and is one of the most racially harmonious countries in the world.

FRIENDS & NEIGHBOURS

Relationship with Britain

New Zealand's closest ties are with the UK, which is the 'mother country' for most Kiwis. However, these ties were severely weakened (and some New Zealanders were left feeling like orphans) in the '70s, when the Brits threw in their lot with the European Economic Community, which meant that they could no longer give preferential treatment to New Zealand's butter, meat and wool – the country's most important exports. The result was traumatic, both psychologically and economically, as the UK was the major market for New Zealand's food products. Although closer, Asia wasn't a viable alternative market, because lamb, butter, cheese and apples aren't a big part of the Asian diet.

Ties with the UK have been loosened in other, more symbolic ways: New Zealand now has its own national anthem; the words 'British subject' were removed from Kiwi passports in 1977; and there's even talk of changing the Union Jack-bearing New Zealand flag. Despite these developments, the bond with the UK remains strong, and many Kiwis still have close connections to the country, although there's an whiff of republican feeling in New

Zealand (although not nearly as strong as in Australia).

New Zealand is more willing to acknowledge its British roots than Australia, which is unsurprising in a country whose people are sometimes still regarded as more British than the British. Many Kiwis remain fond of the Queen and have an attachment to British cuisine. Despite competition from international fast-food chains, traditional British food is still tops, including meat pies, fish and chips and roast dinners. They also love beer, although they favour ice-cold lager rather than the warm bitter drunk by Brits.

Although American programmes dominate Kiwi television, British offerings such as the legendary, long-running soap opera *Coronation Street* are hugely popular; as are other British cultural and sporting institutions, including architectural styles, country shows, pantomimes and, of course, rugby. And the UK remains the most popular first stop for young New Zealanders on their big Overseas Experience (OE).

> 'New Zealand was colonized initially by those Australians who had the initiative to escape.'
>
> Robert Muldoon (New Zealand politician)

Relationship with Australia

New Zealand's closest relationship is, not surprisingly, with Australia (often referred to as West Island by Kiwis), its only near neighbour of any significance. The two countries aren't next door to each other – as is commonly assumed – and the mainlands are over 1,600km (1,000mi) apart, similar to the distance between southern England and North Africa. Each country provides the most visitors to the other, they're important trade partners and there's even a lot of inter-marriage, which is at odds with the two countries' apparent healthy disdain for each other. Australians think of Kiwis as country bumpkins who are 20 years behind the times, while Kiwis regard Aussies as inferior stock descended from convicts (unlike some Australian colonies, New Zealand was never a penal colony but was settled by free men, much to Kiwi delight). Aussies regard Kiwis as second-rate, South Sea Poms, while Kiwis think of Aussies as vulgar, second-rate Americans.

Despite this thick vein of mutual suspicion and mild contempt, New Zealanders and Australians generally accept each other as cousins. Indeed, their relationship is typically familial, a mixture of affection and insults. The former New Zealand Prime Minister Mike Moore once remarked that Australians and New Zealanders have more in common than New Yorkers and Californians.

This is reflected in the fact that the prime ministers of the two countries

hold formal talks annually, as do the defence and trade ministers and treasurers, while the foreign ministers meet twice a year.

> One thing you can rely on is that no matter where you are in the world, you can almost always count on there being an Aussie or Kiwi there as well.

Australia is New Zealand's most important trading partner; an estimated 450,000 Kiwis live in Australia (or across the ditch, as the Tasman is referred to), mainly in Sydney, Brisbane, Melbourne and Perth (a mere 60,000 Aussies live in New Zealand – it's much too blustery for them). This a huge number for a country whose population is just over 4m. In fact, it's significant enough for Kiwi prime ministerial candidates to canvas for votes in Australia in the same way that some British politicians sometimes visit Spain, to ingratiate themselves with that country's burgeoning number of British expats. Since the Trans-Tasman agreement of 1973, Kiwis and Aussies have been able to live and work in each other's countries without restriction, although many more Kiwis do so than Aussies and they're often accused of stealing Aussie jobs or bludging off Australian social security payments (but since 2001, Kiwis have had to wait two years to qualify). There are two sides to this argument, and New Zealanders counter by accusing the Aussies of poaching some of their brightest and best people (which

they do with abandon).

The love/hate relationship between New Zealand and Australia probably stems from the fact that they're too similar – opposites attract and likes repel, as the cliché has it. Kiwis resemble quieter, more taciturn Aussies, and use a lot of the same (often colourful) slang, which the Kiwis embellish with local inventions and Maori words. Both have the same love of drinking, similar food ('tucker'), the same pioneer spirit, a similar suspicion of anything that smacks of being too sophisticated, and the same geographical isolation from the rest of the world.

The competitive, jostling relationship between New Zealand and Australia is encapsulated in their sporting duels, notably in rugby and cricket. The New Zealand All Blacks are currently in the ascendancy in the former sport, but the Aussies have been far superior to the Kiwis (and everyone else) on the cricket pitch for many years. Kiwis don't regard Aussies as good losers – this 'fact' is a particular target for ribbing. They've never forgiven Australia for cricketer Trevor

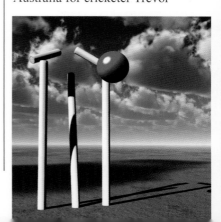

Chappell's infamous underarm delivery, which was seen as totally against the spirit of the game – in other words, 'not cricket'.

While there are undoubtedly many similarities between New Zealand and Australia, there are also many differences. While Australia's early settler population had a significant Irish Catholic element which was hostile to the British authorities, New Zealand was mainly settled by the English (with large Irish and Scots minorities), who were loyal to the home country. As a result, the two countries developed very different attitudes to authority: New Zealand didn't experience the revolts that Australia did, and hasn't developed a serious republican movement.

One of the most significant differences between New Zealand and Australia has been in the treatment of their indigenous peoples. Australia was claimed for the UK as a result of discovery and conquest; but New Zealand joined the British Empire via the Treaty of Waitangi (see **Chapter 2**), which gave the Maori rights not enjoyed at that time by Australia's Aborigines, including legal equality, property rights and the vote: the lot of the Maori has been far superior to that of the Aborigines.

After the Second World War, New Zealand and Australia turned to the US rather than the UK for security, but Australia has maintained a much closer relationship with the US, especially since New Zealand's anti-nuclear policy caused a rift with the Americans. The Australians tend to think that New Zealand doesn't pull its weight in terms of defence, while New Zealanders regard Australia as America's lap dog in the region.

Strange as it may seem, quite a lot of Kiwis and Aussies have never visited each other's countries (for many years Australia was the only affordable place Kiwis could go) and more have visited Europe. Matters might have been very different – the 1901 Australian Constitution included provision for New Zealand to join Australia as its seventh state, even after the Kiwi government had decided against such a move. One reason for this was concern that the Maori would suffer, as at the time Australia had a strict whites-only policy and the Aborigines were treated as non-citizens (almost non-people).

The idea of New Zealand joining Australia raises its head every now and again, but opinion polls show that Kiwis are almost totally opposed, and the Australian government no longer seems to have much interest in the idea either.

Relationship with the USA

New Zealand also has a close relationship with the US, dating back to the Second World War when the country was a base for American forces on their way to the various Pacific war zones. Good relations between the two were sorely tested in the '80s when New Zealand adopted an anti-nuclear policy, which meant that nuclear-powered American vessels were barred from New Zealand waters.

The US reacted badly, suspending New Zealand from the three-party ANZUS defence alliance. Since then, relations between the two have recovered, and New Zealand welcomes many American tourists, but – to its credit – has maintained its anti-nuclear stance. In fact, if anything, this stance has hardened, especially after France's resumption of nuclear testing at Moruroa Atoll. Australia shared New Zealand's feelings of outrage about this and the two joined forces to demand that the French carry out their tests in their own back yard.

> 'A lot of people quote the fact that only 10 per cent of Americans have a passport. They say it's a bad thing.'
>
> Jimmy Carr (British comedian)

ICONS

Every country has its icons – people, places, structures, food (and drink) and symbols – which are revered or are unique to a country and have special significance to its inhabitants. The following is a list of some of New Zealand's icons – the most important of which are also known as Kiwiana – that you can expect to come across or hear reference to.

Sky tower, Auckland

Icons – People
Jean Batten (1909-1982) – One of New Zealand's greatest aviators, Batten flew solo from England to Australia in 1934 in a record time and was subsequently the first pilot to fly from England to Australia and back again. She was created a Dame Commander of the Order of the British Empire (CBE) in 1936.

Sir Peter Blake (1948-2001) – A New Zealand yachtsman who won the Whitbread Round the World Race in 1989, the Jules Verne Trophy in 1994 (in a record time) and led his country to two successive *America's Cup* victories in 1995 and 2000. He was murdered by pirates in 2001 during an environmental exploration trip in South America.

> 'In some ways, I believe I epitomise the average New Zealander: I have modest abilities, I combine these with a good deal of determination and I rather like to succeed.'
>
> Sir Edmund Hillary (New Zealand mountaineer & explorer)

Russell Ira Crowe (b 1964) – New Zealand born (Wellington) film actor, rabble-rouser and sometime musician raised in Australia (where he still lives). Among his box-office hits are *Gladiator*, for which he won an Academy Award (Oscar) for best actor in 2001, *The Insider*, *A Beautiful Mind*, *L.A. Confidential* and *Master as Commander*.

Barry Crump (1935-1996) – A best-selling author and bushman who wrote humorous books loosely based on his experiences, such as *A Good Keen Man* (one of the most popular books in New Zealand history) and *Hang on a Minute Mate*.

Fred Dagg – An archetypal iconic farming character created by Kiwi comedian John Clarke (b 1948) in the mid to late '70s.

Neil & Tim Finn (b 1958 and 1952 respectively) – New Zealand's most successful musicians and songwriters, the Finn brothers were members of the country's two seminal pop/rock groups, Split Enz and Crowded House (both now defunct).

Sir Charles Alexander Fleming (1916-1987) – Ornithologist, palaeontologist and environmentalist, Fleming was the pre-eminent scientist of his generation. In the '60s he led a campaign to stop New Zealand Forest Products destroying the remaining native bush on the Mamaku plateau.

Janet Paterson Frame (1924-2004) – One of New Zealand's best-know novelists, Frame wrote 11 novels, four collections of short stories, a book of poetry, a children's book, and a three volume autobiography.

Sir Richard John Hadlee (b 1951) – One of the best fast bowlers of all time, all-rounder Hadlee played 86 tests and took 431 test wickets, a world record at the time, and scored 3,124 runs. He was knighted in 1990 for services to cricket.

Peter Jackson (b 1961) – Film director, most famous for the brilliant and wildly successful *Lord of the Rings* trilogy, which together won 17 Academy Awards (Oscars), including 11 (all those it was nominated for) for the final part, *The Return of the King*.

Dame Kiri Te Kanawa (b 1944) – World-renowned opera star of mixed Maori and European descent, Kanawa has long been popular in New Zealand. She courted

Mt. Everest

Sir Edmund Hillary

A notably down-to-earth Kiwi mountaineer and explorer, and one of the first two people to scale Mount Everest in 1953 (the other was Sherpa mountaineer, Tenzing Norgay).

controversy in 2003 when she suggested that there's a culture of dependency among the Maori. She was created a Dame Commander of The Order of the British Empire (CBE) in 1982.

Lucy Lawless – Leather-girded, sword-wielding female star of *Xena: Warrior Princess* and every Kiwi man's fantasy.

Bruce Leslie McLaren (1937-1970) – Formula one racing driver, race-car designer, engineer and inventor, and New Zealand's most successful international racing driver. He died in 1970 when his CanAm car crashed at Goodwood in England. His name lives on in Team McLaren, which he founded in 1963, and which is one of the most successful in Formula One history.

Katherine Mansfield (1888-1923) – New Zealand's most famous writer and a noted exponent of the short story.

> 'The pleasure of reading is doubled when one lives with another who shares the same books.'
>
> Katherine Mansfield (New Zealand writer)

Dame Ngaio Marsh (1895-1982) – Author and theatre director, Marsh is best known for her 32 detective novels published between 1934 and 1982. She was created a Dame Commander of the Order of the British Empire (CBE) in 1966.

Sam Neill – An actor who was born in Northern Ireland but raised in New Zealand. In addition to his film work (including roles in *The Dish* and *Jurassic Park*), Sam Neill is a successful winemaker in Central Otago (his Pinot Noir is widely praised).

Lord Ernest Rutherford (1871-1937) – A nuclear physicist of international repute, known as the 'father' of nuclear physics. He won the Nobel Prize for chemistry in 1908, was knighted in 1914 and created a baron in 1931.

Icons – Physical

Bach – A bach (plural baches) is a basic (even primitive) holiday or weekend home usually situated near a beach, which occupies a hallowed place in the national psyche. It's a retreat, a place to relax, and above all, a place where the rules are relaxed, social distinctions blur and routines and formalities have no place.

Beehive, Parliment Building, Auckland

Bath House Rotorua – The Bath House was built (in essentially Elizabethan style) as a therapeutic spa in 1908, and is a Category 1 Historic Building and one of the most beautiful in New Zealand – it's certainly the most photographed. Today it houses the Rotorua Museum of Art & History.

Beehive, Parliament Building – The 'Beehive' is the popular name (after its appearance) for the Executive Wing of the New Zealand Parliament buildings in Wellington, designed by Scottish architect Sir Basil Spence and completed in 1981.

Cape Reinga – The north - westernmost tip of the Aupouri Peninsula at the northern end of the North Island of New Zealand, Cape Reinga (*Te Rerenga Wairua* in Maori) separates the Tasman Sea from the Pacific Ocean. The name comes from the Maori word '*Reinga*' (the 'underworld') and '*Te Rerenga Wairua*', meaning the *leaping-off place of spirits*. It refers to the Maori belief that the cape is the point where their spirits enter the afterlife.

Kemp House – Built by the reverend John Butler as a mission house in 1822 at Kerikeri Basin (Bay of Islands), Kemp House is New Zealand's oldest surviving European building. Together with the replica Maori village, Rewa's village, on the opposite bank, it's regarded as the 'Cradle of the Nation'.

Marae – A sacred meeting place that has both religious and social purposes in Maori and Polynesian societies. It's generally an area of cleared land roughly rectangular (the *marae* itself), bordered with stones or wooden posts and containing a central stone and sometimes terraces. In Maori society the *marae* remains an important part of everyday life.

Mount Taranaki/Mount Egmont – **A** dormant volcano in the Taranaki region on the west coast of the North Island, the 2,518m (8,261ft) mountain is one of the most symmetrical volcanic cones in the

---

Milford Sound

Known as Piopiotahi (meaning 'first native thrush') in Maori, Milford Sound is a fjord situated 15km (9mi) inland from the Tasman Sea in the south-west of the South Island. It's the most famous tourist site in New Zealand and is situated in the Fiordland National Park, which in turn is part of the Te Wahipounamu World Heritage site.

Milford Sound

world. Because of its resemblance to Mount Fuji (Japan), it provided the backdrop for the film, *The Last Samurai* starring Tom Cruise.

Museum of New Zealand –The National Museum of New Zealand (*Te Papa Tongarewa* in Maori), commonly known as *Te Papa* (Our Place), was opened in 1998 on the waterfront in Wellington. It contains six storeys of exhibitions, cafés and gift shops dedicated to New Zealand's culture and environment, including outdoor areas with artificial caves, native bushes and wetlands.

Waitangi Treaty Grounds – Overlooking the Bay of Islands, the Waitangi Treaty Grounds is New Zealand's pre-eminent historic site. It was here on February 6th, 1840, that the *Treaty of Waitangi* (see above) was signed between Maori and the British Crown.

ANZAC Day

Icons – Symbols

ANZAC Day – ANZAC (Australian and New Zealand Army Corps) Day, commemorated on 25th April, is New Zealand's most important national occasion, marking the anniversary of the first major military action fought by Australian and New Zealand forces during the First World War. The soldiers in those forces quickly became known as ANZACs and the pride they took in the name endures to this day.

Bungee jumping

A 'sport' for loonies, involving throwing yourself head-first off a frighteningly-high platform supported only by an elasticised rope tied (hopefully securely) around your ankles. It was 'invented' in New Zealand in the '70s by A. J. Hackett who copied the idea from the people of Vanuatu in the Pacific, who have been throwing themselves off tall towers with only vines tied to their ankles for centuries.

The Colour Black – An iconic colour in New Zealand, given its association with national sporting teams such as the All Blacks (rugby), the Tall Blacks (basketball), the Black Caps (cricket) and Black Magic (yachting). It's also associated with the black singlet (vest) which is often matched with a pair of black gumboots – a combination made famous in the '70s by the comic character, Fred Dagg (see above).

Buzzy Bee – A popular red and yellow children's wooden toy, whose wings turn and make a loud clicking noise. It was created by brothers Hector and John Ramsey in the '40s and remains an iconic New Zealand symbol today.

Cricket – New Zealand's most popular summer sport played by all ages, the New Zealand national team (the Black Caps) is one of the world's top-ranked nations.

Footrot Flats – A famous cartoon strip designed by Murray Ball set in rural New Zealand on Wal's farm in a small town called Rangipo. The cartoon appeared in newspapers across New Zealand and around the world from 1975 until 1994.

Gumboots – Rubber or Wellington boots are considered essential footwear for New Zealand farmers, and are often referred to in Kiwi popular culture such as Footrot Flats. The farming town of Taihape (North Island) proclaims itself 'Gumboot Capital of the World'.

Jandals – Thonged rubber sandals, called flip-flops by the British and Americans and thongs by the Australians, jandals (short for Japanese sandals), were inspired by the traditional woven soled *zori* or Japanese sandals, and the modern design was created in Auckland in the '50s. An essential part of Kiwi national dress.

Jet boat – A high-adrenaline means of exploring New Zealand's hitherto inaccessible waterways.

Maoritanga – *Maoritanga* means Maori culture: a way of life and view of the world. According to Maori beliefs, their ancestors and all living things are descended from the gods, who are often embodied in specific mountains, rivers and lakes, which is why kinship and links with the land are so important.

Overseas Experience (OE)

The Kiwis love to travel and it's almost obligatory for young New Zealanders to travel the world, termed the Overseas Experience or big OE. Traditionally most have travelled to the UK and Europe, but they are increasingly travelling further afield to the USA, South America and Asia.

Tâ Moko – The traditional permanent body and face markings of Maori, *tâ moko* is distinct from a tattoo in that the skin was carved by *uhi* (chisels) rather than punctured, which left the skin with grooves rather than a smooth surface. In pre-European Maori society most high-ranking people had moko, although the practice stopped in the 1860s after the arrival of Europeans. However, there has been a resurgence of the practice in the last few decades, for both men and women, as a sign of cultural identity.

Number 8 wire – A once endlessly useful, all-purpose wire, which became a symbol of Kiwi ingenuity

(hence the term 'number-eight-wire mentality' – see above); sadly, it's no longer in common use.

Racing – Along with rugby and beer, racing – or more correctly – gambling on racing, is an obsession with the Kiwis. However, horse-riding has always been popular (or essential) in New Zealand, and it's one the world's leading equestrian nations.

RSA – The Royal New Zealand Returned and Services' Association (RSA) is one of the largest voluntary welfare organisations in New Zealand with over 130,000 members. It is one of the longest established ex-service organisations in the world, with affiliated social clubs throughout New Zealand which are also open to non-members.

Rugby

New Zealand is the greatest rugby (union) nation in the world and the National team, the All Blacks, are legends of the game. Rugby is a national obsession in New Zealand and it's essential for newcomers to have some knowledge of the game, even if you aren't an aficionado.

Swandri – Usually referred to as a 'Swannie', the swandri is a woollen, waterproof, hooded coat, often green, favoured by hunters and Kiwi farmers – or those wishing to masquerade as Kiwi outdoorsmen.

Team New Zealand – A sailing team based in Auckland which won the *America's Cup* consecutively in 1995 and 2000, thereby cementing New Zealand's reputation for top-class sailors and boat designers.

Icons – Food & Drink

ANZAC biscuits – A type of biscuit made from rolled oats, coconut and golden syrup. The name derives from the belief that they were made by Australian and New Zealand women for the ANZAC troops in the First World War. A British equivalent would be flapjacks (not pancakes).

Beer – Beer is the national beverage in New Zealand, where the average male drinks over 500 cans annually or around 10 per week. Kiwi's are beer connoisseurs and most cities have their own breweries and make their own real ale, made the traditional way in casks by relatively small boutique breweries. The nation's favourite beer is Speights, brewed in Dunedin.

Bluff oysters – Reputed to be New Zealand's best, hailing from Bluff in the South Island.

Chesdale – A processed ('plastic') cheese made back in the unsophisticated days when cheese was simply cheese, Chesdale was the only cheese known to Kiwis growing up in the mid-20th century. It's chiefly remembered due to its popular advertising jingle featuring gum-booted, black-singleted Ches and Dale.

Edmonds cookbook – New Zealand's best-selling book and its culinary bible. More copies of this book, published by the makers of Edmonds 'Sure to Rise' Baking Powder, have been sold than any other book in New Zealand.

Fish & chips – One of New Zealand's favourite foods, which might explain why many Kiwis are overweight.

Kiwi fruit – A small, hairy fruit of Chinese origin (it was formerly called the 'Chinese gooseberry'), the kiwi fruit comes in green and gold varieties. They are a triumph of marketing over substance as they have little taste and are awkward to eat – but are exotic.

Lemon & Paeroa – Usually referred to simply as 'L & P', this lemonade-like soft drink was invented in Paeroa (North Waikato region) in the early 20th century, using carbonated mineral water found in the area; its slogan 'World famous in New ealand' has become a universal joke among Kiwis. Like many soft drinks, it's now owned by Coca Cola.

Manuka honey – Made by bees who feed on the nectar from the flowers of Manuka bushes, Manuka honey is delicious on toast, in porridge and as a natural sweetener, and is much prized throughout the world (particularly 'active' Manuka honey which has antibacterial properties).

Meat Pie – The Kiwi's favourite fast food, individual meat pies are consumed in their millions each year, usually containing meat such as chicken, lamb or beef, and traditionally served with tomato sauce from pie carts. There are even 'gourmet' pie shops, which you may think is oxymoron until you taste them.

Recipe for Pavlova

Ingredients:
4 egg whites
1 tspn vanilla essence (5 ml)
2 tspns vinegar
1 cup sugar

Instructions:
1. Preheat oven to 150°C (300°F).
2. Grease oven tray.
3. Beat the egg whites until very stiff.
4. Fold in vinegar and vanilla.
5. Add sugar, and beat until smooth.
6. Pile the mix onto oven tray about the size of a medium cake.
7. Place the pavlova in the oven, and immediately reduce temperature to 100°C and cook for 90 minutes.

If cooked correctly the 'pav' should be crunchy on the outside and like marshmallow on the inside. Do not open the oven while cooking.

To serve:
Arrange sliced kiwifruit or any other fresh fruit you like (strawberries are popular) on the top of whipped cream (250ml of full cream per pav), with icing sugar added to the cream during whipping to personal taste (about half a cup is sufficient). If this fails, you can buy one from most supermarkets!

Pavlova – A dessert made of meringue filled with whipped cream and topped with seasonal fruits, usually kiwi fruit and/or strawberries. The 'pav' is named after the ballerina Anna Pavlova, who toured down under in the '20s (the Aussies also claim it as theirs).

Tip Top – New Zealand's most famous make of ice cream for over 70 years.

V (Vitalise) – Although a relative newcomer on the scene, 'V' is New Zealand's favourite energy drink, with over 60 per cent of the market.

Icons – Flora & Fauna

Greenstone – Nephrite jade in known as greenstone in New Zealand (*pounamu* in Maori) and is highly valued, playing an important role in Maori culture. Maori weapons and ornaments were traditionally made from greenstone, which is considered a treasure (*taonga*) and is protected under the Treaty of Waitangi.

Kauri Tree – New Zealand's native giant tree, the most famous specimen is Tane Mahuta (lord of the forest), named after the Maori god of the forests, and found in the Waipoua Kauri Forest in Northland, North Island (just north of Dargaville). It stands over 51m (167ft) high with a girth of almost 14m (46ft) and is believed to be over 2,000 years old.

Kowhai – The national flower of New Zealand, the kowhai (*Sophora Microphylla*), is the yellow flower of the kowhai tree.

Paua shell – The paua is a type of abalone found only in New Zealand, whose shell changes colour when viewed from different angles. The shells are commonly used in jewellery and in decoration in Maori carvings, although many New Zealand households use them as ashtrays!

Kiwi

New Zealand's national symbol, the kiwi (usually written with a lower case 'k'), is a small, flightless, mainly nocturnal bird, which has given New Zealanders their nickname, Kiwis (usually written with an upper case 'K'). It's the only bird with nostrils at the end of its bill. There are five species of kiwi: brown, great spotted, little spotted, rowl and tokoeka, which are the smallest of the ratite family which includes emus, ostriches and the extinct moa. Once common, kiwis are currently threatened, their numbers having been decimated by habitat destruction and introduced predators. Efforts are currently being made to boost their numbers, as New Zealand without the kiwi is inconceivable.

Pohutukawa – A tree with bright red flowers, which is a feature New Zealand's coastline; it's sometimes called New Zealand's Christmas tree, as it flowers around Christmas time.

Silver fern – A specie of New Zealand fern, also called a Ponga (punga) tree, which is a symbol of New Zealand used by the army and many Kiwi companies, and, most famously, by the All Blacks on their rugby shirts. New Zealand's netball team is called the Silver Ferns.

Sheep – New Zealand is home to over 40m of these small, woolly beasts with trusting faces, although this is well below the peak of 70m in the '80s. New Zealand sheep have a shorter, wiry staple in their fleece (good for carpets), compared with the long silky merino of Australia.

There are countless sheep jokes aimed at New Zealanders, especially by Australians, although ironically Australia has the largest sheep industry in the world (New Zealand is in second place).

Wild boar – The wild boar was introduced in New Zealand in the 1700s and is found throughout the country. Its iconic status is as game for New Zealand hunters, and there are a number of magazines for 'pig' hunters.

> **'Altogether too many sheep.'**
>
> George Bernard Shaw (Irish dramatist, when asked of his impressions of New Zealand while visiting in 1934)

Bath House at Rotorua

Punting on the Avon, Christchurch

3.
GETTING STARTED

One of the most difficult stages of adjustment to a new country is arrival and those first few days when you have a million and one things to do. This is stressful enough without the need to cope with cultural differences. This chapter helps you prepare for some aspects of daily life, such as getting to grips with bureaucracy, finding accommodation, renting or buying a car, and obtaining utilities, council services, healthcare and education for your children, as well as information about New Zealand's media, banking, taxation and cost of living.

> Immigration is a contentious issue – some Kiwis wish to increase it while others want it reduced – as a consequence you should take care when discussing the subject with Kiwis you don't know well.

IMMIGRATION

New Zealand is keen to keep pests (of the multi-legged variety) out of the country, and its bio-security laws are strict. As a result, the pre-entry form that visitors are required to complete includes lots of questions about what you might be trying to bring into the country – notably food and natural products such as feathers, seeds, soil and wood.

New Zealand's immigration philosophy used to be based on ethnicity and nationality, but now it's more pragmatic and based on age, business, education and experience, irrespective of race or nationality. Immigrants are divided into three main categories: those bringing in business and skills, those with family ties in New Zealand, and those immigrating for humanitarian reasons. Around 60 per cent of immigrants fall under the business and skills category, 30 per cent under the family-sponsored category and only some 10 per cent under the humanitarian category, including refugees.

New Zealand isn't a soft touch and doesn't accept anyone and everyone. You must have English language proficiency to immigrate to New Zealand, and must prove that you and your family are of good character and health, supported by a police certificate, medical certificates and X-rays. If you've been imprisoned for five years or longer at any time, or for 12 months or more during the ten years prior to your application, you'll be refused entry. New Zealand may also refuse entry to anyone they consider likely to be a burden on society, and you must show that you have sufficient funds to maintain yourself and your family for your first two years in New Zealand. The recent insistence that immigrants have good English language and business skills has seen a reduction in the number of Asian immigrants.

Kiwis generally welcome immigrants of the 'right sort' and realise that their small population needs to increase and broaden its skills base in order to maintain its competitiveness; the cheapest and quickest way to do this is to attract skilled immigrants.

Residence Permits

A residence visa is usually issued outside New Zealand and allows you to enter the country once only. It's usually valid for 12 months from the date of issue and cannot be renewed or extended, therefore if you don't travel to New Zealand within this 12-month period, the visa expires and you must apply again.

When you arrive in New Zealand with a residence visa in your passport, you'll be given a residence permit. A residence permit allows you to remain in New Zealand

indefinitely but expires when you leave the country permanently.

You'll need a returning resident's visa to re-enter New Zealand, unless you're a citizen with a New Zealand passport. If you're granted residence in New Zealand, you can apply for citizenship after three years.

BUREAUCRACY

Every country has at least some 'red tape' and requires a certain amount of form-filling, but New Zealand is far from being one of the world's most bureaucratic countries and doesn't seek to torment people with paperwork (although some business people grumble that they have to deal with too much of it). New Zealand is one of the world's least corrupt countries and Kiwis rarely resort to bribery – indeed you would be foolish to try it – or use relatives or friends in high places to get things done (greasing palms certainly isn't a way of life in New Zealand).

Civil Servants

A positive aspect of officialdom in New Zealand is that authority is delegated. When dealing with civil servants, you're unlikely to be pushed from pillar to post and constantly referred to somebody else higher in the chain of command.

Most Kiwis are urban creatures and some 75 per cent live in urban areas with a population of over 10,000, and over half live in just four cities: Auckland, Hamilton and Wellington in the North Island and Christchurch in the South Island.

The people you first see when dealing with government institutions usually know the rules and have the authority to make decisions.

ACCOMMODATION

New Zealand has a strong home-ownership culture and some 70 per cent of Kiwis own their own homes, one of the highest rates in the world. However, there's a huge disparity between home ownership by indigenous Maori and Pacific Islanders, among whom there's a much higher percentage of renters, and other New Zealanders. New Zealand doesn't have a culture of property speculation and Kiwis generally buy a house to live in rather than as an investment, although, as in many other countries, investing in real estate has become much more popular in recent years.

There has been a huge influx of foreign buyers in recent years, particularly British, Canadians and South Africans, which has driven up prices in many areas, particularly for land and properties with a sea or lake view. Property prices in the major cities have also spiralled in recent years, particularly in Auckland.

Of the Kiwis who live in rural areas, most are European or Maori. Asians and Pacific Islanders usually live in the cities, particularly Auckland, a third of whose population was born overseas, compared with a mere one in 15 of the population of the South Island.

A tenant is required to give 21 days' notice to end a tenancy, but a landlord must give 90 days, except in exceptional circumstances, such as when he wishes to move into the property himself (in which case he must give only 42 days' notice).

Kiwis aren't keen apartment-dwellers: 80 per cent of private properties are detached, single-family houses (although more 'multi-family' homes are being built, particularly in Auckland, where land is in short supply). Many of New Zealand's houses reflect the Kiwi character. They are practical and unpretentious rather than fancy or grand – although many spectacular, architect-designed houses have 'sprung up' in recent years, particularly in Auckland.

Some foreigners find New Zealand's houses unimaginative and small, although they have the advantage of being easy and inexpensive to build. All homes are referred to as houses even though most are bungalows, but two-storey houses are becoming more popular.

The Kiwis' liking for travel and new horizons is reflected in the fact that a lot of New Zealand homes are made of wood and are movable (on special lorries) to an owner's new plot or 'section', as it's usually known. New Zealanders like to move (or 'shift') home and do so on average every five years. As a result, the country has many estate agents, even in small towns.

> The down-to-earth, thrifty strand of the Kiwi character is seen in the popularity of furnishing your home with items picked up at garage (yard) sales, which are common most weekends. Note that you need to arrive early to bag the best items.

Holiday Homes

There's plenty of space in New Zealand and many Kiwis take advantage of this and own a holiday home, usually called a 'bach' (a 'crib' in Otago and Southland).

The name is short for 'bachelor' and stems from a time when these properties were home to single men such as (kauri) gum diggers or gold miners. Later they were handy for men-only fishing and drinking trips. In the old days, the bach was by definition a basic, makeshift property, without modern conveniences such as electricity and running water.

Today, although much-loved and well-worn utilitarian family baches survive, the 20th century is conspiring against their unique 'style' continuing. Local authorities and building inspectors no longer turn a blind-eye to rules being bent or broken, and the soaring price of coastal land has meant that many primitive baches have been demolished to make way for residences more in keeping with the land value. Kiwis have also become more sophisticated and house-proud, and most no longer wish to inhabit a tumbledown makeshift 'hut' that may fall down any minute.

Rented Property

Only some 25 per cent of New Zealand property is rented, although in recent years there has been an increasing tendency to rent rather than buy, particularly in Auckland. Rented property in towns and cities consists mainly of apartments, although houses are also available to rent. Unless a newspaper advertisement specifically states that a property is a house or cottage, you should assume that it's an apartment. Two-bedroom apartments are the most highly sought-after properties in the main towns and cities.

When renting property, it's usual to sign a tenancy agreement; the Department of Building and Housing provides a standard agreement for landlords and tenants, which most landlords use. If your landlord uses this agreement and you're happy with the details, it isn't usually necessary to have it checked by a lawyer, as the terms and conditions

Home can mean dome or high rise

are simple and written in non-legal language. (If he doesn't use a standard form, you may have reason to be suspicious.) Most tenancy agreements are for an indefinite period and the tenancy continues until either party gives notice.

Landlords

When you take up a tenancy, you must pay a bond to the landlord, which is usually the equivalent of one or two weeks' rent, although legally it can be up to four weeks rent. The bond isn't held by the landlord but by the Bond Processing Unit (BPU) of the Tenancy Services Centre (Department of Building and Housing), and the landlord must pay your bond to the Unit within 23 working days of receiving it.

At the end of the tenancy, the BPU refunds your bond less the cost of any damage (for which you're responsible under the tenancy agreement). Rent is usually paid fortnightly.

Buying a Home

If you're a permanent resident of New Zealand, there are no restrictions on buying property, although you're sometimes limited by the Overseas Investment Act, 1973 (OIC Act – the Overseas Investment Commission is the government body that oversees foreign investment policies) to buying a home with less than 5ha (12.5 acres) of land. If the land is on or adjacent to a 'sensitive' area (e.g. an island or nature reserve), overseas buyers and those with work permits are sometimes limited to 0.4ha (1 acre) of land. Buying apartments, houses and land in urban areas generally isn't affected by OIC Act restrictions. Your solicitor will advise you if you need to seek approval from the OIC for a purchase and, if you do, will insert a condition in the contract making the purchase conditional on obtaining OIC consent.

When you find a house you wish to buy, you need to make a formal offer (even if you wish to pay the advertised price) in writing, and most estate agents have a standard form for this purpose. The offer is conditional upon certain factors, which may include the approval of finance (e.g. a mortgage), a satisfactory independent valuation and title search, or the sale of another home. Unless you've agreed to pay the asking price, a bargaining process follows. When a price is agreed, a sales contract is signed which commits you to the purchase – this can happen on the same day you view a property!

Some exclusions apply to this commitment (e.g. you aren't obliged to go ahead with the purchase if you find out that a new road is to be built through the living room), but you cannot back out because you decide that you don't like the house or cannot afford it, without paying compensation. You also cannot subsequently reduce the price you've agreed to pay.

> In New Zealand, estate agents' fees are entirely the responsibility of the vendor, and the buyer doesn't pay anything (although the fees are effectively included in the price). This underlines the fact that the agent is working for the seller, not for the buyer, therefore you cannot expect him to do you any favours.

A deposit of 10 per cent must be paid when the sales contract is signed. This is usually non-refundable, but most contracts include a clause requiring its return if the title to the property isn't 'clear' or the land is subject to government requisition (compulsory purchase).

When buying a property in New Zealand, it's the exception rather than the rule to have a survey carried out – unless you're borrowing over 80 per cent of the value of the property, in which case the bank usually insists that a survey and valuation is carried out to protect its interests.

BUYING OR HIRING A CAR

If you live anywhere other than in the middle of a city, you'll almost certainly need a car in New Zealand.

Car Hire

A variety of companies in New Zealand hire out cars by the day or week, including the ubiquitous multinationals such as Avis, Budget and Hertz, plus a large number of local companies. The multinationals offer better insurance and the newest cars but are more expensive than local firms, which usually offer older cars (sometimes with 100,000km/62,000mi or more on the clock). One big advantage of hiring from a national is that you can pick up a car in one town and drop it off in another, whereas with local companies you usually have to return a car to where you got it from. If you book a hire car via the internet, bear in mind that some companies take a few days to confirm the booking, therefore you need to ensure that you receive a confirmation email.

The minimum age for hiring a car in New Zealand is usually 21 and a full licence must have been held for at least 12 months, although some companies have a minimum age of 25. Companies may levy a supplement for larger vehicles when the driver is under 25, and under-25s usually incur a higher insurance excess (deductible).

Hiring a Camper Van or Motorhome

Many visitors to New Zealand buy or hire a camper van or motorhome (RVs or recreation vehicles), which is the cheapest and best way to see the country. A camper van can be anything from an ancient Volkswagen camper or a converted van, to a luxury 6-berth motor home with all the bells and whistles.

Rental fees are from as little as $30 a day for a small 2-berth camper van to over $300 a day for a six-berth luxury motorhome; there are usually discounts for longer than 21 days. Rates should include goods & services tax (GST),unlimited kilometres, insurance, all drivers' fees, a one-way fee (if applicable), cleaning fee, full equipment (usually includes a camping table and chairs), full gas bottle(s), 24-hour breakdown assistance and a travel information pack. Check the cost and desirability of any options, particularly regarding CDW insurance.

There's usually a minimum rental period of around 3 days (which may depend on the kind of vehicle) and a minimum age limit of 21; some companies offer discounts to those

aged over 55. Vehicles may be diesel or petrol, 2WD or 4WD, and manual or automatic (many vehicles are only available with a manual gearbox/stick shift). All companies offer one-way hire.

Buying a Car

Reductions in the price of new cars in New Zealand have had the knock-on effect of reducing used car prices and accelerating depreciation, therefore you should shop around when buying a car and be prepared to haggle over the price. Although new cars are officially sold at list price, a discount is often possible, e.g. by inflating the part-exchange value of a trade-in vehicle or in the form of a cash reduction. Ensure that the price you're quoted includes GST (12.5 per cent) and registration costs. The best selling car magazine in New Zealand is Auto Car, which reports motor industry news, previews new models, performs road tests and provides a survey of prices. The AA magazine Directions also contains a comprehensive list of new car prices.

The easiest way to buy a used car is from a dealer, although it's wise

Many car hire companies don't allow you to take a car from the North to the South Island (or vice versa) on the ferry, and those that do impose a stiff surcharge.

to ask a colleague or neighbour if they can recommend one. When buying a car from a dealer, you should check that he's a member of the Motor Trade Association (Inc) New Zealand (MTA), which has 4,500 members who must abide by a strict code of ethics. The best cars to buy for value for money, economy and reliability tend to be Japanese models.

As in most countries, buying a used car privately in New Zealand requires a great deal of caution, and the vehicle and seller should be carefully scrutinised, including the following:

● Ensure that the seller owns the vehicle or is entitled to sell it. Ask to see the vehicle registration certificate and proof of the seller's address; if the addresses match, this suggests that the seller is who he says he is.

● Inspect the bodywork carefully for damage, as many cars in New Zealand have been involved in accidents. A car with a few minor knocks is preferable to one that looks immaculate but which has been repaired following a major accident.

● Try to confirm that the odometer (km) reading is correct, as odometer tampering is common. Service records from a main dealership and repair invoices showing the km reading are a good way of doing this.

EMERGENCY SERVICES

The emergency number in New Zealand is 111, which can be dialled free from any telephone; you're connected to the emergency operator who connects you with the police, fire or ambulance service, as required. You don't need any money, even when calling from a public telephone, whether it accepts coins, PhoneCards or credit cards. Be ready to tell the emergency operator which service you require and your name.

> You don't need to give your location, as the telephone from which you're calling automatically 'sends' its location.

HEALTH SERVICES

In Kiwi culture, it isn't done to complain about feeling ill (or 'a bit crook' as it's usually described).

Nevertheless, New Zealand has a long tradition of caring for its citizens – dating back to the time when the country was regarded as a test bed for social welfare and, as well as good healthcare, the sick Kiwi would enjoy all kinds of sickness and invalidity benefits. In these days of budget cuts and administrative belt tightening, however, healthcare services have been trimmed and the state is less generous. Unless you have private health insurance, you're likely to have to join a queue for non-urgent surgery and must also pay $45 to $55 for each visit to a doctor, although there are reductions for children and those receiving social security benefits.

The New Zealand healthcare system is comparable to those in European countries such as France and Germany, where the state covers the bulk of the cost of medical treatment but expects most patients to make a contribution or take out private insurance to cover the difference. 'Free' care isn't as comprehensive, for example, as that provided by the British National Health Service, but it's also nothing like the US, where every last pill, potion and sticking plaster must be paid for.

New Zealand is trying to encourage individuals to take responsibility for their health, and Wellness Clinics have been established throughout the country. Kiwis have taken notice

– particularly in response to the country's high rate of skin cancer – but many remain overweight and unfit, despite the country's outdoor life and sporting culture. Their diet of butter, cream, fish and chips, and lamb (a fatty meat) accounts for this, as does the increasing tendency to watch rather than play sport, while guzzling beer.

One notable area of healthcare-related success is smoking. New Zealand has become one of the leading countries in the battle against the habit, which has resulted in a lower death rate from lung disease and other smoking-related diseases than in most European countries.

Rates are much higher among the Maori, however, 47 per cent of whom smoke, compared with just 20 per cent of Pâkehâ.

> The average life expectancy in New Zealand is 77 for men and 82 for women.

State Healthcare

New Zealand citizens and permanent residents are automatically entitled to state healthcare and it isn't necessary to establish a contributions record. If you're a visitor or temporary migrant and a national of a country with which New Zealand has a reciprocal agreement (such as Australia, Canada, Denmark, Greece, Guernsey, Ireland, Jersey, the Netherlands and the UK), you can also receive state health benefits. Otherwise, you must pay the full cost or have private insurance.

The principle of state healthcare in New Zealand is that hospital inpatient treatment is provided free, whereas the cost of outpatient and non-hospital treatment (e.g. consultations with a family doctor and prescribed medicines) must be paid for by patients (although services are subsidised). Those on low incomes can apply for a Community Services Card (CSC), which entitles them to a discount on healthcare costs, and free doctors' services are provided for children under six. Pensioners aren't automatically entitled to reduced-cost services unless they have a low income.

Dental treatment and optical services are largely outside the scope of the state health scheme.

Doctors

New Zealand has a community-based system of healthcare, where your first point of contact is your family doctor or general practitioner (GP), who treats minor conditions and refers more serious cases to specialists or hospitals. It's advisable to find and register with a doctor as soon as you arrive in a new area, although it isn't compulsory to do so and you can just turn up at any doctor's surgery, where you'll usually receive prompt attention. You are free to choose your own doctor.

> Among OECD countries, New Zealand's suicide rate is the sixth-highest for males and the fourth-highest for females.

Emergency Treatment

In a medical emergency in New Zealand, simply dial 111 and ask for an ambulance, which will be despatched to take you to the nearest hospital. The ambulance service (provided by various organisations depending on the region) is free and includes paramedic teams and helicopter ambulances. In remote areas, specially trained search-and-rescue teams are provided, which usually include a doctor who can administer treatment and perform minor operations on the spot.

Medicines

Medicines are sold in pharmacies, known in New Zealand as chemists, which may be part of another business. They sell prescription and non-prescription medicines and other products such as cosmetics and toiletries, but don't usually carry such an extensive range of goods as a North American drugstore. Normal opening hours are 9 am to 5.30 pm Mondays to Fridays (occasionally later on Thursdays or Fridays) and sometimes Saturday mornings. In most areas a duty chemist is open longer hours or an emergency telephone number is provided for those needing medicines in an emergency (details are displayed in chemists' windows).

Hospitals

You can go to a hospital for treatment in the event of an accident or emergency without a doctor's referral, but in all other cases your first point of contact is your family doctor, who will refer you to an appropriate hospital as necessary.

The main criticism of healthcare reforms in recent years has related to the increase in hospital waiting lists, which are long and growing longer. There have been many horror stories of patients requiring urgent hospital treatment having to wait ten hours or more for a bed (not that this makes New Zealand any worse than many other countries). Under the current system, regional health authorities must 'buy' the services you require (e.g. an operation) from the most cost-effective source, which is usually your local hospital.

> **'Besides death, constipation is the big fear in hospitals.'**
> Robert McCrum (English writer)

However, if you're willing to travel to another (or any) hospital, you should inform your doctor, as he may be able to book you into a hospital where the waiting list is shorter.

Once you're allocated a bed in a public hospital, the standard of medical and nursing care is as good as you're likely to find anywhere.

New Zealand hospitals provide free in-patient healthcare, which includes medical and nursing care, medicines and accommodation. (The government experimented with a $50 per day 'hotel charge' in hospitals between 1991 and 1993, but this was dropped after public opposition.) Out-patient treatment in accident and emergency departments isn't free, and is paid for in the same way as visits to a family doctor (CSC holders pay reduced fees).

INSURANCE

New Zealand has an innovative approach to insurance, which is quite different from that in, for example, the USA and most western European countries. In these countries there are state schemes that pay health, sickness and unemployment benefits; however, unlike most other countries, New Zealand's system isn't largely insurance based and individuals aren't required to make contributions in order to benefit.

(Although, as the substantial costs are funded by general taxation, they cannot be said to be free to taxpayers.)

Accident Compensation

The Accident Compensation Scheme (ACC) is a government-operated insurance system, financed through taxes and a levy on earnings. It compensates people who have been injured in accidents, thereby discouraging them from suing whoever they think 'caused' the accident. If you're involved in an accident, you receive whatever payment is awarded by the ACC. Although you're unlikely to receive a multi-million dollar payout, the system ensures that a lot of money isn't wasted on long-drawn-out court cases – and it ensures that New Zealand doesn't have the insidious, vindictive compensation culture found in the US.

> As a consequence of the state Accident Compensation Scheme (ACC), some 40 per cent of cars on New Zealand's roads are 'uninsured'.

Everyone who's resident in New Zealand or a visitor from a country with which New Zealand has a reciprocal agreement (such as Australia, Canada, Denmark, Greece, Guernsey, Ireland, Jersey, the Netherlands and the UK) is covered by the national healthcare scheme, which provides either free or reduced cost medical treatment (see above). However, while treatment under the state health scheme is considered adequate, many people also have private health insurance. The main purpose of this is to pay the cost of doctors' consultations, prescriptions and dentistry, which aren't covered by the state healthcare system.

Insurance also pays for treatment in private hospitals, thus circumventing public hospital waiting lists. Private health insurance schemes provide other benefits, such as cover for loss of earnings due to illness. Almost 50 per cent of New Zealanders have some form of private health insurance.

House Insurance

Premiums are modest in most areas, particularly for home contents insurance (a reflection of the country's low crime rate).

However, your insurance company will probably claw back the savings on buildings insurance, as damage caused by severe weather (particularly flooding) is common in some parts of the country; subsidence is also a risk in some areas.

When insuring your home (rather than its contents) you're offered a choice between comprehensive insurance (known as 'accident damage insurance'), which covers all risks, and 'defined risk insurance', which covers specific risks only.

Napier was destroyed by an earthquake in 1931

Earthquake Insurance

New Zealand is in an earthquake zone, and minor (usually unnoticeable) tremors occur frequently, although records show that serious earthquakes occur, on average, only once every 200 years or so. As the consequences of a major earthquake would be catastrophic and no insurance company could possibly cover them, the New Zealand government assumes the responsibility of providing earthquake insurance.

The Earthquake Commission operates an insurance scheme that's funded by a small levy on property insurance policies. If your home is insured for less, you'll receive only the sum insured. The Earthquake Commission pays no compensation for boats, jewellery, money, vehicles or works of art. This scheme ensures that, in the event of an earthquake, most property owners are compensated, even if the government goes bust as a result.

Because $100,000 is unlikely to be sufficient to rebuild anything other than a very modest home, most insurance companies offer top-up insurance to cover the difference between the $100,000 paid by the government and the value of your home, which is essential for owners of valuable properties.

Car Insurance

In most countries, motorists are required to have at least third-party insurance, so that if they injure or kill another road user their insurance company pays compensation.

This isn't legally required in New Zealand because of the country's innovative Accident Compensation Scheme (see above), whereby anyone who suffers an accident or injury is compensated directly by the government. The system works reasonably well, although it isn't free as everyone pays for it through their taxes. One effect of this system is that it isn't possible to sue anyone who causes an accident or injury for compensation.

In the event that an earthquake devastates your property, the Earthquake Commission will pay you compensation of up to a maximum of $100,000 for a property and $20,000 for contents.

The scheme doesn't, however, compensate drivers for damage to their cars and it's therefore wise to have insurance which covers this; most people with anything other than a worthless heap take out insurance. The cost of car insurance varies depending on the extent of cover (e.g. fully comprehensive, third-party fire and theft or third party), the make and type of vehicle, the drivers (you can obtain a 20 per cent discount if you don't allow drivers under 25), and where you live (Aucklanders pay up to 30 per cent more than country dwellers). A no-claims bonus system operates in New Zealand and you should obtain a letter from your previous motor insurance company stating your no-claims bonus.

EDUCATION

Education is compulsory in New Zealand between the ages of 6 and 16, and free between the ages of 5 and 19, although many state schools ask parents to make financial contributions to compensate for shortfalls in their budgets or for 'extras'. The majority of Kiwi schools are co-educational.

There are three types of schools in New Zealand: state, private and state integrated schools, which are former private schools that have been 'integrated' into the state system.

State and state integrated schools (some 95 per cent of the total) are government funded, while private schools receive about 25 per cent of their funding from the government and rely on tuition fees for the rest.

The country's education culture is quite laissez-faire in some respects, and primary and secondary schools set their own dates for the four terms of the school year, which can make life awkward for families with children at different schools.

The government has introduced a system called 'Tomorrow's School', which gives parents more influence over their child's education. It was a smart move on the part of the government, as it has meant that parents have become involved in certain administrative and fund-raising jobs, thereby reducing government education costs.

New Zealand's schools often take an informal approach to education (reflecting the informal way of doing most things in the country), and strive for cooperation between teachers and pupils, rather than the strict us-and-them approach favoured in some countries. Some foreigners find this approach too informal, but the quality of education provided in New Zealand is generally good or very good, so it seems to work – certainly for children of average or above average ability (see below).

Despite all this, there isn't a strong culture of educational excellence in New Zealand, where there's a suspicion of anything that smacks of intellectualism or cleverness,

> 'The only time my education was interrupted was when I was at school.'
>
> George Bernard Shaw (Irish dramatist & literary critic)

and where school 'swots' tend to be mocked rather than admired.

There's increasing concern about this phenomenon, as recent statistics have shown that the gap between New Zealand's best and worst performing students is the largest in the developed world, and it's estimated that a quarter of Kiwi students leave school lacking many of the basic skills needed to live and work in the modern world.

> While the country's informal approach to education works for pupils of average and above average ability, it's generally unsuitable for less able students.

Private Schools

New Zealand has a flourishing private school sector, although it serves only some 5 per cent of the school population. In recent years, a number of state schools have effectively become private schools, as the government now gives greater autonomy to state schools and several have been encouraged to join the commercial market. Private schools range from nursery schools to secondary schools, both day and boarding, and from traditional-style schools to those offering 'alternative' education such as Montessori and Rudolf Steiner schools.

Private education includes schools sponsored by churches and religious groups (known as parochial schools), educational foundations and private individuals, schools for students with learning or physical disabilities, and for gifted children. In addition to mainstream parochial (e.g. Catholic) schools, there are also schools for religious and ethnic minorities, for example Muslims, where there's a strict code regarding the segregation of boys and girls. Most private schools are single sex, although some have become co-educational in recent years. There are also private boarding schools, although few accept only boarders and many accommodate day students and boarders.

Universities

New Zealand's universities vary from good to excellent and cater for thousands of foreign students. In recent years they've attracted increasing numbers of students from Asia, many of whom come to study English and/or business studies, drawn by the high quality and reasonable costs.

New Zealand has eight universities: Auckland University of Technology, Lincoln University (near Christchurch), Massey University (at Albany between Auckland, Palmerston North and Wellington), the University of Auckland, the University of Canterbury (Christchurch), the University of Otago at Dunedin, the University of Waikato (Hamilton) and Victoria University (Wellington). All offer a wide choice of courses, although most are regarded as 'centres of excellence' in certain subjects.

> **'I chose a single-sex Oxford college because I thought I'd rather not face the trauma of men at breakfast'**
> Theresa May (British politician)

No university is regarded as better or worse than any other, although a degree in a subject from a university that's a centre of excellence in that subject is more highly valued than a degree from a university which isn't. Auckland is the largest university in terms of student numbers (over 30,000) and offers the widest range of courses. It's also more cosmopolitan, whereas the others, both geographically and intellectually, are more provincial. Honours degree programmes last for three or four years.

Entry requirements depend on the individual course, and some courses, such as medicine, demand nothing less than the best grades. Each university controls its own admissions and most distribute an enrolment pack in the first week of September, with applications to be submitted by the end of the first week of December. The university and polytechnic academic year runs from February to November.

UTILITIES

Utilities is the collective name for electricity, gas and water supplies. Electricity and gas are used for cooking and heating in cities and towns throughout New Zealand, although most new homes are all-electric and if owners want to use gas they must buy it in bottles.

Electricity

To have an electricity supply connected (or the bill transferred to your name when moving into a new home), simply call a local electricity company on the number shown in the telephone directory.

Connection charges are around $40, but if the electricity hasn't been disconnected you won't be charged. Unless you own the property, you may need to pay a bond, which can be around $250 if you don't meet the company's credit criteria or $100 if you rent a property. You'll be billed every two months (most people pay by direct debit from a bank account) and the typical bill for an average house is around $200 for two months.

Gas

Natural gas is available everywhere in the North Island except for a few remote corners, but not in the South Island. Liquefied petroleum gas (LPG) is distributed nationally.

If you buy a home in North Island without a gas supply, you can usually arrange with a local gas company to install a line between your home and a nearby gas main (provided there's one within a reasonable distance – otherwise the cost will be prohibitive). If a home already has a gas supply, simply contact a local gas company to have it reconnected or transferred to your name (there's a connection fee of around $40). A security deposit (e.g. $100) is usually payable if you're renting. You must contact your gas company to get a final reading when vacating a property. In areas where mains gas is unavailable, some properties are plumbed for bottled gas.

In some areas, properties (generally newer homes) have a water meter and you're charged according to use. It's generally cheaper to pay for your water on the rated system, although modest users living in large properties find it cheaper to have a meter fitted.

Telephone

To have a telephone connected, simply call your chosen telephone company (the number will be in your local telephone directory). Before connecting your line, Telecom (or another operator) require the following:

● your name and address;

● proof of your address (such as your driving licence);

● details (and proof) of your previous address and your employer;

● your date of birth;

● the address of a relative or friend in New Zealand as a reference.

If you've just arrived in New Zealand, your immigration documents should be acceptable as proof of identity; otherwise ask your employer (if you have one) to confirm your identity.

Once your application has been approved, the telephone will be connected within 24 hours if your home has an existing line, or within 48 hours if it hasn't and there are lines nearby. If you need a line installed or you live in a remote area, you'll be quoted a price for the labour costs and materials involved.

Water & Sewerage

Mains water is available throughout New Zealand except for the most remote areas, where it sometimes shoots up in boiling form directly out of the ground! All tap water is drinkable, although it's heavily chlorinated in towns. Water is supplied and billed by a local water company, which may be a division of your local council. Usually, you pay an annual water rate, which is set according to the size and value of your property. In most areas water rates are included in local property taxes, but in some water is billed separately; e.g. in Auckland some households pay several hundred dollars a year.

Mains drainage is found throughout New Zealand, with the exception of remote rural areas, where properties usually have a septic tank.

STAYING INFORMED

Television

Watching television is New Zealand's major 'cultural' activity,

although Britons will find much of its output dire (on a par with Australia's) and mind-numbing. There are three terrestrial, national free-to-air TV stations – imaginatively named TV One, TV2, and TV3. There are also many local television stations and a government-funded Maori television channel, which promotes Maori culture and language. TV One and TV2 are state owned, while TV3 and C4 are owned by the Canadian company, CanWest. The government has long-term plans to sell TVNZ, the state broadcasting company, although this has been delayed for years.

> **The TV Guide is square-eyed New Zealand's best-selling magazine.**

All stations, even those that are state owned, carry advertising, although the amount of revenue the state-funded channels can raise from advertising is restricted. The TV advertising market in New Zealand is extremely lucrative, with annual revenue of around $500m. There are also state- and privately-owned regional TV stations in some areas (e.g. Triangle TV in Auckland, Channel 7 in Wellington, Canterbury TV and Channel 9 in Dunedin), although TVNZ has closed its five Horizon Pacific regional channels.

Terrestrial TV doesn't cater well for the New Zealanders' passion – sport – because the major sporting events have been sold to the highest bidder, which is invariably a satellite or cable TV company, although a recent agreement between Sky TV and TV3 means that more sport is shown on that channel. Otherwise, if you like watching sport, you need to invest in a satellite dish or cable connection to watch the big matches, although you can watch them free at hotels (pubs) that show live sport on large-screen TVs (but the drinks aren't free).

> TV One is TVNZ's most popular channel, with an audience share of around 40 per cent, and provides a staple diet of news broadcasts, home-produced and imported dramas, and 'lifestyle' programmes. TV2 broadcasts children's programmes, drama series and films, while TV3 claims to target the 18 to 49 age range and offers a mix of home-produced programmes and imported drama and soaps. Both TV2 and TV3 have around 20 per cent of the TV audience, while C4 has just over 1 per cent.

Television in New Zealand has a poor reputation. The small population and limited budgets mean that there are few home-produced programmes (around 20 per cent, the lowest percentage in the developed world and a cause for growing concern). Most programmes are imported from other English-speaking nations (mainly Australia, the UK and the US) and many seem to be the cheapest and worst available.

As in many countries, Kiwis enjoy soap operas, and lovers of America's Friends and South Park and the UK's Changing Rooms, Coronation Street and Eastenders will be delighted to discover that they're all shown on New Zealand TV.

On the plus side, the quality of local documentary programmes is high, and wildlife programmes such as Meet the Real Penguins and Mount Cook have won New Zealand programme-makers top awards in Asia and Europe. News programmes are also presented professionally, although they tend to focus on national rather than international news, and coverage can be rather superficial (making BBC World, CNN and Sky News good value for those who want to know what's happening in the wider world).

The government-funded organisation NZ On Air 🖳 www.nzonair.govt.nz) promotes New Zealand culture and provides funding for home-produced programmes, such as documentaries, drama series and children's programmes, which account for some 20 per cent of total broadcasting. In a recent survey, over 60 per cent of New Zealanders claimed they would like to see this proportion substantially increased.

The percentage is even higher among the Maori population, whose culture is given top priority by NZ On Air, leading to the establishment

in 2004 of a state-funded channel, Maori Television, broadcasting partly in Maori.

Radio

Radio broadcasting in New Zealand follows the model of the TV industry, with state-operated and commercially-run stations. Radio New Zealand (RNZ) operates three national stations: Concert FM and National Radio, which are similar to the BBC's Radio 3 and 4 (i.e. highbrow music and talk respectively), and the AM Network, which relays Parliamentary proceedings (unsurprisingly, not the most popular station). These stations, which are entirely state-funded and don't carry advertising, have a good reputation for the quality of their broadcasting, although they're rather staid and have a mainly older (and declining) audience.

Art installation, Christchurch Botanical Gardens

RNZ also operates a network of local radio stations throughout the country, which are partly state-funded and partly funded from advertising. They broadcast mainly rock, pop and easy listening music, local and regional news, and sport. CanWest (the owner of TV3 and C4) operates RadioWorks, the second-largest national radio network, which broadcasts mainly pop music.

> Most radio stations broadcast in English, although there are a number of state and private radio stations broadcasting in Maori, particularly in regions with large Maori communities, such as Auckland and the north-west region of the North Island.

A wealth of national commercial radio stations broadcast in New Zealand, mainly pop music, and there are several special interest stations such as Radio Sport (whose commentaries have been widely acclaimed) and religious stations. A student station, b.NET, broadcasts from universities and polytechnics around the country. An abundance of local commercial radio stations are on the air, with 100 FM stations alone, plus others broadcasting on the AM frequency. Stations are closely involved with their local communities, play pop or easy listening music, and broadcast local news and sport. Because there are so many commercial stations competing for a limited amount of advertising revenue, stations often go to extraordinary lengths to attract listeners.

Internet

Due to its geographical isolation, New Zealand has enthusiastically embraced the communications revolution and has become highly internet-oriented; many business, entertainment and retail transactions are carried out online. Most companies and all government bodies are online and internet time is free (provided you have free local calls and your service provider has a local access number).

Internet service providers (ISPs) are numerous, mainly based in the large cities, including Telecom's Jetstream and Jetstream Xtra, and TelstraClear's Clear.net. Most companies offer broadband connection via ISDN or ADSL lines, although these aren't available in all areas. Prices are competitive and limited free access (e.g. two hours per month) is available from a few dollars per month or unlimited access from around $30 per month. The monthly magazine NZ PC World regularly publishes a comparison of rates and packages.

Newspapers

Major newspapers include the New Zealand Herald (Auckland), the Dominion Post (Wellington), the Waikato Times (Hamilton), The Press (Christchurch) and the Otago Daily Times (Dunedin). Most daily newspapers are published from Mondays to Saturdays and separate titles are published on Sundays, e.g. the Sunday Star Times in Auckland. Other popular publications include the weekly National Business Review, New Zealand's main business magazine, and The Truth, a weekly 'shock-horror' tabloid.

Press

New Zealand doesn't offer a wide choice of daily newspapers – a situation that has been exacerbated by the closure of a number of

long-established newspapers in recent years. There are no national newspapers in New Zealand, where most are regional and centred on the major cities. As a result, most New Zealand newspapers tend to have a provincial feel, although they contain national and international news. Like the outward-looking Kiwis, New Zealand's press isn't parochial (unlike, say, the US, where most people aren't much interested in what happens in the next state, let alone in other countries) and has good coverage of international news.

Politically, most newspapers take an even-handed approach, as they're mainly independently owned. The content of most newspapers is fairly standard and includes news, business, sport and TV programmes, while the Thursday, Friday and Saturday editions are the best for advertisements for jobs ('Situations Vacant'), property and cars. Friday editions of most newspapers include a substantial entertainment section ('What's On').

Newspapers are sold by newsagents and from street stands (where you leave the money in an honesty box) and vending machines,

where depositing your money opens the door, giving you access to the newspapers inside (a concept developed in America, where honesty boxes would be empty). A daily newspaper costs around $1.10 and Sunday papers around $1.70.

You can also have newspapers delivered to your home. Free local newspapers are distributed to homes in most cities and are useful for finding services, jobs, property and cars.

Expatriates will be pleased to hear that you can buy Australian, American and British newspapers (e.g. the Observer and Sunday Times) in major cities a day or two after publication. There are also several Chinese newspapers in New Zealand, serving the local Chinese community of around 110,000.

A wide range of magazines is for sale in New Zealand catering for most tastes, including sports, hobbies, and home and business topics. However, due to the country's relatively small population, many are imported from abroad, particularly from Australia, the UK and the US. Nevertheless, there are still hundreds of local titles, of which The TV Guide has the largest circulation (around 225,000), followed by New Zealand Woman's Day (160,000).

> New Zealand has the highest per capita number of bookshops in the world.

Books

Kiwis are great book readers, and most bookshops stock a good selection of books, including a wide choice of titles published in Australia, the UK and the US.

However, due to the relatively small print runs of New Zealand publishers and the cost of shipping books from other countries, they're relatively expensive (Americans will be shocked).

Post

The New Zealand Post Office (known as NZ Post) is embedded in the country's culture – it's a national institution with a rich past, similar to the American 'Pony Express'. Tales abound of how postmen in bygone days struggled through forests and over mountains to ensure that the mail was delivered. Today the postal service remains a mainstay of New Zealand life, particularly for those living in remote regions. In addition to delivering (and collecting) letters and parcels, rural posties (postmen and postwomen) deliver a variety of goods, including bread, milk, newspapers and even animals.

BANKING

There are officially just two kinds of financial institution in New Zealand: registered banks and what are euphemistically known as 'other financial institutions'. The main exception is the Reserve Bank of New Zealand (⌨ www.rbnz.govt. nz), which doesn't fit into either of these categories and is the country's central bank, performing a role similar to the Bank of England or the Federal Reserve Bank in the USA.

Bank Charges

Banks in New Zealand make charges for most transactions, which are highly unpopular with clients (a recent survey showed that some 75 per cent of bank customers find bank charges excessive) and are the main reason why people change banks. Most banks charge a monthly 'base' fee for some accounts of at least $5 unless you meet certain conditions, such as maintaining a certain minimum monthly balance.

Electronic transaction and cheque fees are around 50¢ and staff-assisted transactions cost around $2.50. Most banks also charge

around $1.50 for the use of another bank's ATMs.

Cheques

Cheques in New Zealand are similar to those in most other English-speaking countries; you enter the name of the payee, the date, and the amount in words and figures, and sign it. All cheques should be crossed (non-negotiable), as a crossed cheque can be paid only into a bank account in the name of the payee and cannot be cashed.

> The use of a cheque incurs cheque duty (a kind of stamp duty) of 5¢ cents, which is automatically deducted by your bank – bear this in mind when reconciling cheques you've written with the amounts that appear on your bank statement.

Cheque clearing in New Zealand is highly efficient and a cheque paid into your account is usually credited the next day (occasionally the same day if it's at the same branch or bank). A cheque drawn on your account and given to someone else may also be debited from your account on the same or next day – there isn't a delay of between three and ten days as in some other countries. Nevertheless, when paying a cheque into your account, it's probably best to wait a few days before spending the money in case the drawer didn't have sufficient funds to cover the cheque (in which case it will be returned to you by post, which may take a couple of days). On the other hand, you should

> Credit card fraud is a huge problem in New Zealand. If you lose your credit or charge card, you must report it to the issuer immediately by telephone. The law protects you from liability for any losses when a card is lost or stolen unless a card has been misused 'with your consent' (e.g. by a friend you've lent it to), in which case you're liable.

assume that a cheque drawn on your account is debited from it on the same day.

Credit & Charge Cards

New Zealanders are enthusiastic users of credit and charge cards, although many prefer debit cards, where payments are immediately debited from their account. Credit and debit cards are issued by most banks, although some will only give you a credit card if you have a certain type of account with them, e.g. a mortgage loan. Credit and debit cards are accepted almost anywhere, although small businesses such as convenience stores may not accept credit cards. They can also be used to withdraw cash from ATMs or over the counter at banks, but bear in mind that this costs from $1.50 to $4 and interest is charged from the day of the withdrawal if you're using a credit card. To use ATMs you require a personal identification number (PIN).

Most international credit and charge cards are widely accepted in New Zealand, including American Express, Diners Club, MasterCard and Visa, as is the local Bankcard, which can also be used in Australia. Most businesses in New Zealand accept all major credit cards, so you're unlikely to be stuck if you possess only one card.

Opening an Account

To open a bank account in New Zealand, simply choose a branch of any of the registered banks that is convenient to your home or place of work (or where you hope to live or work). Different banks require different documentation, so you should check exactly what's required beforehand; typically you'll need two forms of identification, your IRD (tax) number and possibly statements from your current or previous bank. If you don't have an IRD number when you open an account, you'll be charged resident withholding tax (RWT) at 39 per cent on any interest earned.

Opening Hours

Normal banking hours are from 8.30 or 9 am until 4.30 pm, Mondays to Fridays, although banks may stay open for half an hour later one evening a week (which is the exception rather than the rule). Banks don't open at weekends and are closed on public holidays,

although bureaux de change open at weekends.

TAXES

New Zealand's tax system is relatively straightforward and there are no local income taxes, capital gains tax, wealth taxes or estate (inheritance) taxes. The income tax system is designed so that most people can prepare and file their own tax returns, although if your tax situation is complicated you may need to obtain help from an accountant. A goods and services tax (GST) is levied in New Zealand, which is essentially the same as the value added tax (VAT) levied in European Union countries and sales tax in North America. New Zealand also has property taxes (levied by local authorities, based on the rateable value of properties), gift tax and fringe benefits tax.

COST OF LIVING

It's useful to try to estimate how far your dollars will stretch and how much money you will have left (if any) after paying your bills. The inflation rate in New Zealand is low (around 3.2 per cent in 2006) and the government is committed to reducing it to around 2 to 2.5 per cent. Prices of many imported goods have fallen in real terms in recent years, particularly cars and electrical appliances. In general, New Zealanders enjoy a relatively high standard of living, although salaries are lower than in Australia, North America and most Western European countries.

It's difficult to estimate an average cost of living in New Zealand, as it depends on where you live as well as your lifestyle. If you live in Auckland, drive a BMW and dine in expensive restaurants, your cost of living will be much higher than if you live in a rural part of the South Island, drive a small Japanese car and live on lamb and kiwi fruit. You can live relatively inexpensively by buying New Zealand produce when possible and avoiding expensive imported goods, which are more expensive, not only because of the distance they have to travel but also because they're considered fashionable.

Examples of typical salaries, housing costs and the cost of many everyday items can be obtained from Statistics New Zealand (🖳 www. stats.govt.nz), the statistical office of the New Zealand government.

4.
BREAKING THE ICE

One of the best ways to overcome culture shock and feel more at home in New Zealand is meeting and getting acquainted with Kiwis. Making new friends anywhere is never easy, but it's much easier in New Zealand than in many other countries, as Kiwis are informal and usually happy to chat and socialise with strangers. This chapter provides information and advice about important aspects of New Zealand society such as sexual attitudes, meeting people, how to behave in social situations, topics to avoid, and dealing with confrontation.

NEIGHBOURS

Kiwi society has a healthy attitude to neighbours and neighbourliness, especially in country regions and small towns. People in these communities tend to know everyone else in their area and quite a lot about their business. This is a legacy of the pioneering days, when it was important to your survival to keep in touch with those around you and to help each other out in times of crisis. Even in New Zealand's cities, people often know their neighbours and have contact with them. In this respect, Londoners and Parisians can learn a lot from the Kiwis.

New Zealand's culture of neighbourliness might have been encouraged by the fact that most people live in detached houses. If you live in an apartment block or a terraced (row) house, you're often exposed to your neighbours on a daily basis, living cheek by jowl and being forced to listen to the sounds of their daily life – which means that

> 'If there's one thing nearly everyone who lives and works abroad has to get right, it is this: they must be able to get along with the local people.'
>
> Craig Storti, *The Art of Crossing Cultures*

you may want to avoid them socially. On the other hand, homeowners who live in detached house often miss this daily contact – and have the luxury of choosing whether or not to see (and hear) their neighbours.

Community Regulations

In cities where apartments are most common – particularly Auckland, where the shortage of space has encouraged the building of apartment blocks – the most frequent cause of disputes between neighbours is noise, even though most blocks have community regulations designed to minimise such problems. These include the requirement to keep noise to a minimum after 11pm and before 7am, the restriction or banning of pets (especially noisy ones, primarily dogs) and even regulations concerning the type of flooring allowed (laminated and wooden floors transmit sound to the apartment below much more than carpeted floors and may be prohibited).

Unruly people who persistently disturb and harass their neighbours can be evicted.

> Even more shocking to the inhabitants of some European cities than neighbours knowing your name, is that in New Zealand neighbours and friends tend to drop in on each other informally and unannounced (the impertinence!); these informal visits are often via the back rather than the front door.

SEXUAL ATTITUDES

New Zealand is a liberal country, particularly regarding attitudes to sex and marriage. But moral attitudes vary according to people's gender, age and background: the older generation, those from rural areas and certain immigrants are much more conservative and less 'tolerant' than the younger generation in the major cities, where there's a cosmopolitan culture.

The age of consent is 16 and, to most New Zealanders, premarital sex is acceptable, although extramarital sex is not. Most Kiwis aren't shocked by the sight of naked flesh – the country has a number of

beaches where nudity is accepted – and are tolerant of homosexuality. Prostitution and brothels are legal in New Zealand, provided prostitutes are aged 18 or older, and the country has liberal laws on the sale of pornography (to anyone aged 18 or over), although extreme and violent forms of pornography are illegal.

Films are graded by censors, with some restricted, e.g. to those aged at least 16 or 18, depending on their level of explicit sex and/or violence. New Zealand's television output is monitored by the Broadcasting Standards Authority, which has guidelines regarding sexual material, when it can be broadcast and what warnings must be given.

Sex education is a part of the curriculum in schools, although the Education Act gives parents of students under 16 the right to exclude their children; children aged 16 or older can excuse themselves.

Results from the 2005 Durex Global Sex Survey indicate that Kiwis are an active lot when it comes to sex but put their health at risk by having unsafe sex. New Zealanders rank fourth in the world for having unsafe sex (of the 41 nationalities surveyed, only Norwegians, Greeks and Swedes were more reckless) and have the third-highest number of sexual partners, with 13.2, behind Turkey (14.5) and Australia (13.3). But quantity doesn't always translate into quality: the survey also found that only 49 per cent of New Zealanders are happy with their sex lives – perhaps they have too many one-night stands: they apparently have the second-highest number in the world, beaten only by the Norwegians. (There's just one small problem with all this interesting data; people are often 'economical with the truth' when answering questions about their sex lives, and therefore the results of surveys need to be taken with a large pinch of salt!)

Men

The stereotypical Kiwi male is a heavy-drinking, rugged pioneer type with little time for high culture. He's traditionally seen as unemotional, resourceful, non-intellectual, tough, rural, good with animals and machines, and practical (able to turn his hand to almost anything), attributes which he shares with stereotypical pioneer men in other colonial countries such as Australia, Canada, South Africa and the USA.

On average Kiwis lose their virginity at 16.4 years, the global average being 17.3, and adults have sex 114 times per year, ahead of the global average of 103 (and the Aussies, who manage only 108).

This image has persisted – not least because Kiwis still see themselves as practical country men – even though most New Zealanders have been urban dwellers since the late 19th century and fewer and fewer earn their living from the land. Male culture was traditionally said to centre around rugby, racing and beer, although the three Rs (there's an 'r' in beer) no longer dominate male attitudes and pastimes, although beer and rugby remain very popular.

As a hangover from the pioneer days, when physical strength and dexterity were not only valued but vital, Kiwi men have tended to be macho and to do physical work. Although Kiwi women are liberated and are often found doing traditional men's jobs (which was essential in the past when their men-folk were working away from home or at war), the same cannot always be said of Kiwi men when it comes to helping around the house. However, although many unreconstructed Kiwi men stick religiously to their 'traditional' tasks of DIY, tinkering in the shed, gardening and car maintenance, the modern Kiwi man is much more likely to help with the household tasks such as cleaning, cooking, shopping and

child-rearing (particularly driving them to and from sporting events).

The New Zealand male's macho side can have disturbing consequences and their desire to be seen as 'strong, silent types' means that they can be repressed and uncommunicative, which is thought to have contributed to the country having one of the highest suicide rates among young males in the industrialised world.

Women

As well as running most homes and looking after children, New Zealand's women are involved in many areas of public life and are often more independent than women elsewhere. Although not as forthright ('in your face') as some nationalities (Australians, for example), Kiwi women are certainly not afraid to speak their minds and stand up for themselves. The country's egalitarian culture is illustrated by the fact that it was the first to give women the vote (in 1893) and it also has more than its fair share of high-achieving women in many different walks of life, including many of New Zealand's top jobs (see box).

However, this tends to ignore the century since female emancipation, in which New Zealand was far from progressive on women's rights; for example, rape within marriage was only criminalised in the mid '80s.

New Zealand women have traditionally been required to take on a wider range of jobs and learn more skills than was the case in the 'mother country', because in the pioneer days their men-folk were working away from home for days or weeks at a time and later were off at war. This has led to a society in which it's common to find traditional male activities – everything from driving trucks to piloting airliners – undertaken by eminently practical Kiwi women.

New Zealand women have a undeserved reputation for being 'unfeminine', due to their penchant for wearing masculine clothing and spending little time on their makeup and personal grooming. However, although they may not be particularly interested in high fashion (or can afford it) – or are as easily taken in by clever advertising as others – they are as feminine as

New Zealand is the only country in the world where all the most important constitutional roles have been held simultaneously by women, in 2004: the Governor-General (Dame Silvia Rose Cartwright), the Prime Minister (Helen Clark), the Speaker of the New Zealand House of Representatives (Margaret Wilson) and the Chief Justice (Dame Sian Elias).

women anywhere when they wish to be. As with most things, they are practical in their approach to fashion and buy clothes because they are well made, comfortable, durable and won't go out of vogue overnight, rather than simply because they have been endorsed by the latest 'supermodel'.

Abuse of Women

Domestic violence is sometimes described as New Zealand's 'dark secret' and the country has a shocking record of domestic violence and child abuse. Violence against women is a growing problem, especially among Maori and Pacific Islanders. Half of those sentenced for assaults on women in recent years have been Maori, although they comprise some 10 per cent of the country's population. Social workers argue that this is the result of disproportionate numbers of Maori being at the lower end of the socio-economic scale and because men in 'colonised cultures' feel 'disempowered' and take out their feelings on those closest to them.

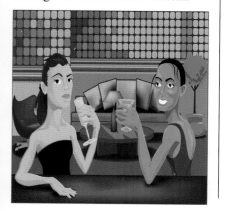

Studies indicate that one in three Kiwi women experiences violence from a partner in her lifetime. In 2006, New Zealand police attended nearly 11,000 incidents of family violence. Some commentators disagree that these figures demonstrate that New Zealand has one of the worst rates of domestic violence in the developed world, but feel that the country is simply better at identifying and monitoring the problem than others.

Homosexuals

New Zealand is tolerant of gays and lesbians, although this is quite a recent development. Same sex activity between men wasn't legalised until 1986 and in December 2004, civil union laws were passed (and implemented in April 2005) that gave legal recognition to gay and lesbian relationships. New Zealand now has one of the world's most liberal attitudes to the immigration of gay couples.

New Zealand's gay scene is centred in Auckland and Wellington, and although it isn't as established or vibrant as Australia's, there are still plenty of 'gay-friendly' bars, cafes, hotels, restaurants and saunas. The limited gay scene is partly the result of New Zealand's small population (and hence modest number of gay inhabitants) and partly because of the general acceptance of gay people, which makes a separate gay scene less necessary.

Some homophobia lingers in macho New Zealand, but most of it is low-level, often unthinking.

MEETING PEOPLE

Meeting people in New Zealand isn't usually a problem as most people are friendly, although they may appear reticent at first; and most people are happy to socialise with their colleagues and business associates, unlike people in many other countries. You'll usually be invited to have a drink or a meal with your colleagues after work (if you aren't, there's something wrong), and even if you find this strange or inhibiting, it's unusual to refuse. You don't have to accept all the time and can make an excuse and leave early, but it's considered an important way to bond with your fellow workers.

> **Singles Scene**
>
> There's an active singles scene in all New Zealand and it's generally easy for young people to meet. However, it isn't so simple for middle-aged or mature people and, as in other developed countries, there are dating agencies and organisations that arrange social events for single people. However, the best way to meet like-minded people is to join a club, particularly a sports club.

Kiwis may not be very forthcoming about themselves, their background, and what they think with new acquaintances, but will gradually open up as they get to know you better. By the same token, they're unlikely to ask personal questions and won't be too familiar or inquisitive (unlike Americans and Australians). New Zealanders prefer to get to know people gradually, in an understated way, and will certainly not try to become your new best friend immediately and appreciate the same approach from others. They also like people to wait their turn in conversations rather than butt in, and not to stand too close (Kiwis don't like their personal space to be invaded).

Although they like to get to know people gradually, Kiwis are sociable people and often strike up conversations with strangers. On the other hand, they can be shy – like their namesake, the kiwi – when it comes to approaching people who are obviously of a different race or from a different culture. This is rarely a sign of xenophobia so much as uncertainty as to how to behave and a desire not to offend. If this is the case, you might have to take the initiative. Because they're such inveterate travellers, Kiwis will be sympathetic to those who are suffering from culture shock because they will invariably have suffered it themselves, probably in a number of countries. In fact, many of the Kiwis you meet may have visited your home country and even lived there for a while (this applies particularly to the British).

Among the many ways to meet people and make friends in New Zealand are:

- **At work** – Meeting people isn't a problem if you're an employee, although you may have to take the initiative and ask others to join you for lunch or coffee, or a drink or meal after work. Office parties aren't common, although most companies organise Christmas lunches and farewell get-togethers for employees leaving their jobs.

- **Expatriate networks** – Expatriates from many countries run a variety of associations, clubs and organisations in cities (ask at embassies and consulates for information). Clubs organise a wide range of social activities including art and music classes, bridge and chess evenings, local history tours, cookery and wine-tasting classes and evenings, sports activities, and theatre and cinema outings.

- **Clubs** – If you want to integrate into your local community or New Zealand society in general, one of the best ways is to join a local club. You can find out about local clubs and societies from town halls, libraries and local newspapers. Sports clubs such as tennis and golf clubs are ideal for meeting people and keeping fit at the same time. Many social clubs allow visitors to use their bars and restaurants, which are usually the best value places to eat, particularly in country towns.

- **School or childcare facilities** – These, or rather the area immediately outside them, provide a ready-made meeting place for parents. Check the school notice board for news about forthcoming events and meetings. Most schools have parents' associations, which are worth joining, and welcome offers of help. Many associations

If you're invited to a Kiwi's home in a rural area, you should offer to remove your shoes before entering. This custom dates from the time when most people worked on the land and their footwear was habitually covered in all sorts of carpet-unfriendly, animal-related substances.

organise social events for parents as well as fund-raising activities.

Paying

If you arrange a get-together, you aren't generally expected to pay. Kiwis don't automatically pay the bill when they invite someone to coffee, lunch or dinner, except when it's a special occasion, when they will offer to pay either before the meal or at the end. Kiwis usually assume they will 'go Dutch', i.e. each person pays for what he has had, when making casual arrangements to eat out (although it isn't such a rigid rule as in Australia). On more informal occasions, those present invariably take it in turns to pay for a round of drinks – make sure you pay for at least one round or offer to share the bill.

INVITATIONS

Receiving Invitations

New Zealand doesn't have a great tradition of home entertaining and Kiwis don't tend to invite people to their homes unless they know them well. If you receive an invitation to a New Zealander's home, it's more likely to be an informal occasion such as a barbecue (barbie) than a formal dinner party. Rather than entertain in the home, many Kiwis socialise in pubs, restaurants and at sporting events. Lunch invitations usually mean you should arrive around 12 or 12.30pm and lunch is usually served around 1pm, although this varies. Dinner is usually served between 7 and 8pm and you're normally asked to arrive half an hour earlier for drinks. You should never arrive earlier than suggested, but equally, arriving very late is considered bad manners in New Zealand. Invitations usually extend to your partner or spouse, but if your host isn't aware you have a partner, it's acceptable to ask for him or her to be included.

If you have children, you shouldn't take them with you unless your host specifically mentions it, e.g. invitations to a barbie may include the whole family.

Vegetarian Guests

Vegetarians used to be rare animals in New Zealand, although nowadays they're fairly common. Most restaurants (particularly ethnic restaurants) provide vegetarian options or are happy to make up something. If you're a vegetarian, your hosts won't be shocked and will usually take this into account and provide an alternative dish, although you should inform them beforehand if possible.

Dress Code

Kiwis are casual dressers and you can generally wear anything in most public places. The standard dress in summer is shorts and jandals (or even shorts and no jandals) – a reflection of the country's egalitarian philosophy, in which dressing up or draping yourself in designer labels to show how wealthy (or insecure) you are is uncommon. Even in the country's better restaurants, the dress code (and the decor) tends to be casual (but **not** shorts and jandals).

However, some restaurants and private clubs have dress rules which may exclude jeans, T-shirts, trainers and shorts, requiring instead 'smart casual' dress, i.e. long trousers (slacks) and a short- or long-sleeved shirt (with a collar) for men and a dress or skirt and blouse for women.

If you're expected to wear anything more formal – such as a suit or a tie – it will be indicated on the invitation card or you'll be told. For social events during the day (such as a barbie), particularly in summer, shorts are *de rigueur*, with jandals and a T-shirt.

However, Kiwis do dress up for formal occasions such as weddings, celebration parties or big public events, but these are exceptions.

Gifts

You may wish to present your hosts with a gift as thanks for their hospitality. Usual gifts include a good bottle of wine (it doesn't need to be New Zealand wine), which is standard practice if you're invited to a dinner party. If you know your hosts well you may wish to give something more personal, e.g. a box of chocolates or a bouquet of flowers for a special occasion such as a birthday or anniversary (always gratefully received by ladies).

Sometimes an invitation will ask you to 'bring a plate', which means a plate of food; this is common for barbies and informal lunches (or a 'pot luck' dinner), where food is pooled and everyone helps themselves.

> 'A man who is sick of chips is tired of life.'
>
> Cilla Brown, Coronation Street

The Meal

Most Kiwis serve two courses plus dessert at lunch and dinner, although many people have two rather than three courses. Portions for guests are invariably generous and the host may insist on serving you extra – it's rude to decline, as it looks as if you don't like the food. Bread and water may be provided, although they aren't customary among Kiwis and you may have to ask for them (don't expect fresh bread to be served at meals).

You should keep your hands above the table at all times, and in common with many countries, cutlery is used from the outside inwards, e.g. the cutlery on the extreme left and right is for the first course. Kiwis tend to use a knife and fork in the British fashion, holding the fork upside down in their left hand and the knife in their right. (They don't generally cut up their food first – as is the custom among Americans – and then eat it with a fork.)

Drinks are usually offered on arrival and may consist of cocktails, beer or wine, which may be accompanied by appetizers (nibbles). Beer or wine may be served with the meal, although wine is more common. Water is also usually served (usually tap water, which is excellent in New Zealand). The host may serve coffee after the meal, which may be anything from strong espresso to weak instant coffee, and may also offer tea. You should remain seated while the meal is served, although it's considered polite to offer to help clear up.

For more information about table etiquette, see **Chapter 8**.

Extending Invitations

If you invite Kiwis to your home for a meal, you should clearly state the occasion, dress code (if anything other than casual) and the time.

When guests bring wine it should usually be served with the meal (unless it's entirely inappropriate or plonk). Most guests will expect drinks and light snacks (e.g. chips and nuts) when they arrive, followed by two courses and dessert – and large portions, so make sure you prepare sufficient food.

> 'It is not true that I don't eat vegetables. I once ate a pea.'
>
> Beau Brummell (English 19th century arbiter of fashion)

A typical dinner consists of meat (barbecues are popular), potatoes and vegetables. Seafood is also usually well received, as New Zealand has some of the best fish and shellfish in the world. If you aren't a great cook, it may be better to buy ready-prepared food, which is widely available in New Zealand's cities. It's advisable to avoid spicy recipes and exotic dishes unless you're preparing typical food from your home country and your guests know what to expect. You should provide salt and pepper, serviettes, and plenty of bread (not ready sliced) and water.

In conversation, Kiwis are generally positive and tend to suggest that everything will turn out all right; there's an air of optimism, confirmed by the common use of positive expressions such as 'she'll be right', 'good as gold' and 'right as rain.'

A simple dessert is fresh fruit, such as bananas, mangoes, pawpaws (papayas), pineapples, pears, apples and citrus fruits. A well-known dessert is pavlova, made with meringue, cream and kiwi or other fruit (see the recipe in chapter 2 – or buy one from a supermarket). Offer coffee after the meal, but serve the coffee and milk separately as some people prefer black coffee. You should also offer decaffeinated coffee and tea, as many people prefer these.

TABOOS

Kiwis don't respond well to people who boast about their achievements or level of wealth, as this is seen as getting above yourself. Traditionally, the average New Zealander hasn't set much store by fame or wealth. To be contented with your life and lot is more important – and most Kiwis are. They don't feel the need to constantly compete and achieve, and they have difficulty understanding people who do. In fact, there's still a tendency to knock success (the 'tall poppy' syndrome, mentioned elsewhere). Behaving in a flashy or pushy way is therefore frowned upon, as is pretending to be an expert in things you obviously

know little about. However, this is changing, and the yuppie way of thinking has begun to permeate (or pollute) New Zealand – particularly Auckland, where the thrusting and aspirational members of society tend to congregate.

Not many subjects are taboo – the word comes from the Maori/Polynesian *tapu*, meaning sacred and therefore not to be touched – but those to avoid until you understand the subjects intimately and are well acquainted with the people you're talking to include: Maori land claims and rights, immigration and the country's high rate of domestic violence.

One of the worst things you can do is to treat New Zealand as if it's a colony or state of Australia, or to compare it unfavourably with Australia. Either of these is akin to treating a Scot as if he's English, or a Canadian as if he's American. Nor is it the done thing to compare New Zealand unfavourably with your home country (as Poms are apt to do), grumble about the weather (the

Kiwis like to do this themselves) or say that New Zealand is a backwater. It's also considered bad form to ask people how much they earn or how much any of their possessions cost. Like the British, many Kiwis are uncomfortable talking directly about sex and favour euphemisms.

Swearing (apart from 'bloody') isn't common in general Kiwi society, especially the 'f' word, although you'll encounter swearing in pubs and at sporting occasions if things are going badly for the local team. You should definitely avoid swearing in front of older people and in 'polite' company. Public drunkenness is frowned upon in New Zealand, as is drinking and driving, although the latter is widespread, particularly in rural areas.

TOPICS OF CONVERSATION

Although usually sociable, Kiwis aren't usually talkative, especially men. You'll notice the frequent use of the words 'you know' in Kiwi conversation – a useful bit of filler when they don't know what to say. Unless the average New Zealand male has had a few drinks and/or the conversation turns to the subject of the All Blacks, it can be an uphill struggle prising many words out of him. As well as administering alcohol and steering the conversation around to the subject of rugby, you can encourage a Kiwi to talk by asking him for advice – which will make him feel useful and valued.

Kiwis like to hear compliments, so feel free to say positive things about their homes and possessions. You'll also be well received if you heap (understated) praise on New Zealand and its achievements. Be particularly complimentary about the country's sporting successes, especially in rugby or netball (the latter when talking to women) and try to keep up with the latest sporting developments, especially the results of the All Blacks and the Super 14 rugby competition. Mocking Australians and yourself will also help you fit in, as will learning something about Maori customs and perhaps a handful of Maori words (see the **Appendices**).

> New Zealanders are noted grumblers, although their grumbling is usually good-natured. The most common things they complain about are politicians and weather

As in the UK, the weather is a common and safe topic of conversation with New Zealanders. In fact, it's a national obsession – perhaps understandable in a country where farming has always been important. There's an ever-changing array of weather to talk about, owing to New Zealand's geographical position – stuck in the middle of a huge body of water, a long way from any large landmass.

Weather forecasters are therefore well-known figures in New Zealand, and Kiwi farmers are especially scathing about them and the inaccuracy of their predictions. Mind you, there has been plenty to complain about in recent years, such as the effects of *El Niño*, alarming holes in the ozone layer, and global warming, which are making life even more difficult for forecasters than usual.

Sport is another favourite topic of conversation in New Zealand and you're advised to keep abreast of the latest sporting developments if you want to join in. Rugby is the main sport to acquaint yourself with, but whenever there's any type of international sporting contest in which New Zealand has some chance of success, most of the country will follow the action with rapt attention and talk about it *ad nauseam*.

Kiwis also like to discuss politics and politicians, particularly if any scandal or impropriety occurs.

MEETING MAORI & PACIFIC ISLANDERS

The best place to experience traditional Maori protocol is at an aforementioned *marae,* and visits are organised by many tour operators (although this obviously isn't as authentic as being invited privately). At a *marae*, the *powhiri* or traditional Maori welcome, begins with a *wero* (challenge). A warrior from the *tangata whenua* (hosts)

challenges the *manuhiri* (guests) – one of whom may be invited to be the group 'leader' for the day.

He might carry a *taiaha* (spear) and lay down a small token, such as a small branch, which the leader of the *manuhiri* will pick up, to show that they come in peace. Then *kuia* (women) from the *tangata whenua* perform a *karanga* (call or chant) to the *manuhiri*. Women from the *manuhiri* respond, as they move onto the *marae* in front of their men.

Once inside the *wharenui* (meeting house) on the *marae*, *mihimihi* (greetings) and *whaikorero* (speeches) are made. To reinforce the good wishes expressed in the speeches, *waiata* (songs) are sometimes sung.

The guests then usually offer a *koha* (present) to the hosts, after greeting them with a *hongi*, the ceremonial touching of noses. After the welcome, hosts and guests may share *kai* (food).

There is little violence in New Zealand and aggressive or confrontational behaviour in public is unusual.

Maori culture differs from *Pâkehâ* ways, and there are a number of rules you should observe when socialising with them, including the following:

- Never touch a Maori's head with your hands because the head is regarded as the most sacred part of the body.

- Maori find it offensive if people sit on a table where food has or will be served.

- You must be careful regarding the *marae* (see **Chapter 2**) and always obtain permission; remove your footwear before entering and refrain from chewing gum, drinking, eating or smoking.

- Obtain permission before photographing Maori buildings and Maori or Polynesian people.

- Polynesians tend to be modest, so avoid making too much eye contact.

- Don't sit higher than a Polynesian as this is regarded as rude.

CONFRONTATION

Kiwis tend to be laid-back and understated and to avoid confrontation, preferring to negotiate. For example, in the event of a disagreement over a question of law (e.g. a business contract), Kiwis prefer to discuss the matter and reach a compromise rather than calling in lawyers.

Kiwis don't tend to become excited or emotional about things – except sport (particularly rugby) – drunken brawls and confrontations at sporting events have been cited as one reason for the slowness in liberalising New Zealand's licensing laws.

DEALING WITH THE POLICE

Despite being dogged by some recent controversies ('inappropriate' emails, sexual misconduct, alleged mistreatment of prisoners and the falsification of crime statistics, etc.), New Zealand's police officers have a good reputation. The Kiwi police force is considered to be one of the least corrupt in the world, and officers are generally helpful, friendly and easy to deal with (provided you behave the same way).

If the police ask you to stop (on the street or while driving) you must do so, but if they ask you to accompany them to a police station, you aren't obliged to do so unless you're formally placed under arrest. The police also cannot search your home or vehicle without your consent or a search warrant.

5.

THE LANGUAGE BARRIER

English is the official language of New Zealand and it's universally used in all aspects of Kiwi life. However, even if English is your mother tongue, you shouldn't expect to understand everything Kiwis say as most Kiwis speak *Newzild*, or New Zealand English, which contains a lot of slang and colloquialisms. These may be unfamiliar to other English speakers (particularly Americans) and those for whom English is a second language.

'Language is the source of misunderstandings.'

Antoine de Saint-Exupéry (French writer).

New Zealand also has a second official language, Maori, the language of indigenous New Zealanders, which is also described in this chapter. Learning to speak a foreign language is never easy and is full of potential pitfalls – all expats have stories to tell of when they have said 'the wrong thing', often with embarrassing consequences. To help keep your own collection of anecdotes as small as possible, this chapter gives an insight into communicating in New Zealand English, Maori and body language (and its importance in communication), as well as forms of address and greetings.

ENGLISH IS ESSENTIAL

A good knowledge of English is a pre-requisite for living and working (or even holidaying) in New Zealand. If you cannot speak and write English well, not only will you find it extremely difficult to get a job, but you probably won't qualify for any sort of work visa in the first place. You will, however, be relieved to hear that you won't be required to speak Maori (which was made an official language in 1974) as well. Although New Zealand is officially bilingual and there have even been proposals to replace some English place names with Maori names, English is the major language of business and is spoken by everyone.

New Zealanders aren't generally adept at speaking foreign languages – though some shrewd New Zealanders with an eye to the future have made great strides in Chinese, Japanese and other Asian languages.

NEW ZEALAND ENGLISH

New Zealand English, often colloquially referred to as *Newzild*, is close to Australian English in pronunciation, but has several subtle differences which usually go unnoticed by people from outside these countries. Some of these differences show New Zealand English to have more affinity with the British English, as spoken in London and south-east England, than Australian English does, and also reflect the influence of Maori. The New Zealand accent also has some Scottish influences, particularly in the southern region of the South Island, as a result of the large number of Scottish settlers in the early 19th century.

A distinct Kiwi variant of the English language has been in existence since the late 19th century, although it probably goes back further than that. From the beginning of British settlement on the islands, a new dialect began to form, due to the need to adopt Maori words to describe the flora and fauna of New Zealand, for which English didn't have any words of its own.

The most striking difference from Australian and other forms of English (although shared partly with South African English) is the flattened 'i' of New Zealand English.

There's also a tendency to shorten words (a characteristic shared with Australia) so that they end in o, y or ie; for example, afternoon becomes 'arvo', kindergarten 'kindy', position 'pozzy' and mosquito 'mozzy'.

> The world's longest place name is found in New Zealand; in southern Hawke's Bay, 44km/27mi south of the Waipukurau, there's a sign marking a hill: 'Taumatawhakatangihangak-oauauotamateaturipukakapikimaun-gahoonukapkaiwhenuakitanatahu', roughly translated means 'the hilltop where Tamatea with big knees, conqueror of mountains, eater of land, traveller over land and sea, played his koauau to his beloved'.

New Zealand English invariably follows British English spelling rather than American English spelling, for example 'colour' rather than 'color' and 'travelled' rather than 'traveled'. However, some American English forms have managed to creep into the country, for example 'thru' rather than 'through', although these are informal, non-standard spellings.

New Zealand English has a few other spelling quirks, e.g. 'fiord' rather than 'fjord', but Brits will be relieved to learn that Kiwis pronounce the last letter of the alphabet 'zed' rather than 'zee', e.g. the initials of the country, NZ, are pronounced 'en-zed'.

Kiwis of all origins often use Maori words (see below); for example the friendly Maori greeting *kia ora* is frequently heard, although the usual informal greeting is

'g'day'. For those who wish to learn more about New Zealand English, the *Reed Dictionary of New Zealand English* and the Oxford University Press's *Dictionary of New Zealand English* are useful sources of information about definitions and pronunciation.

Differences from British English

New Zealand English has experienced what linguistics experts call a 'vowel shift' in relation to the 'parent' language: front vowels are invariably pronounced higher in the mouth than in British English. 'Pan' tends to sound like 'pen', 'pen' like 'pin', 'pin' like 'pun', 'pair' like 'peer' and 'ferry' like 'fairy'. Some New Zealanders insert a so-called 'schwa' into words such as grown, mown and thrown, which become grow-en, mo-wen and throw-en. But groan, moan and throne don't suffer this fate, which means that these words can be distinguished by the ear, unlike in British English – how helpful of the Kiwis.

On the other hand, in stronger New Zealand accents, words like 'chair' and 'cheer' are pronounced in the same way, i.e. like 'cheer' in American, Australian and British English. The same is found with share and shear, bear and beer, and spare and spear. But some New Zealanders pronounce such words differently from each other.

> 'Howareyou' is often said to strangers, as you might say 'good morning' or 'hello' to somebody you pass when out walking the dog; in these circumstances, a smile or nod is the usual response.

A curious modern development Kiwis share with Australians is a tendency to end their sentences on a rising inflection (known to linguistics' experts as a 'high rising terminal'), which makes statements sound like questions. They also tend to end sentences with 'eh'; for example, 'we're off to the airport, eh', making the statement open rather than an order, and inviting the other person to reply or disagree.

New Zealanders also have a tendency to use the third person feminine 'she' to replace the third person neuter 'it', especially when the subject is the first word of a sentence, e.g. 'she's a beaut, your car, mate' (i.e. 'what a splendid motor vehicle you have, my fine fellow' in British English). This is most commonly found in the favourite Kiwi expression 'she'll be right', which means 'it will be all right' or 'it's near enough to what's needed'.

Differences from Australian English

New Zealand English is similar to Australian English in pronunciation, but has several differences that often go unnoticed by people from outside the two countries. Kiwi English is more similar to the English spoken in southern England than is Aussie English, and it has been influenced by the Maori language as well as by the pronunciation of the Irish and Scots, who settled in the country in large numbers in the 19th century.

The most obvious difference between New Zealand and Australian English is the former's flattened or clipped 'i' (also found in South African English), which can make 'fish and chips' sound like 'fush and chups', or even 'f'sh and ch'ps.' In contrast, the 'i' in Aussie English is lengthened, even when set against British English, perhaps because of the influence of Italian immigrants; thus, 'fish and chips' becomes 'feesh and cheeps' in some areas. It's thought that the Kiwi shortened 'i' might come from a combination of a Scottish English influence and from the way that native Maori speakers pronounce English vowels.

New Zealand English's short 'e' sounds like a short 'i' to other English speakers; for example 'eggs for breakfast' becomes 'iggs for brickfist' and 'collect' becomes 'collict.' The Kiwi pronunciation of words such as 'dance' uses the vowel sound of 'a' in 'far,' like British English's broad 'a'. Aussies, in contrast, would rhyme it with 'ants.'

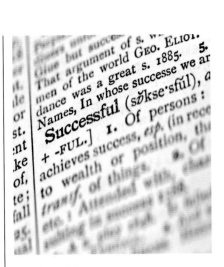

Regional Accents

Geographical variations in New Zealand English are small and generally restricted to specialist local words. However, one group has a distinct way of speaking: the so-called 'Celtic fringe' of people in the south of the South Island, who have a 'Southland burr' characterised by a trilled 'r'. This part of New Zealand received a lot of immigrants from Scotland and locals use typically Scottish words such as 'wee' (small – heard throughout the country nowadays) and phrases like 'to do the messages' (to go shopping). Many of the region's place names also display Scottish Gaelic origins, including the two largest cities, Dunedin and Invercargill.

> Some Kiwis from the west coast of the South Island have an Aussie twang to their accent, a legacy of 19th century gold-rush settlers from New Zealand's nearest neighbour.

MANNERS & GREETINGS

New Zealanders, are generally polite and it's usual to say 'sorry' when you bump into someone or block their path (Kiwis say it all the time, even when they aren't at fault). It's also considered polite to say 'please' and 'thank you' when requesting something or asking a question (or when being served in a shop) irrespective of the situation or the 'rank' of the person you ask.

This differs considerably from the practice in many other countries, where please and thank you may be implied but are often omitted from speech.

When meeting Kiwi men, a firm handshake and eye contact are expected. As for greeting Kiwi women, follow their lead: take a hand if one is extended, but some Kiwi women greet new acquaintances with a smile. In fact, it's an appealing feature of Kiwis that they tend to smile in public, even at strangers – the type of behaviour that can get you arrested or assaulted on the London underground. A common greeting is 'How are you' (which tends to be delivered as if it's one word), to which the expected reply is 'Fine thanks' – don't launch into an extended account of how you actually are.

MAORI

The Maori language was brought to New Zealand by Polynesians, most likely from Cook Island and Tahiti. An Eastern Polynesian tongue, it's closely related to Tahitian and Cook Islands Maori, slightly less closely to Hawaiian and Marquesan, and more distant from the West Polynesian languages, Niuean, Samoan and Tongan.

In the last 200 years it has gone from being the predominant language of the country for 500 years or more, until the arrival of *Pākehā* (whites) in the 19th century, to becoming a minority language. Maori is the second most widely-spoken language in New Zealand and is an official language, although it's rare to hear it spoken outside the Maori community (except on ceremonial occasions). It's spoken mainly in the North Island, particularly in the far North, Central & Eastern areas, where there

> The Maori call their language either te reo Māori (the Maori language) or simply Māori, which means 'normal', 'natural' or 'ordinary', and is used to refer to both the Maori people and their language. In legends and other oral traditions, the word Maori distinguished ordinary mortal human beings from deities and spirits (wairua). There's no word in Maori for a Maori-speaking person or a non-Maori speaking person.

are sizeable Maori communities.

It's estimated that in the early 21st century, Maori was spoken by some 130,000 people – or around a third of all Maori – or 4 per cent of the total population of New Zealand (nearly all of Maori descent). However, the level of competence of those claiming to be Maori speakers is unknown, and it's estimated that the number of fluent speakers is less than a quarter (mostly aged over 50) of the total number of speakers (very few people speak only Maori). There are a few dialects of Maori, but they are nothing like the barrier to comprehension that many non-speakers believe. There are also some regional variants of pronunciation and accent, and a small number of lexical differences – but it's basically a single language throughout the country.

Pronunciation

Like other oral languages, written Maori is phonetic, and was first recorded by English missionaries, prior to which there was no written language. Every letter represents a sound and is pronounced, and there are no silent letters (as in English).

at a time. Individual vowels are pronounced separately and somewhat slurred into each other. Some examples of pronunciation are:

Letters	Pronunciation
Te	tay
Wai	why
Tapu	tahpu
Mana	mahna
Iwi	eewee
Haka	hahka

Maori has five vowel sounds: a, e, i, o and u. The 'a' is as in car, the 'e' as in egg, the 'i' like ee, the 'o' as in four and the 'u' like the 'o' in to. Maori has eight consonants similar to the English h, k, m, n, p, r, t and w and two others: wh and ng. In many Maori words 'wh' is pronounced like the English 'f', while 'ng' resembles the English 'ng' as in sing, the difference being that in Maori, words can begin with ng.

Contemporary English-language usage tends to avoid pluralising the word 'Maori' (i.e. 'Maoris'); the standard Maori language has no 's' sound and generally expresses plurals using preceding articles. Note that the word Maori is written Māori in Maori, with a macron (a line) over the letter 'a' to denote a long 'a' sound.

Maori Influence on English

There are many words in New Zealand English which have been taken from Maori, particularly animal, place and plant names, although important Maori cultural terms are also known and used by

Pākehā. This process of borrowing slowed in the early 20th century, but has been revitalised in the last few decades, particularly in the North Island, with the revival of Maori culture and increased interest in it.

Many native animals and plants retain their Maori names in New Zealand English, including birds (e.g. kakapo, kea, kiwi, moa, pukeko and weka), fish (such as hapuku and tarakihi) and plants (e.g. kanuka, kumara, manuka, rimu, totara and tutu). There are regional variations; for example, in much of New Zealand the native wood pigeon is called the kereru, but in Northland it's known as the kukupa or kuku, and it's called the parea on the Chatham Islands.

The odd hybrid word has come into use, part-English and part-Maori, the best known being half-pai (often written as half-pie), which means incomplete or of inferior quality – pai is Maori for 'good'. In similar fashion, the Maori ending 'tanga' (which is similar to the English ending 'ness') is sometimes used in hybrid words like kiwitanga, which means the state of being a New Zealander.

There are also hundreds of words in Maori which are derived from English. In the 19th and much of the 20th century, many Maori place names suffered the indignity of inelegant Anglicisation. The Maori revival in recent years has seen a reversion to correct pronunciation, although the Anglicised versions (e.g. Otahuhu is usually shortened to Otahu) have tended to endure among local inhabitants, and correct pronunciation marks you as an outsider.

See **Appendix D** for a list of Maori words in common general use.

Official Use

The Maori language enjoys the equivalent status de jure as English in government and law, although it continues to be marginalised in mainstream use. Most public services are available only in English, although some government departments provide translations or Maori-speaking translators on request. Citizens have the right to conduct business with government agencies in Maori, although in practice this almost always requires an interpreter. This restricts its everyday use to the limited geographical areas of high Maori fluency (e.g. Auckland, Gisborne, the Bay of Plenty and Northland)

and to more formal occasions. New Zealand citizens can request to be addressed in Maori in a court of law, and the court is expected to provide a translator, although the proceedings will be recorded only in English. However, key government documents, such as the census and other important documents, are usually translated into Maori.

Most government departments and agencies now have bilingual names, for example, the Department of Internal Affairs is known as Te Tari Taiwhenua; local government offices and public libraries also have bilingual signs, as do all national and local government services (such as the police and ambulance services).

> ### Kia-ora
>
> The Maori greeting, kia-ora, has entered New Zealand English; it means literally 'be well/healthy' and in a more formal sense is a traditional greeting of 'good health'. It's used today both as 'hello' and 'goodbye', and is a popular phrase (it has also been adopted by a number of businesses and is the name of a well-known concentrated orange drink).

Education

In the late 19th century, the English school system was introduced for all New Zealanders, and from the 1880s the use of Maori in school was forbidden. Increasing numbers of Maori people learned English, though most Maori still spoke Maori as a native language until World War II. Worship was in Maori and it was the language of the Maori home and political meetings, and some

literature and many newspapers were published in Maori.

However, by the 1970s fewer than 20 per cent of Maori spoke the language well enough to be considered native speakers, and even for many of those it was no longer the language of the home. Maori educators became concerned that their language might be lost, and initiated a Maori language recovery program. There has been an increase in Maori language revitalisation efforts in recent years, and many people, both Maori and Pākehā, have learnt Maori as a second language at universities, polytechnics and other organisations.

To preserve the language, a network of Kōhanga Reo (language nests) was established; these are basically pre-schools where children (tamariki) learn the Maori language and culture, but which became a movement promoting Maori self-determination. There are also Kura Kaupapa (Maori immersion schools) as well as bilingual units attached to many mainstream schools. In 2004, a government-funded TV station committed to Maori-language programmes, began broadcasting.

> The Maori name for New Zealand is Aotearoa, which is generally translated as 'the land of the long white cloud'. It originally applied only to the North Island but nowadays is generally used to refer to the whole of New Zealand.

FOREIGN LANGUAGES

It isn't unusual to hear foreign languages in New Zealand, especially in expatriate communities in the major cities. Many migrants predominantly use their mother tongue on a day-to-day basis and some may have only a smattering of English. New Zealand isn't a multicultural country in the way Australia, Canada and the UK are, but has significant East Asian and Pacific Island communities whose mother tongue is Maori or another Polynesian language.

New Zealand also has a significant number of speakers of east Asian languages, notably Cantonese, Japanese, Korean and Mandarin. Some two-thirds of Asian immigrants live in the Auckland region, while most of the rest live in the Wellington area and Christchurch. New Zealand also has smaller numbers of speakers of other languages, notably Arabic, Russian and (former) Yugoslavian languages.

BODY LANGUAGE

Kiwi body language is similar to that of the UK. Physical contact between heterosexual men is minimal and New Zealanders don't generally hug or kiss one another unless they're from a culture where this is common practice (or they're gay). Similarly, putting your arm around the shoulder of another person or on their arm may be considered too intimate, unless it's a close friend or someone who needs physical help. Kiwis tend to like more personal space than those in many other cultures – at least two or three feet is normal.

It's usual to shake hands on meeting – in formal situations you should wait to be introduced – and men should wait for a woman to offer her hand first (although women usually shake hands with other women). You should maintain eye contact when conversing; people who don't are said to be 'shifty-eyed', and betray a lack of confidence or sincerity. You should cover your mouth when yawning or using a tooth pick.

Common gestures generally include the following:

- shrugging the shoulders – meaning 'I don't know' or 'maybe';
- nodding – 'yes';
- shaking the head – 'no';
- thumbs up – agreement;

- thumbs down – disagreement;
- pointing – generally aggressive, and to be avoided;
- raising one or two fingers – insulting, and definitely to be avoided.

The traditional Maori greeting is to press noses (hongi, literally smell), and often the forehead, together. This isn't, as is often assumed by westerners, a rubbing of noses but a 'sharing of breath', with participants inhaling nasally in a single breath. The hongi is considered a sacred act by Maori and is performed between the same and opposite sexes. It isn't, however, usually performed between Maori and Pākehā (non-Maori) business partners.

You must take care not to touch a Maori's head – which is regarded as the most sacred part of the body – with your hands. Polynesians tend to be modest, therefore you should avoid making too much eye contact.

Pokarekare Ana (love song by Paraire Tomoana)

Maori	English Translation
Pokarekare ana	How placid are the ripples
Nha wai on Waiapu	Of restless Waiapu
Whiti atu koe hine	Dear, they know of your returning
Marino ana e	From far across the sea
Ehine e	Dear heart of mine
Hoki mai ra	I'll wait for thee
Ka mate ahau	My love is thine alone
I te aroha e	To eternity

Auckland at night

6.

THE NEW ZEALANDERS AT WORK

One of the most common mistakes foreigners make when moving abroad to work or start a business, is to assume that they can continue working in the way they did in their home country, particularly if they had a successful business there. Many expatriates completely underestimate the dramatic differences in business culture between countries. Depending on where you come from, working in New Zealand can involve a fairly steep learning curve – professionally, linguistically and culturally.

This chapter provides information on working for or with the Kiwis, setting up a business and business etiquette.

The most difficult part of working in New Zealand for many people isn't finding a job – it's obtaining a work permit.

WORK ETHIC

Kiwis are not live-to-work people and the country isn't awash with high-achieving wheeler-dealers; added to which, a long history of full employment and a generous welfare state have created a laid-back 'weekend' culture. In recent decades, New Zealanders have had to become more entrepreneurial to adapt to the changing world and increasing competition, and have become more business-minded and adventurous since the '80s. The proportion (around 15 per cent) of Kiwis who are self-employed or run their own business is now one of the highest in the world.

That said, Kiwis tend to avoid talking about business and the economy, mainly because not many know much about either (certainly outside their particular field) – an ignorance which is reflected in the low readership figures for business publications in New Zealand. This attitude to business is an extension of the country's tall-poppy syndrome: business success isn't lauded in New Zealand in the way that it is in, for example, the US. That doesn't mean that business success is frowned on – if you start from scratch, battle against the odds and succeed, but are modest about it and don't flaunt the trappings of success, you'll be highly regarded – the appropriate cliché here is 'It isn't what you do but the way that you do it that counts'.

New Zealand's informality is carried into the workplace, where the atmosphere is invariably laid-back and relaxed, with everybody on first-name terms. A loud, pushy or rude approach to work will get you nowhere. Kiwis' predominantly work-to-live attitude means that workers know their entitlements and take all available holidays. Nevertheless, everybody is expected to do his share, which is an expression of the Kiwi preoccupation with fairness.

When you start a new job, it's quite likely that you'll be teased for the first week or two. This is a light-hearted test to see whether you can fit in and are a 'good sport'. The best way to respond is to laugh at yourself and not be offended. If you're from an Asian country you may find this 'ribbing' difficult to handle, but bear in mind that in Kiwi culture, allowing yourself to be mocked doesn't involve a loss of face but rather the opposite: an increase in your standing.

WORKING WOMEN

As might be expected in a country with a female prime minister, New Zealand has an egalitarian approach to women in the workplace. This stems from the country's long tradition of women doing jobs that in most other western countries have traditionally been in the male domain; this dates back to the pioneer days when men were digging out stumps, fording rivers and generally being tough guys, and women had to take care of everything at home. So it isn't unusual in New Zealand to come across female factory workers, lorry drivers and politicians: the country has had two female prime ministers and over a quarter of New Zealand's politicians are women.

> The official rate of unemployment in New Zealand is among the lowest in the world – in March 2006 it was just 3.9 per cent.

Nearly half of Kiwi women work, which is a reasonably high percentage compared with other countries. This is possible partly because of New Zealand's excellent system of nursery education; but female employment has also been boosted by the growth in service industries, which include careers popular with women.

There's no reason why women shouldn't take jobs in almost any industry, although, as in other countries, women tend to prefer the caring professions and education. Women have also made good progress in professions such as law, medicine, advertising and publishing, although few reach the higher echelons. For more information, contact the National Advisory Council on the Employment of Women (NACEW, 🖳 www.nacew.govt.nz) or the Ministry of Women's Affairs (🖳 www.mwa.govt.nz).

> The Equal Employment Opportunities Trust (EEO, 🖳 www.eeotrust.org.nz) is a non-profit organisation that promotes equal opportunities in the workplace. It has around 300 member organisations from a wide range of employment sectors who are committed to EEO policies and ideas, and their employees generally enjoy greater equality at work.

All members of the workforce are entitled to equal pay for equal work under the Equal Pay Act 1972. In practice, the average wage tends to be marginally lower for both female and ethnic minority workers. A recent survey by Statistics New Zealand revealed that women's wages were, on average, much lower than men's, but this is partly because women and ethnic minorities are more likely to do unskilled or semi-skilled work, and because they often work part-time. Discrimination in the workplace is illegal under the Human Rights Act 1972, which protects employees against discrimination on all grounds, including their sex, that are irrelevant to the performance of a job.

WORK VISAS & PERMITS

The three main categories (known as 'streams') of residence in the New Zealand Immigration Programme are: the Skilled/Business, the Family Sponsored and International/Humanitarian streams. The Skilled/Business stream makes up around 60 per cent of the places under the New Zealand Immigration programme (around 27,000 per year), an indication that the country's priority is to attract immigrants who will benefit its economy. There are a variety of sub-streams within the Skilled/Business stream, with strict criteria that must be met. Nevertheless, work visas are granted to foreigners only when no suitable New Zealand citizen or resident is available to do a job. They aren't based on a points system and each case is treated on its merits, taking into account the availability of local labour.

To obtain a work visa you must have a firm offer of a job in writing and apply to the New Zealand immigration Service (NZIS), which

the type of job you're seeking– the more skilled the position, the better your English must be. When you apply for residence in the Skilled/Business stream (see above) you must prove that you have an English-speaking background, and/or must pass a test set by the International English Language Testing System.

> Work and Income provides help with job applications, writing CVs and training, and provides many helpful brochures such as Getting Work Skills and Experience and Need Help to Find Work?, which can be downloaded from its website (💻 www.workandincome.govt.nz).

can be done from abroad or in New Zealand (if, for example, you arrive as a visitor and then wish to work). The visa fee is between $150 and $300 (depending on where it's issued) and isn't refundable if your application is rejected. A work visa allows you to travel to New Zealand to undertake a period of temporary work. It isn't applicable to those planning to take up permanent residence in the country, and applies mostly to contract workers and other short-term employees. On arrival in New Zealand you're issued with a work permit, which applies to one job for a specified period – in most cases a maximum of three years but often for a much shorter period.

FINDING A JOB

Qualifications

The most important qualification for a job in New Zealand is a good level of spoken and written English. All employers expect their staff to have adequate English, which varies with

With regard to formal qualifications, it's a condition of employment for most jobs in New Zealand that overseas qualifications must compare with New Zealand's standards, and be accepted by local employers. An organisation called the New Zealand Qualifications Authority (NZQA) assesses foreign qualifications to determine whether they meet New Zealand standards. Information and forms are available from the NZIS, or direct from NZQA, PO Box 160, Wellington (💻 www.nzqa.govt.nz).

Registration

For certain jobs, you must register with the appropriate New Zealand professional organisation, which involves an assessment of your professional or trade qualifications and leads to membership of the appropriate body, thus allowing you to work in New Zealand. If your trade or profession is one where registration is required, you should contact the appropriate body well in advance, as you may need to take an examination or undergo a period of retraining, for which you must pay. In some cases, examinations can be taken in other countries, although they may be held on one or two days a year only. Since January 1996, it has been necessary to obtain registration (where applicable) before applying for permanent residence.

Government Employment Service

The New Zealand government employment service is run by an agency called Work and Income, which is part of the Ministry of Social Development (MSD). The MSD was established in 2001 to provide social policy advice to the New Zealand government and provide income support and employment services to New Zealanders (which it does to over a million people). Work and Income has, in government-speak, 'a focus on getting people into employment and gaining independence'.

Salaries in the major cities of Auckland and Wellington are markedly higher than in the rest of the country, where they're around 20 per cent lower. This reflects not only the fact that living costs are higher in these cities, but also the tendency for jobs there to carry more responsibility (i.e. stress).

It recommends that job applicants should spend at least 11 hours a week looking for work and should contact Work and Income at least once every two weeks. When people enrol with Work and Income, they are sometimes asked to make a Job Seeker Agreement, which sets out their responsibilities in an agreed plan to help them prepare for work.

Those caring for a child under 14 aren't asked to look for full-time work but might be asked to seek part-time employment or prepare for future work.

Work and Income operates a Job Bank, an online tool which job seekers can access from computers at Work and Income service centres. It's updated every half an hour with new job vacancies submitted by employers throughout New Zealand.

Salary

It's quite easy to determine the salary you should command in New Zealand, as they're usually quoted in job advertisements. However, New Zealand employers can be rather coy when quoting salary figures, using terms such as 'salary to' – for example, 'salary to $60,000' usually means you're highly unlikely to receive $60,000 and the employer is probably thinking in terms of paying $45,000 (he just wants to attract as much interest as possible). The term 'negotiable' is frequently used in job advertisements, e.g. 'salary $60,000 negotiable', which means that you'll need to work hard to convince the employer that you're worth $60,000. However, if you have qualifications or skills that are in short supply, you may be able to negotiate an even higher salary. For example, the wool industry was thrown into turmoil when shearers began flocking to Australia in their hundreds in search of higher pay, and the Shearing Contractors' Organisation was forced to raise pay rates by 20 per cent.

A national minimum wage applies in New Zealand, which is currently $9.50 per hour. This doesn't, however, apply to those aged under 18, to whom the 'youth minimum wage' of $7.60 an hour applies. A recent survey carried out by Statistics New Zealand revealed that some 40,000 adult employees received less than the legal minimum wage but that most (over 1m) earned at least 30 per cent more than the legal minimum wage. The average hourly wage in December 2006 was

> Until Britain joined the European Economic Community (now the European Union), the UK was New Zealand's major export market, but it's now only the fifth-largest after Australia, the US, Japan and China.

$22.36. However, as few wages in New Zealand are negotiated on a collective basis, a huge variation in pay occurs in different industries and areas.

Executive and professional salaries are much lower than in other developed countries, such as Australia, France, Germany, Japan, the UK and the US, although a lower cost of living (particularly housing) compensates to a certain extent. The average salary for top company bosses is around $250,000. Executive salaries are often subject to much greater annual rises (e.g. 10 per cent) than average wages, which are around 2 or 3 per cent annually (in line with inflation).

New Zealand's employers don't traditionally shower executives with fringe benefits on top of their basic salary package, but may offer certain benefits to lure an outstanding applicant. Nevertheless, company cars are widespread at executive level, as are health insurance benefits (around 55 per cent of posts) and superannuation or pension schemes (around 60 per cent). Productivity bonuses and profit sharing may also be offered. Relocation costs and contributions towards housing expenses are usually offered only to employees with particularly rare skills (but it's worth asking).

STARTING A BUSINESS

Many of New Zealand's businesses are small or of medium size and are therefore able to respond quickly to changing market conditions than larger operations. Kiwis tend to concentrate on niche areas, as the country has a small economy and population; the country excels in certain specialist areas, including biotechnology, earthquake-resistant engineering (the country's geographical position astride two tectonic plates provides engineers with plenty of opportunities for research), electrical engineering, film production, food, tourism, wine production, wood processing, and yacht design and manufacturing. Farming and related industries remain important but less so than in the past.

Other areas in which New Zealand excels are information technology and export. Many businesses in New Zealand have benefited greatly from the information technology revolution, which has minimised the negative effects of New Zealand's geographical isolation; the country manufactures most of the tools that make the computer chips used used in California's Silicon Valley.

New Zealand business has long been geared towards exporting – not surprisingly, given its small domestic market. Dairy produce, meat and wool are still significant exports, but they've been joined by many of the country's specialised products, including children's cots, green-lipped mussels, Pinot Noir and Sauvignon Blanc wines, shark cartilage and racing yachts.

New Zealand promotes itself energetically abroad, with a campaign called 'The New Zealand Way', which spreads the word that the country is thrusting and vibrant, with a creative, innovative way of doing business.

Trades Unions

New Zealand doesn't have such as strong a trades union culture as it used to. At the end of the '80s, almost half of the workforce belonged to one of the country's 175 trades unions, which has now fallen below 20 per cent.

Business Entities

The simplest form of business entity in New Zealand is an individual trading on his own, which involves unlimited liability. There are no accounting, auditing or reporting requirements other than the need to keep accounts for the IRD (tax authorities). You can also form a partnership, which is governed by the Partnership Act, 1908, where it's usual to have a formal written agreement between parties. This doesn't need to be drafted by a lawyer, as the rights and responsibilities of each partner are governed by the agreement rather than by employment law. A partnership can be special, where some partners have limited liability but may not be involved in the management of the business, or general, in which case all partners have unlimited liability.

A limited company or corporation can be established under the Companies Act, 1993, which makes no distinction between a public and a private limited company. There's no requirement to appoint a secretary, and directors can be held personally liable for the debts of their company if they're found not to have carried out their duties properly. Registration of a company is a relatively simple procedure (costing between around $100 and $200) and involves making an application to the New Zealand Companies Office (⌨ www.companies.govt.nz) giving details of the directors, the registered address and the company's constitution.

Legislation

New Zealand's business legislation is halfway between that of the UK and US (lightly regulated), and France and Germany (heavily

> If your business involves practising a trade or profession that requires registration in New Zealand, you must register before you can start trading.

regulated). It has one of the least regulated economies in the Pacific region and few restrictions on businesses, where market forces dictate the location, size and type of businesses, rather than government regulations. New Zealand also offers a well-developed infrastructure, skilled labour force, low levels of corruption and low tariffs, which all adds up to a business-friendly environment.

On the other hand, the country has a plethora of employment legislation regarding matters such as annual leave, minimum wages, public holidays and compassionate leave. Since 1st April 2007, the culture of fair treatment entitles workers to at least four weeks' annual leave plus 11 paid public holidays. Both parents are entitled to leave when a child is born, as are those who adopt children under the age of five. New Zealand grants paternity leave of two weeks and maternity leave of 14 weeks, plus ten days during a pregnancy for pregnancy-related matters.

SELF-EMPLOYMENT

Restrictions

There are few restrictions regarding the kind of business that can be started or purchased by new migrants in New Zealand. Foreign involvement in telecommunications and transport used to be restricted, but this is no longer the case and American investors raced to snap up New Zealand companies the minute ownership controls were relaxed. Restrictions have also been eased in broadcasting, which was the last bastion to be protected by law. Government approval via the Overseas Investment Commission (🖳 www.oic.govt.nz) is required in the case of foreign investments (at least 25 per cent of a business), when the business or property is worth over $50m, or when the land occupied is over 5ha (12 acres) and/or worth more than $10m.

Government Help

The Ministry of Economic Development (33 Bowen Street, PO Box 1473, Wellington, 🖳 www.med.govt.nz) operates several schemes to help and advise those wishing to run their own business (whether starting from scratch or buying an existing business) and also to help small businesses grow. They can help with planning and preparation; understanding the law regarding business names, taxation and other financial regulations; locating premises; finding staff; marketing; and management. As with free government services in any country, the help provided is limited, but you're directed to other sources of help. The Ministry publishes *Connectionz*, a quarterly newsletter containing business news and information. If you know the kind of business you wish to

start it's advisable to contact the relevant trade association (your local chamber of commerce can put you in touch).

> It's legal (under certain circumstances) to arrive in New Zealand on a tourist visa, find a job and then apply for residence, although most other countries don't permit this.

Finance

You should usually plan on providing at least 50 per cent of the cost of a business purchase or start-up. New Zealand banks look more favourably on an application for a loan if you have a substantial sum to invest, not to mention good business experience and a well thought-out business plan. As with banks elsewhere, they also expect security for a loan – preferably in the form of property in New Zealand.

BLACK ECONOMY

New Zealand used to have a reputation as something of a 'soft touch' when it came to illegal working, particularly among immigrants who had been turned

away by countries such as Australia, Canada and the US, which had stricter immigration regulations. New Zealand's work regulations and enforcement were lax in comparison, and a blind eye was often turned to those working without the necessary visa. Many people who worked illegally had been refused a permit or didn't bother applying at all, and simply settled in New Zealand as 'permanent visitors'.

In the last few decades, however, the New Zealand government has become increasingly concerned about the country becoming an immigration 'dustbin' for those refused by other countries, particularly the unskilled from poor Asian countries, who have tended to regard the country as a promised land. High unemployment in the early '90s meant that a blind eye could no longer be turned to illegal workers – even those doing unpleasant and poorly paid jobs, which in the past New Zealanders wouldn't consider. As a result, new laws were introduced that provided stiffer penalties for illegal workers (including fast-track deportation) and fines for anyone who employed them. The police and immigration authorities have begun to enforce the regulations, mounting periodic dawn raids on companies likely to employ illegal workers, such as fruit farms and large factories.

> **Kiwis are impressed by visitors who are aware of Anzac Day and Waitangi Day (see below) and what they commemorate.**

Despite tougher immigration regulations, many employers still won't ask to see your visa or immigration papers before taking you on. They will, however, usually expect to see your IRD (tax) number.

This can be obtained from the nearest IRD office by producing your immigration papers and proof of your permanent address in New Zealand, such as a utility bill or driving licence.

BUSINESS ETIQUETTE

In the workplace, as in any other environment, there are unwritten rules that must be observed if you're to avoid upsetting others – particularly Kiwis – and be accepted by your colleagues and clients. You should wear a suit, shirt and tie for a first business meeting, but thereafter follow the lead of the people you're dealing with. Women can wear a trouser suit for a first meeting – an outfit popular with New Zealand's prime minister. In the more creative industries, such as advertising, computers, the media and publishing, people usually dress more casually, often in jeans and T-shirts.

Business meetings in New Zealand are usually friendly and informal, and are conducted on a first-name basis. But it's important not to be over-friendly – Kiwis are more reserved than Australians (a trait inherited from the British).

As in social relations, you should work towards getting to know potential business partners gradually rather than at top speed. A meeting might begin with small talk before getting down to business, often involving current affairs or the Kiwi obsessions of sport and the weather, therefore it's best to keep up with all three.

New Zealanders expect and respect people with strong beliefs and opinions, but you should never get personal or make insults, and avoid controversial subjects such as immigration and race relations.

Also bear in mind that there's a fierce rivalry between Kiwis and Australians, so you should avoid praising Australia or Australians to Kiwis and never confuse the two countries.

When talking business, New Zealanders like directness, integrity and professionalism. Don't meander, waffle or oversell yourself or your product or service, but stick to evidence, facts and figures. Do your homework about the New

> The solemnity with which Anzac Day is commemorated is illustrated by the fact that there have been debates in New Zealand about repealing the laws preventing shops from opening on Christmas Day, Good Friday and Easter Sunday, but not on Anzac Day morning.

Zealand market and its needs and peculiarities. As in social relations, a dry, understated sense of humour goes down well when doing business, but you should avoid swearing.

New Zealand doesn't have a haggling culture, but Kiwis want value for money, so quote what is nearly your best price or offer early in negotiations. Don't improvise or promise things you cannot deliver. New Zealanders will take what you say at face value, unless given cause to change their minds. They're naturally trusting, but if that trust is lost, it can be difficult to regain.

Kiwis don't like being forced or hurried into making decisions, so bide your time. Don't pester them with too many follow-up emails or telephone calls. All forms of high-pressure selling techniques are inadvisable; Kiwis don't like being presented with tight deadlines. An understated rather than a forthright approach is best; present the facts succinctly and let them decide in their own time.

WHEN TO AVOID DOING BUSINESS

New Zealanders take their holidays seriously and the vast majority of employees take all their annual leave. There are therefore certain times of the year when it's best to avoid doing business.

Public Holidays

New Zealand has ten statutory annual public holidays, as follows:

Public Holidays	
1st January	New Year's Day
2nd January	New Year's Observance
6th February	Waitangi Day
March or April	Good Friday and Easter Monday
25th April	Anzac Day
First Monday in June	Queen's Birthday
Fourth Monday in October	Labour Day
25th December	Christmas Day
26th December	Boxing Day

Each region also has an Anniversary Day, which has the status of an official public holiday in that region.

New Zealand's most important holiday is Christmas, which falls during the school summer holiday – from before Christmas to the end of January. This is when the majority of Kiwis head for home. As a result, many people travel over the Christmas period (and in January), which means it's important to book flights, train seats, etc. well in advance.

Whereas most public holidays are simply days off, Anzac Day is solemnly observed in New Zealand. ANZAC is an acronym for Australia New Zealand Army Corps, and the holiday commemorates New Zealand's participation in the disastrous Gallipoli offensive in Turkey in 1915. Anzac Day is when New Zealand's casualties in all conflicts are remembered, and when Kiwis attend remembrance services held at the war memorials throughout the country.

Another significant New Zealand holiday is Waitangi Day, which takes place on 6th February and commemorates the signing of the Treaty of Waitangi; the occasion is celebrated mainly by Maori and sometimes becomes the focus of Maori protests about topical issues.

Other Holidays

New Zealand's main holiday periods are in late December and early January, and over Easter. Many people are away at these times, and you're unlikely to get much business done or be able to hold any meetings.

A lot of Kiwis like to escape New Zealand's winters (which can be cloudy, damp and depressing in much of the country – despite what the New Zealand tourist authorities might tell you) and jet off to the sun, notably Queensland's Gold Coast and the Pacific islands.

7.

ON THE MOVE

Travel in New Zealand is dominated by the car, and the country has one of the highest rates of vehicle ownership in the world, at around 700 per 1,000 people, which is second only to the US. Many families have two or more cars. The main reason for this devotion to the motor vehicle is that driving is simply the most convenient way of getting around the country, and many places aren't accessible by public transport or services are infrequent.

> New Zealand's love affair with the car results in almost three-quarters of Kiwis driving to work, leading to ever-increasing congestion in New Zealand's cities, particularly Auckland.

A car is highly recommended if you live in a rural area, where you'll find getting around difficult without one. Long-distance public transport is generally reliable and reasonably priced, but city transport isn't good, particularly as bus services have been reduced in many cities.

Even in Auckland and Wellington people make use of their cars a great deal, as traffic congestion and parking aren't yet bad enough to make driving a headache with the exception of rush hours. However, traffic density is increasing, along with the resultant pollution, which is an important issue in this environmentally-minded country; the government and motoring associations are now considering traffic reduction measures for Auckland. Motoring is more expensive than taking a coach (bus) or train, but much cheaper than flying, particularly over long distances.

DRIVING

You can get a probationary licence in New Zealand at the dauntingly young age of 15 – a tradition dating back to a time when people began work much younger than today. Japanese cars are popular, as they're invariably economical and reliable, and have largely replaced the American, Australian and British cars that most Kiwis used to drive.

New Zealanders drive on the left and left-hand drive cars aren't usually allowed to be used on a regular basis.

Roads

In the absence of a comprehensive rail network, roads are the mainstay of the transportation system in New Zealand. The road network covers over 90,000km (56,000mi), over 60 per cent of which are sealed (tarmac)

roads. The country has no national motorway (freeway) network, however, and those that exist are short – e.g. in and around Auckland and Wellington – although more are planned. Most New Zealand roads have just one lane in each direction, but they're invariably well surfaced and maintained, even when they traverse rugged terrain (which is frequently). All New Zealand roads are toll-free, but that's set to change: the Orewa-Puhoi motorway (due to open in 2009) will be a toll road, and new roads planned for Auckland area are also likely to be toll roads.

> There were 384 road deaths in New Zealand in 2006, the lowest total for 40 years.

The travel brochures portray motoring in New Zealand as an idyllic pursuit, where roads are traffic-free and the scenery breathtaking. To some extent, this is true in rural areas, particularly outside the main tourist season, when it's possible to drive for miles without seeing another motorist (or having to crawl behind a caravan). However, it disguises the fact that the country has moderately dangerous roads. In a recent survey, New Zealand was ranked 14th among 28 OECD countries, with a road death rate of 10.3 per 100,000 people, similar to the OECD average of 10.8. New Zealand's death rate was lower than that of the US at 14.9 per 100,000, but worse than Canada's (8.9), Australia's (8.8) and the UK's (6.1).

Rules of the Road

The highway code or rules of the road in New Zealand are contained in *The Official New Zealand Road Code*, available from Land Transport NZ agents (💻 www.ltsa.govt.nz/roadcode) and most booksellers. Some of the most important things to note include:

● Among the many odd customs of New Zealanders is that of driving on the left-hand side of the road, as in Australia, Japan and the UK. You may find this a bit strange if you come from a country which drives on the right; however, it saves a lot of confusion if you do likewise. It's helpful to have a reminder on your car's dashboard (many hired cars have a fluorescent sticker stating 'DRIVE ON THE LEFT' on the dashboard). Take extra care when pulling out of junctions, one-way streets and at roundabouts, and remember to look first to the **right** when crossing the road on foot. If you aren't used to driving on the left, you should be prepared for some disorientation (or blind panic), although most people have few problems adjusting to it.

● At crossroads and junctions where no right of way is assigned, traffic coming from the right has priority. At major junctions, right of way is indicated by a triangular 'GIVE WAY' (yield) sign or an octagonal red 'STOP' sign. There may also be road markings. When faced with a stop sign, you must stop completely (all four wheels must come to rest) before pulling out onto a major road, even if you can see that no traffic is approaching. At a give way sign, you aren't required to stop, but must give priority to traffic already on the major road. You must also give way to traffic coming from your right when entering a motorway or dual-carriageway from a slip road.

● There are many roundabouts (traffic circles) in New Zealand, which, although they're a bit of a free-for-all, speed up traffic considerably and are usually preferable to traffic lights, particularly outside rush hours (although some busy roundabouts also have traffic lights). At roundabouts, vehicles on the roundabout have priority, and not those entering it. Traffic flows clockwise around roundabouts and not anti-clockwise, as in countries where traffic drives on the right. Some roundabouts have a filter lane which is reserved for traffic turning left. You should stay in the lane in which you entered the roundabout, follow the lane markings and signal as you approach the exit you plan to take.

It's a legal requirement to carry your driving licence with you at all times when driving – if you're stopped by the police without it you face a stiff fine.

● Where fitted, seatbelts are compulsory for all passengers, and children must be properly restrained by a child restraint or adult seatbelt when fitted. In the absence of a restraint or seatbelt, children must travel in the back of a car. A child must **never** travel in the front seat without using a child restraint or seatbelt, even when the back seat is fully occupied. Seatbelts and restraints must be approved (to the requisite New Zealand standard) and be appropriate for the age and weight of a child. Babies aged up to six months must use an infant seat and children up to the age of four must use a child's seat. Older children may use either a child seat or an adult seatbelt. It's the driver's responsibility to ensure that children are properly restrained. In addition to risking death or injury, you can receive a fine for ignoring the seatbelt laws. If you're exempt from using a seatbelt for medical reasons, a safety belt exemption certificate is required from your doctor.

● Be particularly wary of cyclists, moped riders and motorcyclists. It isn't always easy to see them, particularly when they're hidden by the blind spots of a car or when cyclists are riding at night without lights. When overtaking, always give them a **wide** berth. If you knock them off their bikes, you may have a difficult time convincing the police that it wasn't your fault; far better to avoid them (and the police).

● If you're planning to stay and drive in New Zealand for over a year, you must apply for a New Zealand driving licence.

Slow Vehicles

There's an unwritten code when travelling in rural areas that if you're driving slowly and there's a build-up of vehicles behind you (e.g. if you're driving a camper van or enjoying the scenery) you should pull into a side lane provided for the purpose (often very narrow) or a lay-by (small off-road parking area) to allow traffic to pass. To do so will generally bring you a friendly toot and a wave; not to do so will incur the wrath of those forced to tootle along behind you for miles.

If you needed spectacles or contact lenses to pass your sight test, you must always wear them when driving (assuming you can see without them). It's wise to carry a spare pair of glasses or contact lenses in your car.

● At the age of 75 and 80 and every two years after that (from age 82), New Zealand drivers must obtain a 'Medical Certificate for Driver Licence' from their doctor. However, it isn't necessary to take a driving test to renew your licence.

● White or yellow markings are painted on the road surface in towns and cities, e.g. arrows to indicate the direction traffic must travel in a particular lane. You should stay in the centre of the lane in which you're driving or, where there are no lane markings, keep to the left side of the road. White lines mark the separation of traffic lanes. A solid single line or two solid lines means no overtaking in either direction. A solid line to the left of the centre line, i.e. on your side of the road, means that overtaking is prohibited in your direction. You may overtake only when there's a single broken line in the middle of the road or double lines with broken line on your side.

- Headlights must be used when driving between sunset and sunrise, and at any time when there's insufficient daylight to be able to see a person wearing dark clothing at a distance of 100m (so keep an eye out for people in dark clothing). It's illegal to drive on side (parking) lights, but headlights must usually be dipped (low beam) when driving in built-up areas where there's street lighting. Headlamps must also be dipped within 200m of an approaching vehicle, immediately an oncoming vehicle has dipped its headlights, and when travelling less than 200m behind another vehicle.

- Headlight flashing has a different meaning in different countries. In some countries it means 'after you', while in others it means 'get out of my way'. It can even mean 'I'm driving a new car and haven't worked out what the switches are for yet'. In New Zealand, headlamp flashing has only one legal signification – warning another vehicle of your presence, although most people use it to give priority to another vehicle, e.g. when someone is waiting to exit from a junction. Note that it's illegal to warn other vehicles that they're approaching a speed trap or police road block by flashing your lights (although many drivers do it). Hazard warning lights – all indicators operating simultaneously – should be used only to warn other drivers

of an obstruction, e.g. an accident or a traffic jam.

Look out for pedestrianised streets in city centres, which are closed to traffic during certain periods – indicated by a sign. Note that bicycles may not be ridden – or sometimes even wheeled – in pedestrianised streets.

- The sequence of New Zealand traffic lights is green, amber, red and back to green. Amber is warning to drivers to stop and you may drive through an amber light when stopping could cause an accident. A green filter light may be shown in addition to the full lamp signals, which means you may travel in the direction shown by the arrow, irrespective of other lights showing. Cameras may be installed at busy traffic lights to detect motorists shooting (running) red lights – a favourite pastime of some Kiwi motorists.

- Always approach pedestrian crossings with caution and don't park or overtake another vehicle

on the approach to a crossing. At some crossings, a flashing amber light follows the red light, to warn you to give way to pedestrians before proceeding. Pedestrians have right of way once they've stepped onto a crossing without traffic lights and you **must stop** (it isn't optional as in many other countries). Motorists who don't stop are liable to heavy penalties. Where a road crosses a public footpath, e.g. at the entrance to a property or car park bordering a road, motorists **must** give way to pedestrians.

● Keep an eye out for animals on roads in country areas, where fields are often unfenced and livestock are free to graze at will. Many motorists are injured following collisions with animals, particularly at night. On country roads, be prepared for the sudden appearance of herds of cows and flocks of sheep, when it's advisable to simply pull over and wait for them to pass.

● Snow chains may be used on snow-covered roads, but should be removed as soon as the road is clear.

Kiwi Drivers

In normal circumstances, New Zealanders are friendly and polite. However, this can change the minute they get behind the wheel of a car, when they can become uncharacteristically aggressive, discourteous and intolerant. Some New Zealanders' only thought is to reach their destination as fast as possible with little regard for whoever they may maim or kill in

Beware of falling trees!

the process. There are, on average, around seven road deaths each week in New Zealand, together with 20,000 convictions annually for careless or dangerous driving.

> Alcohol 'contributes' to some 30 per cent of fatal road crashes in New Zealand.

A significant danger on New Zealand roads, where there are few multi-lane roads, is drivers changing lane and pulling out without looking or without leaving sufficient space. Many drivers have no lane discipline, but young men tend to be the worst offenders.

Road rage is the latest 'trend' to emerge in New Zealand and there have been several cases of motorists who, after having been hit by a car, have remonstrated with the offending driver only to be hit again – this time in the face.

All this shouldn't put you off driving in New Zealand. Kiwi drivers are generally polite and law abiding, particularly when it comes to stopping at red lights and pedestrian crossings; however, this doesn't often extend to letting motorists out of side turnings or parking space into the flow of traffic.

You'll pass through some breathtaking scenery (best admired by stopping the car), even on the most routine trips to the office or the shops. Best of all, roads are relatively uncrowded outside cities, so your chances of meeting many kamikaze drivers are slim.

Motorcycles

Motorcycling is popular in New Zealand, both as a means of transport and as a leisure pursuit. It is, however, a dangerous undertaking, partly because drivers of other vehicles have little regard for motorcyclists (usually they don't even notice them) and partly because many motorcyclists are tempted by New Zealand's open roads to reach incredible speeds.

In general, the laws that apply to cars also apply to motorcycles. Crash helmets must be worn and riders must use dipped headlamps at all times. It also pays to wear bright, fluorescent or reflective clothing, but even then don't expect car drivers to see you.

It's possible to buy or hire (rent) a wide range of motorbikes in New Zealand, ranging from lovingly preserved British classics to the latest German and Japanese superbikes.

Unsafe Vehicles

Police can order vehicles off the road if they believe that they aren't safe. A pink sticker indicates that a vehicle must be removed from the road and may not be driven until it has been inspected and passed as fit to drive. A green sticker is less serious and indicates that a vehicle may be driven to a garage for repairs or be driven for a limited time under certain restrictions.

Car Inspection

All road-going vehicles in New Zealand are subject to an official inspection test, after which (assuming they pass) they're issued with a Vehicle Inspection Certificate (VIC), more commonly known as a Warrant of Fitness (WOF), an old term still in widespread use. Vehicles first registered less than six years ago must have an inspection every 12 months, while other vehicles must have one every six months. VICs are issued at official government testing stations and approved garages (most garages are approved), many of which offer the service while you wait. A VIC inspection costs around $35 (for a car) and is similar to vehicle inspections carried out in most US states: checks are made only for basic roadworthiness, covering such things as brakes, lights and tyres.

The test isn't as stringent as either the British MOT or German TUV inspections, although the regulations regarding corrosion and rust have been stiffened in recent years, and there are large fines for garages that fail to stick to the rules. This has resulted in inspection centres becoming almost obsessed with checking for corrosion and 'forcing' large numbers of old cars off the road.

As well as the VIC, you receive a sticker, which must be displayed behind the windscreen of a vehicle; the penalty for failing to display a valid sticker is $200.

Petrol Stations

There are plenty of petrol stations in towns and cities, but they can be few and far between in rural areas, particularly in the South Island. It's wise to plan your fuel stops on long trips using a reliable map. Bear in mind that many petrol stations close at 6pm and are closed on Saturday afternoons and all day Sundays, although now it's at least possible to buy petrol in New Zealand on Sundays (a fairly recent development).

PUBLIC TRANSPORT

Unless you live in a remote country area, you'll have access to at least some public transport in New Zealand, but city transport isn't good, and bus services have been reduced in many cities in recent years. Probably the most impressive feature of New Zealand's public transport system is that its various elements are closely integrated,

and if you start a journey by bus, continue by rail and then take to the air, you'll usually find that services are planned and timed to connect. One major drawback of public transport is that it tends to finish too early.

Trains

New Zealand's rail network is operated by Tranz Scenic, the country's only passenger rail company. The network is limited, mainly due to the mountainous terrain in many parts of the country and, of course, by the fact that lines cannot cross the Cook Strait which separates the two islands.

Privatisation

Like the disastrous privatisation of Britain's railway (the best in the world for over a hundred years), the New Zealand railway network was sold off to the Americans (for peanuts in the '80s), who promptly stripped it to the bare bones leaving nothing but a few tourist and freight trains in the South Island.

The service itself is modern and comfortable (part of the Auckland-Wellington line has recently been electrified), but neither frequent nor fast, although stops at many small stations on long-distance routes have been eliminated, making journey times shorter. As a result, rail services are widely promoted as a tourist attraction rather than a day-to-day commuter service. In this regard, the rail service is excellent, as many lines pass through native forests, past volcanic peaks and through alpine passes, offering spectacular, panoramic views. The following are the four main railway routes in New Zealand:

Rail Routes	
Name	**Route**
The Overlander	Auckland-Wellington
Capital Connection	Palmerston North-Wellington
TranzCoastal	Christchurch-Picton
TranzAlpine	Christchurch-Greymouth

There's only one class of travel, and there are many special offers on fares – if you're a student or disabled, you qualify for a 50 per cent discount off the standard fare, although you need proof of identity and must book. Given the limited rail network, however, there are no season tickets. If you expect to do a lot of travelling by train, you should consider buying a Scenic Rail Pass.

Some services provide 'free' refreshments and/or a 'free' lunch (and you thought there was no such

thing); on others there are buffet cars selling more substantial meals, and a bar. Some trains have commentaries for tourists (which you must listen to whether you're a tourist or not). If you wish to take a bicycle on a train, you should check when booking, as they aren't allowed on many services and only limited space is available when they are. Smoking isn't permitted on any trains.

Stations have few facilities. This is mainly because, in many cases, there's only one arrival or departure a day, and hence no demand for bars and buffets, or the range of other services you usually find at major railway stations. There's an office open from before the first train leaves (or at least 7.30am) until 5.30pm for information and bookings. Taxis and buses don't stop at stations throughout the day, but tend to congregate when a train arrives. This means that you may have to wait in a queue, although you're unlikely to be left stranded as there's usually a bus timed to meet the last train.

Stations aren't always conveniently situated for city centres; for example Auckland's is on Beach Road, a 15-minute walk from the city centre, and isn't on a regular bus route. On the other hand, Wellington's station is on Waterloo Quay – on the edge of the central area, near one of the city's bus stations – and is served by the city's commuter railway services, and also connected by shuttle bus to the Interislander ferry terminal.

There are no underground railway (subway/metro) services in New Zealand, but there are reliable commuter rail networks in Auckland and Wellington. Auckland's two suburban lines run from the railway station to Waitakere in the west and to Papakura in the south. Wellington's commuter rail network (operated by Tranz Metro, 🚆 www.tranzmetro.co.nz) has four lines, serving Johnsonville, Paraparaumu, Melling and Wairarapa. Tranz Metro services are popular with commuter

Wellington's Cable Car

Wellington has a cable car operating between Lambton Quay and the Botanic Gardens in Kelburn, which is a popular tourist attraction but is also used by local residents to negotiate one of Wellington's steepest hills.

and provide frequent services.

Trams & Trolleybuses

All New Zealand's major cities once had tram networks, but they were abandoned in the '50s or earlier. The only remaining tram line in the country is in Christchurch, where trams were reintroduced – as a tourist attraction rather than a serious form of public transport – in 1995. The single line operates between 9am and 6pm on a city centre loop, stopping at nine points along the way. It attracts mostly tourists but is also handy for commuters and shoppers in the city centre. You can buy a one-hour, half-day or full-day ticket.

There are trolleybuses in Wellington (the only city in Australasia to use them), which were introduced as a replacement for the city's trams. They operate on several routes in the city centre and inner suburbs and cost the same as buses; a Daytripper pass issued for buses can also be used on trolleybuses.

Local Buses

Most towns and cities have a good public bus service and some cities operate double-decker buses, like those in the UK. Bus services have been deregulated and privatised to some extent in recent years, although in many cases the original public bus company is still the largest operator on the majority of routes. One of the drawbacks of the public bus service is that it ends early; on Saturdays and Sundays the last services leave at around 5pm. Even during the week in Auckland (where the main operator is Rideline) you won't find a public bus running after 11.30pm (many routes finish much earlier) and some services are suspended altogether at weekends.

> Check your telephone directory for details of where to obtain information about services and a copy of timetables.

One benefit of bus deregulation is that small private companies have been allowed to enter the public transport business, and some operate services late into the evening and at weekends when the main operators have suspended their services. Some services, using minibuses and cars, can be ordered by telephone when required. Several companies now operate in most towns, although there's no central information office where you can obtain timetable information.

In larger cities there's usually a number of bus stations serving different companies and routes. In Wellington, the main stations are at Waterloo Quay and Courtenay Place; while in Auckland, buses use the Downtown and Midtown terminals, although the latter is just a series of lay-bys rather than a proper terminal. Fares for town bus services are calculated on a zone basis and depend on how many zones you travel through.

Auckland bus services include the Link, which runs at ten-minute intervals around the main areas of the city in a loop. In Wellington, the bus service is run by Stagecoach,

who operate frequent services, including an after-midnight service from the entertainment district to outlying suburbs. Christchurch buses are among the best in the country, with cheap and frequent services, plus a free shuttle bus that serves the city centre at ten-minute intervals.

You usually buy your ticket from the driver as you enter a bus, although some accept the exact fare only.

Long-distance Buses

New Zealand has a comprehensive and reliable long-distance bus (coach) service. Services are provided by two main companies: InterCity Group NZ (operating as InterCity Coachlines) and Newmans, both of which have an extensive network of routes covering throughout the country. There are around a dozen smaller companies, such as Northliner Express Coachlines.

Coach services are well co-ordinated so that they connect, not only with other coach services (even of competing companies) but also with other modes of transport. For example, if you want to take the train from Auckland to Wellington, the Interislander ferry across the Cook Strait and then a coach to

Christchurch, it's possible to plan a timetable which connects smoothly, allowing time to get from one terminus to another.

Unlike trains, there are several coach services per day on the main routes such as Auckland to Wellington.

Coaches are modern and provide facilities such as toilets, reclining seats and air-conditioning. On routes popular with tourists, the driver usually provides a commentary on sights and places of interest. On services operating in more remote areas, you may find that half the coach is given over to freight and parcels. Snacks and drinks aren't available on board but there are regular stops for refreshments, although drivers tend to choose the more expensive places (so it pays to take your own snacks with you).

Smoking isn't permitted on coaches.

It's usually possible just to turn up and travel by coach without booking, except at busy times such as during summer and public holiday periods. However, if you know when you want to travel, it makes sense to book as it costs no extra. When booking, take note of exactly where your service operates from, which depends on the coach company and isn't necessarily the same location as the departure point of local city buses. In Wellington, for example, Newmans' services operate from the Interislander ferry terminal, while

InterCity services depart from the Skytower in Hobson Street, whereas Newmans operates from Quay Street.

Backpackers' Buses

An economical way of travelling for young people is backpackers' buses, which operate throughout New Zealand (similar to those in Australia). Backpackers' buses are operated by a number of companies, of which Kiwi Experience and Magic Bus are the best known. Services operate on a pass basis, whereby once you've purchased a ticket you can switch buses and stop off along the route, whether for a few hours or a few days. Sporting and adventure activities are sometimes offered along the way, such as white-water rafting or kayaking. These services tend to be cheap and cheerful and are targeted at those aged between 18 and 35. You must pay extra for accommodation, although this is usually low-cost and there's also the option of camping. Booking is essential in summer.

There's a wide range of fares and offers, as well as the conditions of travel (see 🖳 www.interislander.co.nz).

Ferries

As a country consisting mainly of two islands, separated by the Cook Strait, New Zealand is highly reliant on the ferry service between the two. The main service is the Interislander, which is highly efficient and employs two roll-on roll-off ferries most of the year – the Arahura (the larger) and the Aratere (the newer), which carry passengers, vehicles and railway carriages. They sail between Wellington in the North Island and Picton, Christchurch and Kaikoura in the South Island, taking around three hours. The ferry route is 96km (60mi), although the Strait is only 20km (12mi) wide at its narrowest point.

The number of daily sailings varies between summer and winter. In summer (December to April) there are usually five daily sailings (four on Sundays and Mondays), while in winter the service is usually reduced to two or three crossings a day, as one of the vessels is taken out of service for maintenance. Summer timetables vary only slightly from year to year: ferries leave Wellington at around 8am, 9.30am, 3.30pm and 5.30pm, and Picton at 5.30am, 11.30am, 1.30pm, 7pm and 9pm.

It isn't essential to book for the Interislander ferry except at busy times, such as the beginning of school holidays, although it can be cheaper as discounted tickets can only be purchased in advance. If you turn up without a ticket, you must pay the full fare, even if you're travelling off-peak. Bookings can be made up to six months in advance. Children under two travel free and groups of 20 or more may be eligible for a group discount.

There are several smaller ferry services linking the two main islands, as well as some serving the smaller islands.

Taxis

Taxis are plentiful in most cities and towns in New Zealand. They're usually ordinary saloon cars (or minibuses) painted in distinctive colours, which vary from city to city. You can pick one up at a taxi rank or order one by telephone; they cannot be hailed in the street and will pick you up only if they're stopping to drop a passenger (so you had better be quick). All taxi fares are metered, with a minimum charge (flagfall) of $2 to $3.50, and you pay only the amount shown on the meter and aren't expected to tip (Americans please note). An extra charge is made for luggage ($1) and when travelling during the evening and at weekends, when taxis are most in demand due to the curtailment of bus services. There's also a surcharge for waiting and for journeys to and from airports (around $5).

Airline Services

Air travel is a popular form of domestic travel in New Zealand and is inexpensive compared with what it used to be. Nowadays, domestic fares are on a par with European scheduled services but not as good value as in the UK or US. Despite this, New Zealanders travel by air as frequently as possible as it's by far the fastest way to get around the country.

New Zealand is served by some 25 international airlines, most of which fly to Auckland or Christchurch. New Zealand's main domestic airline (and also its international airline) is Air New Zealand (ANZ), which was previously state-owned but is now privatised and is regularly acclaimed as one of the world's best airlines.

Air NZ (🖳 www.airnewzealand. com) has a comprehensive route network, with over 470 flights per day to 25 domestic destinations, as well as flights to destinations in Asia, Australasia, Europe and North America (including two in Mexico).

Air NZ's main domestic competitors are Freedom Air, Pacific Blue and Qantas. Freedom

Air New Zealand

In 2001, Air NZ came near to bankruptcy when it attempted to buy the remaining 50 per cent of Ansett Australia (it already owned 50 per cent), which went into liquidation in mid-2001. In an attempt to save the airline, the New Zealand government announced a $500m rescue package, which made the government the majority shareholder in the company. Many New Zealanders believe that the airline shouldn't have been privatised in the first place.

Air serves Auckland, Christchurch, Dunedin, Hamilton, Palmerston North and Wellington (as well as Australia and Fiji). Air Nelson, Eagle Air and Mount Cook also operate domestic services, the latter two of which are owned by Air NZ. A number of other competitors have started up or been proposed over the years, including the inappropriately named Kiwi Air (considering that the kiwi is a flightless bird) and Origin Pacific, although most have fallen by the wayside.

Many domestic services provide in-flight bar facilities, which is something of an innovation in New Zealand, where the sale of alcohol is normally subject to strict licensing hours. Smoking isn't permitted on the domestic services of any airline. Surprisingly, however, the health-conscious New Zealanders haven't banned that other risk to the well-being of air travellers – airline food.

There are a number of mini-airlines serving minor destinations, often using aircraft with as few as four seats. Great Barrier Airlines and Mountain Air both operate services to Great Barrier Island (a paradise-like island, likened to Fiji or Tahiti) in the Hauraki Gulf off Auckland.

Air NZ's services were notoriously expensive until the now-defunct Ansett arrived on the scene, which prompted more competitive pricing. However, standard fares are still high and it's advisable to shop around and compare prices to obtain the best deal. The cheapest fares are to be had by booking at least seven days ahead; one of the best agents is Flight Centre (🖥 www.flightcentre.co.nz) or you can select from a range of agents and airline websites at Cheap Flights (🖥 www.cheapflights.com.au/misc/cheap_flights.html).

Airports

New Zealand's main international airport is Auckland, which is connected by direct flights to most main cities in Asia, several cities in the US and Europe (including London), and several Polynesian destinations. The airports at Wellington and Christchurch also dub themselves 'international' but offer a much smaller number of Australia, although Christchurch serves some other countries, including the UK.

Wellington is the country's domestic air hub. There are also airports at Blenheim, Dunedin, Gisborne, Hamilton, Hastings, Hokitika, Invercargill, Kaitaia, Mount Cook, Napier, Nelson, New Plymouth, Palmerston North, Queenstown, Rotorua, Taupo, Tauranga, Te Anau, Wanganui, Whakatane and Whangerei. These serve mainly domestic flights and private planes, and their facilities range from a modest terminal building to a motley collection of huts.

A departure tax of $25 is levied on passengers on departing international flights, which must be paid before you pass through immigration. At Auckland International Airport it can be paid at the Bank of New Zealand offices on the ground and first floors.

8.

THE NEW ZEALANDERS AT PLAY

Becoming socially adept in a different culture is perhaps the most difficult obstacle to 'fitting in' abroad. It's also the area where you're most likely to make mistakes. To help you avoid social gaffes, this chapter contains information on social customs, dress code, dining, and social and leisure activities.

> 'I find it hard to offer an opinion on New Zealand because when I was there it seemed to be shut.'
>
> Clement Freud (British writer, broadcaster & politician)

APPEARANCE & DRESS

Your appearance and, most of all, how others see you is generally of much less importance in New Zealand than in many other countries. However, much depends on the circles you move in and whether you're trying to make a good impression, e.g. on a prospective boss or a member of the opposite sex. Most people will take you as they find you and expect you to do likewise. On the other hand, Kiwis (at least in the cities) have become much more fashion conscious in recent years and the urban young are now at the cutting edge of fashion.

For informal occasions, shorts, jandals and a t-shirt are acceptable, although for more formal occasions smart casual wear is the order of the day, such as deck shoes (loafers), slacks and a shirt with a collar for men, and a dress or skirt and blouse for women. However, if you're invited to a special (more formal) social occasion, you should inquire about the appropriate dress beforehand.

EATING

New Zealand traditionally had a reputation as something of a culinary wilderness, and although this image may persist among some foreigners, it's no longer borne out by the facts. In recent years, Kiwi chefs and dining establishments have been at the forefront of the foodie revolution sweeping the world, influenced by globetrotting Kiwis, the demands and tastes of tourists, and the culinary diversity and expertise of the country's immigrants (particularly Asians). New Zealand chefs (those that haven't left for Europe and North America) such as

Peter Gordon have played a major part in the creation of fusion cuisine, known locally as 'Pacific Rim', which draws inspiration from Asia, Europe, Polynesia and the country's indigenous people.

> It's a sign of respect to dress modestly when entering a place of worship and if you're wearing shorts and/or a skimpy top you may be refused entry (women may also be asked to cover the tops of their arms). You may also be refused entry to some restaurants and other establishments if you're 'under-dressed'.

The country has always had superb ingredients but didn't always make the best of them (to say the least). Nowadays, cook books regularly feature in the bestseller lists and cookery programmes attract large audiences (large by New Zealand standards anyway). As a result, New Zealand has ever more restaurants and cafes, particularly in the major cities, offering imaginative and expertly-cooked food.

New Zealand's new-found culinary appreciation hasn't, however, dampened their enthusiasm for traditional British-style grub – far from it. Fish and chips, pies (including 'gourmet' pies) and roast dinners remain many Kiwis favourite meals, as is the ubiquitous tomato sauce, which some Kiwis smear on just about everything. Other fast food is also popular and New Zealand is awash with the usual international chains, although they also have some healthier options of their own, such as Burger Fuel (💻 www.burgerfuel.co.nz), which is not only good but excellent value.

Many older Kiwis remain suspicious of new dishes and 'foreign' foods, which they see as 'fancy' or 'pretentious'; for such traditionalists, nothing beats a plate of roast lamb, mint sauce, roast potatoes, parsnips, pumpkin and *kumara* (Maori for sweet potato).

The national pudding is pavlova (or 'pav'), named after the famous ballet dancer, Anna Pavlova (also claimed by Australia), which is an air-filled concoction of meringue and cream topped with kiwi fruit or strawberries (see the recipe in **Chapter 2**).

Meals

New Zealand's eating habits and meals reflect their British heritage. They generally eat three meals a day, breakfast, lunch and dinner, which may be referred to as 'tea' (an English working class expression), which isn't to be confused with its (English upper class) cousin 'afternoon tea'. Eating establishments include restaurants, pubs, cafes and bars, many of which offer dine-in or take-away options.

Breakfast

Breakfast is usually eaten at home in New Zealand, although it's becoming more common to see individuals and families eating breakfast in cafes, particularly in cities. A traditional breakfast may include fresh or tinned fruit, fruit juice, cereal or porridge, eggs (which may be boiled, fried, poached or scrambled), bacon and sausages, with tea or coffee. Toast may be spread with marmalade, Nutella (a hazelnut spread with a chocolate taste originating in Italy) or Vegemite, a concentrated yeast extract (like Marmite but with added sugar). In rural areas, where men need a hearty meal to start the day, breakfast fare may also include steak and chops.

Nowadays, however, many Kiwis eat a light, 'continental' breakfast (i.e. of the type typically eaten on the European continent), consisting of just croissants and/or toast with coffee or tea. Kiwis don't put savoury and sweet foods on the same plate, as is the American custom. Most people drink a coffee (or less often, tea) mid-morning, perhaps accompanied by a snack or a cake.

Lunch

The midday meal, eaten between noon and 2pm, is normally light (and not the main meal of the day, which is eaten in the evening). Most people eat sandwiches or rolls during the working week. Other lunch foods include meat pies (a flaky pastry filled with ground beef or other meat and spices), hamburgers and fried chicken – all of which are usually smothered in tomato sauce and accompanied by chips.

On formal or special occasions lunch is taken at a restaurant, although it's usually a lighter meal than dinner, consisting of two courses, perhaps accompanied by a glass of wine or beer. Many restaurants have a lunch menu or serve lunch 'specials'.

Afternoon Snack or Tea

Most New Zealanders have an afternoon snack, which may consist of a cup of tea or coffee and a biscuit or cake. More formal afternoon tea may consist of sandwiches, cakes and scones, usually spread with butter and jam.

Dinner

Dinner is eaten in the evening and is the main meal of the day, usually consisting of one or two courses and dessert. A typical main course consists of meat or fish, potatoes and boiled or steamed vegetables (or a

green salad) accompanied by beer or wine. Tap water is served free of charge in restaurants, but you may prefer to order bottled water. Dinner is usually eaten between 7 and 8pm, although in rural areas it may be eaten as early as 6pm and may be called 'tea'. (If you're invited to a private dinner, bear in mind that some people don't eat until 8pm or later – if you're used to eating at 6pm, have a snack beforehand.) A formal or grand dinner, whether at a private home or a high-class restaurant, may consist of many courses, each of which may be accompanied by a different wine.

Formal & Informal Dining

During your stay in New Zealand you'll probably receive invitations to meals in informal and formal settings. Knowing which cutlery to use, how to behave at the table and make polite conversation will help you feel more comfortable, and might make the difference between being invited again and being ostracised (although Kiwis are informal and most don't stand on ceremony).

Invitations

When you receive a written invitation to dine, it's always necessary to respond, although not always in writing. A formal invitation will usually have RSVP (*Répondez s'il vous plaît* – literally 'please reply') written on it, and possibly a date by which you should reply. With both formal and informal invitations, if you need to cancel, you should always ring and

have a good excuse if you want to be invited again. It's also usual to ring friends and tell them if you're going to be more than 15 minutes late. On formal occasions you should **never** be more than a few minutes late and it's considered very bad manners to arrive after the main guest or speaker (when it's better not to arrive at all).

If you have medical, dietary or religious reasons for not eating certain foods – or you're a vegetarian – you should explain this to your hosts when accepting an invitation, although you may have no choice with a formal meal and may just have to refuse or leave anything you cannot eat.

> When you're invited to join friends for a meal at a restaurant, you're usually expected to pay for your own meal unless your friends have offered to pay. If in doubt, ask.

Formal Dining

The type and use of cutlery for formal dining in New Zealand is the same as in most other western countries. Cutlery is placed on the right- and left-hand sides of the place setting and you start with the implements on the outside and work in, i.e. the outermost cutlery is for the first course. Dessert cutlery is placed above the place setting. A serviette (napkin) is provided, which you should place on your lap.

You should always use both a knife and fork if they're provided and most food should be eaten using cutlery. It isn't necessary to try to eat all your food off the back of the fork – as is the British style – and it's acceptable to cut up your food with your knife and fork and then eat with a fork, as in the American manner (although this may be frowned upon in some circles). There's no cultural significance in eating with the left or right hand in New Zealand. Chopsticks and other implements aren't usually provided.

Bread isn't automatically served at formal meals in New Zealand, although water is usually provided. On formal occasions you should eat all food without touching it with your hands. The general rule is that fingers shouldn't be used for any food that can be eaten with a fork/ spoon; usually you won't be given 'finger food' at a formal dinner party. If you're served something you would usually eat with your hands, you should wait to see how your host eats it and follow suit – if he uses his hands, it's also acceptable for you to do so.

When you've finished eating, you should place your knife and fork side by side in the middle of the plate. Once you've used cutlery you should never put it back on the table; cutlery isn't reused for another course (as it is in some countries) and any unused silverware is left on the table.

If there's a guest of honour, he or she is usually seated to the immediate right of the host. Other positions aren't generally significant, although if you're seated in 'Siberia' (the worst position miles from the host) you shouldn't count on receiving a Christmas card! At large formal dinners where there are many tables, there's usually a 'top' table where the most important people are seated.

Informal Dining

In informal settings, many Kiwis eat with just a fork (provided it's in bite-size pieces) and use a piece of bread to push food onto the fork rather than a knife. It's also acceptable to eat some food with your fingers – e.g. shellfish, chicken drumsticks, chops/spare ribs, chips, bread and pizza – and take-away (take out) food is often eaten 'on the go' with your hands. You can ask whether your host has chopsticks, although it's unlikely. Many people eat food at home on a tray while watching television and children may eat in their rooms, rather than all the family sitting down to a meal together.

You may receive an invitation to a barbecue (barbie) and be asked to 'bring a plate', which doesn't mean the host hasn't sufficient crockery but that you should bring a plate of food. The food may be pooled or you may be asked to bring something for yourself (e.g. steak or burgers) to cook on the barbie (barbecue food is sold pre-packaged in supermarkets). You always serve yourself at a barbie. It's bad manners to heap your plate to the skies, particularly if you then leave some of it, but it's okay to help yourself to more after everyone else has been served. You may be told that a meal or barbie is BYO ('bring your own') or BYOG ('bring your own grog'), which means that you're expected to bring your own drinks (beer, wine or soft drinks). You may also see BYOGM, which means 'bring your own grog and meat'.

In any case, if you're invited to dinner or a barbie at someone's home it's usual to take a bottle of wine (or some beer for a barbie – at least six cans is normal) – even if you don't drink. You may get away with a cheap bottle for a barbie, particularly if your hosts drink plonk, but if they're wine connoisseurs you should take a good bottle (no wine is too expensive for a good dinner party). Usually wine brought by guests is served by the host, although it may not be if it doesn't complement the food being served. Kiwis aren't wine snobs or parochial in their tastes, so a good bottle of wine from any region of New Zealand (preferably) or Australia is usually acceptable.

You should ask permission before smoking in someone's house and shouldn't be surprised if you're asked to smoke outside. On the other hand, non-smokers should refrain from commenting on other people's personal habits, including smoking.

Table Manners

Table manners – like everything else in New Zealand – are fairly relaxed. However, there are certain conventions that should be followed, particularly when dining formally. You should eat with both hands above the table, use your serviette often to wipe the corners of your mouth (and fingers) and keep your elbows off the table, although diners at informal meals (even in restaurants) often sit with both elbows on the table between courses.

Fingerbowls may be provided when food is to be eaten with your hands, when each guest will have an individual bowl served with a slice of lemon; you're expected to dip your fingers in the bowl during and after your meal and dry them on your serviette. It's considered impolite to use salt and pepper before tasting food as it implies that the host doesn't know how to season correctly (you could say this also applies after tasting, but then you may prefer your food more heavily seasoned than other people).

Grace

Some households say grace before a meal, although this is rare nowadays. If this is the case, you should sit with your head bowed until it's finished. Christians may say 'Amen' at the end of grace and Catholics may also cross themselves.

When to Start

It's polite to wait for everyone to be served (regardless of the formality of the occasion) before starting to eat. At formal meals you should wait for the host to start before you do, unless he gives you permission to start beforehand.

The closest expression in English to the French '*Bon appétit*' or the German '*Guten Appetit*' is 'Enjoy your meal', but these aren't often used in New Zealand and may be considered pretentious.

Noises

Coughing and blowing your nose loudly are considered rude at the table. If you need to cough, do it discreetly into your napkin and if you need to blow your nose, do so quietly in a handkerchief or napkin. Burping is a no-no and should be avoided at all costs. If you cannot hold a loud noise in, say 'pardon' quietly and act as if nothing has happened.

Seating

On formal occasions, guests are usually seated male-female with the hosts at the ends of the table. It's polite to wait for the host to tell you where to sit and not to sit down until you're invited to do so. At large occasions such as weddings or banquets, name cards may be placed at the settings on the tables. It's considered impolite to change places before or during a meal, but after dessert guests are usually free to mingle and sit elsewhere.

Although it's usual to drink a moderate amount of alcohol in New Zealand, which may be more than in many other countries, it's considered bad manners to drink too much or, worse still, get drunk. However, it's also impolite to comment about another person's drinking, which may elicit an angry response. Drinking and driving is naturally illegal, although many people do it.

Conversation

What you talk about depends very much on the occasion and how well you know the host. As a general rule, it's best to let the host do most of the talking and lead the conversation. If you want to make small talk you should stick to neutral and impersonal topics such as the weather, local events and your holidays until other subjects arise. Expect other guests to ask you questions about your home country and your impressions of New Zealand – keep to the positive ones. Avoid asking anyone personal questions unless you know someone well and don't talk about work unless someone else brings up the subject (for other taboo topics, see **Chapter 4**). It's polite to compliment the host on the meal – even if it was terrible.

CAFES, PUBS & RESTAURANTS

New Zealand offers a wealth of eateries from luxury gourmet restaurants (with matching prices) to humble pubs and clubs serving homely fare at bargain prices. The food in an increasing number of New Zealand's restaurants is good or very good and there's a wide choice of ethnic cuisines on offer, although the ambience and decor tend to be lacking, even in upmarket establishments. The dress code for dining out in New Zealand is notably informal (not unlike the standard decor).

> Toasts are common in New Zealand. The host usually proposes the toast and you should raise your glass and say 'Cheers' or 'Good health'. On informal occasions people often clink their glasses together at the same time.

Parents don't usually dine in smart restaurants with their children, although most restaurants have an outdoor eating area where children are welcome, and there are many family-friendly restaurant chains.

Service charges and tips aren't included on bills in New Zealand and tipping isn't traditional, although you may wish to leave a tip when you've had exceptional service or have received good value.

Cafes

There's a strong cafe culture in New Zealand and meeting for coffee and/or snacks is popular with Kiwis. Even small towns usually have a selection of cafes, which are important locations for socialising. Cafes generally serve tea, coffee and soft drinks but no alcohol, though a few have an alcohol (liquor) licence. The following points apply to Kiwi cafes:

● **Opening hours** – Cafes usually open early in the morning and in the cities may remain often open late evening.

● **What they serve** – Cafes serve hot and cold drinks and food, which is usually of the snack and fast food variety ('all-day breakfast' is common) rather than *à la carte* meals. They usually serve food all day, although some may have a special lunch menu. Many people finish their meal in a cafe with coffee and a sweet (e.g. ice cream or pastries).

● **Ordering & paying** – Cafes may have table service and printed menus, in which case you order from a waiter or waitress. When you've finished you ask for the bill (which may be left automatically) and either pay the waiter or pay a casher on the way out. If it's a self-service cafe, you must check the menu board and order from the counter, where you also pay. You may be asked to collect your order at the end of the counter or be given a number to put on your table, where it will be delivered.

● **Prices** – Prices are the same wherever you sit, and you won't be charged more for sitting on a terrace. However, prices at cafes in prominent tourist spots and city centres are usually higher than average. Coffee isn't usually outrageously priced in New Zealand and may cost as little as half that in Europe or the US.

Smoking

In December 2004, New Zealand became the third country (after Norway and Ireland) to ban smoking in bars, casinos, clubs, restaurants and school grounds, and you also cannot smoke in many other places, including in most public buildings and on public transport. What's more, smoking is increasingly considered socially unacceptable in New Zealand and a lot of people won't have smokers in their homes.

Coffee Culture

Coffee is served in a mind boggling variety in a plethora of coffee shops and cafes in New Zealand. If you just want a regular white coffee it's best to stick with an 'Americano' or a 'flat white'. Coffee also comes in various sizes including short (small – large enough for most people unless you want to swim in it) and long (large) and may be served in a cup (usually) or a glass. Philistines can also order decaf coffee (made with decaffeinated coffee beans), low-fat milk (skinny) or soya milk (soy). The most common types of coffee offered in New Zealand include those below, but the list isn't definitive and the names, descriptions and ingredients may vary depending on the establishment.

Restaurants

There's a mind-boggling choice of restaurants in New Zealand cities and large towns, from gourmet establishments to humble fast-food 'restaurants' and cafes.

● **Opening hours** – Restaurants generally open from 11.30am or noon until 3pm, although many remain open until the evening. They generally serve dinner from around 6pm and close between 10pm and midnight (some restaurants open only for dinner in the evening). However, bear in mind that some restaurants take last orders at around 9pm or even earlier. Most restaurants close on at least one day a week and they may also close for holidays in the winter (in some resort areas, restaurants may close for the whole of the winter).

● **Booking** – It's advisable to book a table, particularly if you're planning to dine at a popular place on a Friday or Saturday

Coffee Variations	
Name	Description
Affogato	a single or double espresso poured over vanilla ice cream
Americano	an espresso diluted with an equal portion of hot water (with milk)
Café au lait coffee	coffee and heated milk in latte proportions, but using 'regular' instead of espresso
Cappuccino	a single shot of espresso with frothy milk, topped with a pinch of powdered chocolate
Espresso	a black strong coffee prepared in the Italian way by forcing steam through dark-roast coffee beans – can be short (single shot, also called a short black) or long (double shot, also called a long black)
Filter	a method for brewing coffee which involves pouring water over coffee contained in a filter. Not considered real coffee (except by Americans) and may be left to stew in a jug. It may be available in caffeinated and decaffeinated (decaf) versions
Flat White	made with one-third espresso and two-thirds steamed milk and similar to the ingredients in a latte. Can be a single or double (i.e. an extra shot)
Latte	an espresso with steamed milk and a cap of foam
Long Black	a double-shot espresso topped with hot water
Macchiato	a single espresso with a shot of cold or steamed milk (short macchiato) or a glass filled with hot frothed milk into which a double espresso is slowly dribbled (long macchiato)
Mocha	usually an espresso shot with steamed milk and chocolate
Mochaccino	an espresso with hot chocolate milk
Plunger	a one-person plunger or French press (cafetière) coffee
Short Black	a single-shot espresso
Vienna	a double shot espresso, laced with vanilla and topped with whipped cream

evening (or anytime for some 'in' places) and on Sundays or public holidays, when many people go out for lunch or dinner. Bookings can be made in person or by telephone. It's polite to telephone to cancel a booking if you cannot go or change your mind.

● **Menu** – Most restaurants offer a choice of starters (soups, salads, etc.), main courses (usually meat or fish) and desserts. Most people choose a starter and a main course but have coffee instead of a dessert. It's common to share a starter or a dessert but not a main course. Many restaurants provide half or smaller portions for children under 12 or have a children's menu, and some have a fixed-price menu (which may change daily) comprising two or three courses.

● **Alcohol** – Some restaurants don't have an alcohol licence but you can usually bring your own beer or wine (see **Bring Your Own** below). When a restaurant has a licence it will usually offer a wide range of mostly (or exclusively) New Zealand and Australian wines and other beverages. You

should be offered the wine to taste before it's served.

● **Seating** – When you enter a restaurant, you may need to wait for a waiter to show you to a table, which may be indicated by a sign. If there are several free tables you may be offered a choice.

● **Table settings** – Depending on the type of restaurant, settings range from a knife and fork wrapped in a paper serviette to full silver service with linen napkins. A bread basket or rolls may be brought to the table shortly after you sit down, along with a bottle or jug of water. Bread is usually included in the price and a jug or bottle of tap water is provided free of charge, but if you want bottled water you will have to order and pay for it.

You usually order and pay at the counter in a cafe and are given a number or an 'alarm' (buzzer) to put on your table. Your order is served at your table when it's ready or you may have to collect it from the counter when the alarm goes off (this system may also be used in pubs).

● **Service** – Waiters aren't usually professionally trained in New Zealand and staff are often casual, so you shouldn't expect high standards except in top class restaurants. However, service will invariably be friendly and efficient. If service is slow, it's acceptable to mention this to the waiter and ask politely for faster service, but if a restaurant's busy

this may be impossible. In a good restaurant, food is cooked to order (rather than heated up) and dishes may take at least 15 minutes to prepare – if a dish is expected to take longer than this the waiter should inform you when you order.

● **The bill** – When you're ready for the bill, you should attract the waiter's attention by catching his eye, beckoning to him or calling to him discreetly (shouting for the waiter is bad manners). When you want to pay you ask for the 'bill' rather than the 'check' or, if you can attract the waiter's eye from across the room, you can make the universal air-writing signal with your hands. Few

Portions are invariably huge in New Zealand and a starter is often sufficient as a main dish for anyone with a 'normal' appetite and a main course is usually large enough to feed two people.

waiters will bring you the bill unprompted.

Bring Your Own

Many New Zealand restaurants either don't have alcohol licences, or allow customers to provide their own wine, known as BYO ('bring your own') or BYOG ('bring your own grog') restaurants. There may be a 'corkage' charge of a few dollars for opening bottles and providing glasses, although some restaurants make no charge. Up-market restaurants with alcohol licences may charge around $5 or $10 per bottle corkage, which still saves you money, unless you choose the cheapest plonk on the wine list.

Eating at BYO restaurants is excellent value compared with most of Europe and North America, and you can have a good meal for around $20 a head (plus the cost of your wine).

Maori Cuisine

The Maori have traditionally been hunters, gatherers and arable farmers, and their food (*kai*) reflects this – a blend of produce from the forest, garden, sea and stream, with an emphasis on birds, fish, shellfish, wild herbs and root crops.

There's a lot more to Maori cuisine than the *hangi* (see below), although some foods are an acquired taste, for example the mutton bird, which is favoured by Maori on Stewart Island. Maori foods that are more to the general taste include *puha* (a green leafy vegetable found in streams) and *rewena pararoa* (a potato bread). The

Maori have also been involved in New Zealand's increasingly foodie culture. For example, the Rotorua-based Maori chef Charles Royal produces fine contemporary cuisine from indigenous foods and herbs, including *kuku* patties (made with green mussels) and salmon flavoured with *manu*.

The Maori have also become involved with New Zealand's burgeoning wine industry. Tohu Wines is the first indigenous branded wine to be made for the export market, made from grapes grown in the Gisborne and Marlborough regions.

Choosing the right kind of stones for the hangi is important, as they must be able to withstand high temperatures without chipping or crumbling. Igneous (volcanic) stones are preferred over metamorphic or sedimentary ones, although ancient Maori almost certainly didn't distinguish between these three types of rock and used a much simpler test: if a stone produces a ringing sound rather than a dull thud when you strike it with another stone, it's probably suitable for the hangi.

Hangi

A popular example of Maori cuisine is the *hangi* – food cooked slowly in an earth 'oven' – a hole in the ground lined with hot stones. It's often reserved for special occasions because of the large amount of time and work involved in its preparation.

To 'lay down a *hangi*' or 'put down a *hangi*' involves digging a pit in the ground and constructing a lattice of strong wooden beams inside it on which to heat stones over a fire. The beams need to support the stones for a reasonable period; if they fall, they become buried in ash,

thereby losing heat. The heating time for the stones depends on the size of the *hangi* but is usually between one-and-a-half and two-and-a-half hours. When the stones are hot enough, Hessian cloths, flax or large leaves that have been soaked in water overnight are usually laid on them and wire baskets of food (consisting of layers of meat, fish, shellfish and vegetables) set on top, followed by another layer of cloth or leaves to protect the food from the soil with which it's covered and to provide additional water for steam, which aids the cooking. Everything is then covered with soil for between three and eight hours (depending on the amount of food being cooked) before uncovering (or 'lifting') the *hangi*.

There are several variations on the *hangi*: for example, sometimes food is wrapped in cabbage leaves rather than being put in baskets, or both; rosemary and garlic are sometimes added, and taro leaves can be wrapped around food to add a peppery spice.

The *hangi* remains popular in New Zealand and is seen as a viable (if much more labour-intensive) alternative to the weekend barbecue. It's also popular with tourists, who can experience it at several locations, including the Tamaki Maori Village in Rotorua on the North Island. The taste of food cooked in a *hangi* has been described as 'steamed food with an earthy twist' – which may or may not be to your liking.

DRINKING

New Zealand has a schizophrenic attitude to selling alcohol: on the one hand, drinking is almost an obsession, while on the other, the country still has a strong temperance movement. Although Kiwis aren't quite the inveterate boozers they're sometimes portrayed as, most do enjoy a drink or three and the country has a long-established drinking culture. Wine is still regarded by some as a drink for the better off – although Kiwis drink more every year – and New Zealanders aren't generally big drinkers of spirits, which are relatively expensive (the far south of the country being the exception, as it was settled by the Scots whose whisky-drinking influence remains strong).

A popular brand of sauvignon blanc from Cooper Creek is called 'Cat's Pee on a Gooseberry Bush' – an allusion to the characteristic aroma and taste of sauvignon blanc wines.

Beer

Beer has long been the country's favourite tipple (real men never drink anything else in a pub) and a love of beer is embedded in Kiwi culture: it was the drink of the pioneers and now it's the preferred lubrication for the parched throats of sports fans, made hoarse by cheering yet another Kiwi rugby victory.

There are two main breweries in New Zealand, NZ Breweries and DB Breweries (formerly Dominion Breweries), which together also own the vast majority of drinking establishments and produce a range of beers and lagers. There are also a number of independent breweries and 'boutique' (i.e. small) breweries producing draught and bottled beers (Speights is one of the best). Imported and locally-brewed foreign beers are also widely available, even in small country supermarkets.

Beer is sold in a wide variety of measures, which may vary with the city or region. Glasses are designed to hold metric quantities, although beer can also be ordered in imperial quantities, e.g. if you ask for a pint or half pint you will be served around 500ml to 600ml or 250ml to 300ml respectively. The most common measures are a 'seven' (originally 7oz but now 200ml), a

Hawkes Bay and proud of it!

'twelve' (originally 12oz but now 350ml), a 'handle' (500ml) and a jug (containing one or two litres). If in doubt, just ask for a 'small' or 'large' beer – in any case, in most places 'free pouring' is the norm and measures tend to be somewhat academic.

Wine

New Zealand has become an increasingly respected wine producer over the last few decades. Initial success was with white wine, first with the sauvignon blanc grape, which is closely identified with New Zealand, and latterly with chardonnay.

But the country has also shown that it can make very good red wines, notably from the capricious pinot noir grape (most famous for red Burgundy), but also with Bordeaux stalwarts cabernet sauvignon and merlot.

> Pubs used to be called pub hotels or hotels because they were originally required to provide accommodation, but nowadays most pubs don't offer accommodation. Pubs in country areas, which may be called 'commercials' because guests were traditionally commercial travellers (salesmen), are more likely to offer accommodation than those in cities.

The actor Sam Neill's involvement in the industry (he makes impressive wines in Central Otago) has helped to raise the profile of New Zealand wine, and consumption has doubled since the mid-'70s. The country's current output is quite modest, and wine still isn't seen as an everyday tipple by many people in New Zealand. The future looks bright, however, as New Zealand is well suited to wine production.

Its grape-growing regions span the latitudes of 36° to 45° – equivalent to those between Southern Spain and Bordeaux in the northern hemisphere – and it has a wide variety of soils and different altitudes, providing ideal conditions to make a variety of wine styles.

The regions of Gisborne, Hawke's Bay and Marlborough produce around 90 per cent of New Zealand's wine.

Pubs

The traditional New Zealand drinking place is the local 'hotel', which is roughly equivalent to a pub in the UK or a bar elsewhere, although nowadays an establishment without accommodation is officially known as a tavern. At its most basic, a New Zealand hotel can be rudimentary indeed, with plastic chairs, fluorescent lighting and no music, although the larger

establishments offer a choice between public and lounge bars (a lounge bar is more attractively furnished but more expensive). Some country hotels even have beer gardens.

Most traditional hotels don't serve food and those that do have a rather limited menu. All hotels have a 'bottle sales counter' where you can buy alcohol to take away, a consequence of the licensing laws which allow shops and supermarkets to sell beer and wine, but not spirits.

New Zealand hotels are public houses in the true sense of the word, in that usually all-comers are served. Lone women drinking in a public bar may attract a few stares in remote places but are unlikely to meet with disapproval. In country areas, you may initially feel that you're intruding upon the locals' private territory, but you'll usually be warmly welcomed and engaged in conversation. Indeed, you should make an attempt to talk to the regulars, as it may be considered rude not to do so.

Bars are generally more up-market establishments and are usually found in cities and large towns, where you can choose from French-influenced bars, cafe-bars, brasseries, wine bars and pavement cafes. These places offer none of the traditional New Zealand atmosphere but, as in other countries, are fashionable places to see and be seen. Drinks are invariably more expensive than in a hotel and bars may also serve food. Alcohol isn't served in cafes unless they're licensed cafes or cafe-bars.

As a nation of beer enthusiasts,

Kiwis are keen on their pubs, and spending time in one is a popular pastime in New Zealand, particularly when the All Blacks are live on television. Every town of any size has at least one hotel or bar, and in many town and city suburbs, there's one on almost every corner. Dunedin is generally considered to have the country's best pub scene.

Licensing Hours

Despite (or perhaps because of) the popularity of drinking, New Zealand has some of the world's more bizarre licensing laws. Until 1967, hotels could serve alcohol only until 6pm and, although licensing hours have been liberalised in recent years, 6pm is still often the busiest time for drinking – known as the 'six o'clock swill'. Liberalisation has resulted in a confusing array of licensing hours for different premises in different towns. In theory, drinking establishments can apply for a 24-hour licence, allowing them to open day and night except on Sundays, when they must close by 3am.

In 2005, 99 out of Auckland's 237 bars operated under a 24-hour licence.

In practice, most hotels and bars are open daily from 11am to 10pm and until 10.30pm on Fridays and Saturdays. Even establishments with a 24-hour licence may be closed by 1am, simply due to a lack of demand for late-night drinking. Hotels that don't serve food aren't usually allowed to sell alcohol on Sundays, although Sunday drinking is permitted in nightclubs, private clubs and places of entertainment (in addition to restaurants).

Age Limit

After much public debate, the legal age for drinking in public establishments in New Zealand was reduced in 2000 from 20 to 18, although it has created considerable controversy as statistics have shown teenage drinking to be on the increase. On-the-spot fines for under-age drinking have been introduced and are up to $2,000 for individuals and up to $10,000 for establishments that sell them alcohol. Identity cards, such as a passport or driving licence, must be shown on request.

New Zealand's temperance movement is strongest in a few areas of Auckland, Wellington and Christchurch, whose licensing authorities don't licence **any** establishments to serve alcohol, and which are therefore effectively 'dry'. The main effect of this, however, is to encourage drinking and driving, as drinkers are forced to travel to other areas to quench their thirst.

POPULAR CULTURE

New Zealanders' favourite leisure activities include watching television (particularly sport), shopping, watching and playing sport, DIY and gardening, dining out and going to the beach. Kiwis have a great love of the outdoors and many pastimes revolve around the 'great outdoors' – not surprising when you consider New Zealand has some of the most beautiful and spectacular country in the world and only 4m inhabitants.

DIY & Gardening

At weekends, New Zealand's do-it-yourself (DIY) shops and garden centres are crammed with eager people buying yet more goodies for their latest DIY project or garden remodelling plan. But it doesn't stop at participation: evenings find many Kiwis in front of their televisions, watching programmes about… DIY, home renovation and gardening. DIY is massively popular in New Zealand and almost ingrained in the national psyche. There are few things the average Kiwi enjoys more than building things, fixing things and decorating, which is a throwback to the pioneering days when you literally **had** to 'do it yourself'.

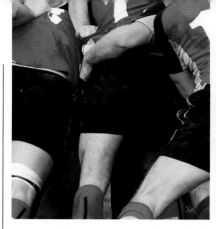

The popularity of gardening is reflected in the large number of gardening competitions and flower and vegetable shows. And you don't need to be particularly green-fingered to succeed as most plants flourish in New Zealand's mild, damp climate.

> Car maintenance and general tinkering is also popular with a lot of Kiwis, particularly men. This often means that New Zealanders keep their cars for years on end, their lives extended by their owner's flair for maintenance. This harks back to the time – not so long ago – when cars were prohibitively expensive and were lovingly cared for and literally kept for decades.

Sport

A love of sport is deeply ingrained in Kiwi culture – yet another legacy of bygone days, when physical fitness and strength was vital to survival. Sport is the country's major leisure pursuit – in terms of both participation and spectating – and Kiwis will happily set their alarm clocks for ridiculously early morning viewings of their countrymen flying the flag in international competition. Rugby, horse racing and cricket are the three most popular spectator sports, although interest in the latter has declined following relatively poor performances by the national team in recent years.

One of the most popular participant sports is golf – partly as a result of the success enjoyed by the Kiwi golfer Michael Campbell. Golf isn't regarded as an elitist sport in New Zealand (unlike in some countries), where there are plenty of opportunities to try your hand at hitting a small ball into a small hole hundreds of yards away: the country has around 400 golf courses, one of the highest numbers per capita in the world.

Tennis is also a very popular participant sport and is likewise non-elitist and open to all, which is New Zealand's philosophy in most sports. The main professional sports are rugby, cricket and – surprisingly – netball, which is the most popular sport among women. The world's most popular sport, football (or soccer, as many people now call it so as not to be confused with other forms of 'football'), is becoming increasingly popular in New Zealand, especially among children. This trend has been encouraged by some parents because the game is seen as less dangerous than rugby, but it's frowned upon by rugby fans who see it as a threat to their game.

Kiwis also like to ski (they would: it's done outdoors and can be dangerous) and Queenstown in the South Island is a world-class skiing destination. Extreme sports are also popular, most famously bungee jumping, which was invented in New Zealand (as Kiwis are fond of telling you at every opportunity).

Getting together to watch sport (especially rugby) on television is an important part of Kiwi social life. If you're invited to such an occasion and you're from the opposing country, expect some good-natured ribbing. Talking about sport is one of the great ice-breakers in New Zealand, in both social and business environments, and if you can demonstrate knowledge of sport or contribute an original perspective, it will be well received. The **least** you should know is the names of New Zealand's leading sports teams (see box).

> Kiwis have an extreme attitude to their sporting heroes: the successful ones are lavished with praise (understated praise, of course), but failure is mercilessly pilloried.

A lot of school sport in New Zealand is played on Saturday mornings and many parents spend much of their Saturdays ferrying their offspring to and from matches and watching them compete. Many Kiwis also take part in organising and running sport, as managers, referees and trainers – sport is central to life in New Zealand and 'sportsphobes' need to be aware of this.

Rugby

It's no exaggeration to say that rugby is New Zealand's 'religion', with a much stronger following than any of the recognised religious faiths. Winter Saturdays find many Kiwi men getting their 'spiritual' fix of rugby – at a live game or watching at home or in a pub. The national men's side – and national obsession – is called the All Blacks, which is probably the most important fact you can know about New Zealand.

Great claims are made for rugby in New Zealand: it has been cited as a unifying force in the country because Maori and Pacific Islanders are an important part of the game – as can be seen by the composition of the All Blacks and, most obviously, by the fact that the All Blacks perform the *haka* (a traditional Maori challenge – see **Chapter 2**) on the pitch before their games.

New Zealand used to dominate world rugby in the days before the game became professional, but in recent decades, other countries have threatened its dominance and sometimes overtaken it. New Zealand hosted and won the first ever World Cup, in 1987, but haven't won since (despite having been favourites to do so on a number

of occasions), although things are improving and the side has been much stronger in recent years. Whereas any loss by the national side used to be treated as a national tragedy, the country plunged into a slough of despair, Kiwis have had to become more philosophical in recent years. Nevertheless, success for the All Blacks results in almost non-stop coverage and national rejoicing, while failure may result in rugby being unofficially purged from the media as if the sport had never existed.

Rugby is also popular at club (rather than national) level, notably the Super 14 competition, which involves 14 teams, drawn from New Zealand, Australia and South Africa (it was known as the Super 12 until the 2006 season, when two more sides joined). New Zealand is represented by five teams: the Blues (based in Auckland), the Chiefs (Hamilton), the Crusaders (Christchurch), the Highlanders (Dunedin and Invercargill) and the Hurricanes (Wellington). Kiwi teams have dominated Super Rugby (the collective term for Super 12 and Super 14), winning all but two of the 11 titles so far contested – the Crusaders six and the Blues three – the other two being won by the Brumbies from Australia, the only non-New Zealand team to have won.

Having these facts and figures emblazoned on your brain will make a good impression with most Kiwi men and ease your social and business life. Rugby is the subject of a great many conversations in New Zealand and keeping abreast of the latest scores and standings is important if you want to be able to

Sports Team Names		
Sport	National Team Names	
	Men	Women
Basketball	Tall Blacks	Tall Ferns
Cricket	Black Caps	White Ferns
Hockey	Black Sticks	-
Ice Hockey	Ice Blacks	Ice Ferns
Netball	-	Silver Ferns
Rugby League	Kiwis	Kiwi Ferns
Rugby Union	All Blacks	Black Ferns
Soccer	All Whites	SWANZ
Softball	Black Sox	White Sox

join in without looking oafish.

The rugby season traditionally lasts from May until September, during which clubs play rugby union and rugby league at all levels, including international, regional, representative, city and local. While primarily a men's game, New Zealand also has a small but enthusiastically supported women's rugby movement and the national women's team won the World Cup in 1998 and 2002.

The South African national team, the Springboks (or 'Boks') are the All Blacks' traditional arch enemy and the Tri-Nations tournament (consisting of the All Blacks, Boks and the Australian 'Wallabies') is one of the country's major sporting events. Tickets to top rugby matches usually cost between $75 and $130.

Anyone with a keen interest in rugby will find that they're warmly welcomed by local clubs and even those with absolutely no interest will find that they're unable to escape the country's passion for the sport.

Touch rugby is a lighter version of 'real' rugby and is popular throughout the country. The game is played on a football pitch and the aim is to score a touchdown by passing the ball backwards and forwards to your team mates.

Touch rugby teams are mixed sex and must include at least two women or 'children' and the game is supposed to be non-contact. Games are essentially social occasions with 'compulsory' beer and BBQ afterwards. Not only is the game good fun, but it's an excellent way to meet people and you don't have to be a sports fanatic to join in.

Boating

Messing about in boats is central to the lives of a lot of New Zealanders – which is understandable given that nobody lives more than 130km (80mi) from the sea – and one of New Zealand's favourite outdoor activities. The country boasts the world's highest per capita boat ownership; it's estimated that around a third of New Zealanders own a boat, even if it's a bottom-of-the-range 'tinny', i.e. a modest aluminium rowing boat – and many

Despite the game's supposedly gentlemanly image, rugby can be a dangerous business in New Zealand. Post-match violence and drunkenness (sometimes associated with soccer in other countries) occurs occasionally and being a rugby referee isn't without its risks; attacks on referees during and after matches is increasing amid demands for greater protection and strike threats from referees.

Kiwis' driveways and gardens are cluttered with boats of various kinds.

Sailing is particularly popular – Auckland has even gone so far as to dub itself the 'City of Sails' (like Wellington, it has a reputation for being windy). Marinas are found throughout the country, the most popular of which include those at the Bay of Islands, Hauraki Gulf and the Marlborough Sounds. More adventurous sailors venture to the Pacific islands, which, with their idyllic climate and unspoilt beauty, make ideal sailing destinations (now that the French have stopped detonating nuclear warheads there).

And sailing – or rather yachting – is the source of one of the country's greatest achievements: winning the world's most important yachting trophy, the America's Cup – not just once, but twice running. New Zealand secured an impressive and unexpected victory in the 1995 America's Cup and successfully defended the title in the Hauraki Gulf in 2000. This caused great celebration in New Zealand, Kiwis being ecstatic that their small, sometimes ignored country had triumphed against the might and wealth of the United States. However, the Kiwis were brought

back down to earth with a bump in 2003, when they lost the second defence of the cup to a landlocked nation, Switzerland. The loss was made more painful by the fact that some of the crew on the Swiss boat were Kiwis, including the skipper, Russell Coutts, who had previously skippered the Kiwis to America's Cup triumph.

Sailing isn't a pursuit just for the wealthy, however, as there are numerous opportunities to hire a boat and spend some time on the ocean waves or pottering around the coastline. A variety of boats are available for 'bare-boating', where a hire company provides the yacht and sailing equipment and you provide the crew and provisions. Alternatively, if you have heaps of money you can hire a professionally crewed yacht.

Fishing

Fishing, whether in the sea, rivers, streams or lakes, is the most popular participation sport in New Zealand; and one of the few that doesn't involve a great deal of exertion (unless you're fighting a 100kg marlin). In fact, New Zealand is

Fishing tackle can be imported into New Zealand without restriction (and can be purchased in the US via the internet at huge savings over local prices), although it's wise not to import fishing flies, as they must be fumigated before passing through customs (at your expense), which can be frustrating bearing in mind their relatively low value.

one of the few countries where women regularly go fishing, albeit on female-only fishing trips – an invasion of a male 'pastime' that would horrify chauvinists and rednecks in Australia, Britain and the US.

Salmon and trout (weighing up to 5kg) are plentiful in the country's lakes and rivers, and are the most popular freshwater catches. There are two species of salmon in New Zealand: landlocked quinnats (which spawn near the sources of the country's main rivers and can weigh up to 11kg), and sea-run quinnats (which emerge from the sea to spawn in river estuaries and rarely exceed 1kg).

The fishing season varies with the area and the catch but usually starts around 1st October and finishes some time between 30th April and 30th June.

All anglers require a fishing licence, which can be purchased from tackle and sports shops, although the Maori claim they have the right ('enshrined in the Treaty of Waitangi') to fish without a licence and this has been upheld by the courts.

New Zealand's clear coastal waters are ideal for sea fishing; deep-sea fishing is popular, although it's naturally more expensive as it requires the hire of a boat and special equipment. The best location for deep-sea fishing is the north-east of the North Island, while other good spots include the Bay of Islands around Russell, Mercury Bay, Tutukaka near Whangarei, Tauranga and Whakatane. Some keen fishermen even venture as far as the Chatham Islands, 850km (528mi) east of New Zealand.

> Boats and tackle can be hired throughout New Zealand and no licence is needed for game or deep-sea fishing.

Popular catches include hammerhead, mako and thresher shark, black, blue and striped marlin, kingfish and tuna (which is the Maori word for eel). It's possible to hire a guide (ask for a quotation first) to find the best local fishing spots.

Tramping

Tramping (or trekking) is the Kiwi term for hiking, which is enjoyed by New Zealanders of all ages, shapes and sizes. It's a broad term, encompassing everything from a relaxed afternoon stroll to a military-style march across challenging terrain lasting several days or even weeks. You can therefore make it as easy or as demanding as you wish, and there are plenty of places to

> ### Going Walkabout
>
> The term 'going walkabout' is generally associated with Australia, notably with its Aboriginal peoples, but Kiwis do it also. In New Zealand the term is used to refer to somebody who wants to change his way of life or take an extended break from work and doesn't usually have anything to do with walking or tramping. It usually involves taking off into the countryside, probably in some kind of mobile home, for a couple of months or even years.

tramp, even close to major cities. A vast amount of New Zealand's land mass is designated as official parks (e.g. national, forest and maritime parks – Fiordland is one of the world's largest national parks) and there's always somewhere new to explore, which in the more remote areas includes many breathtaking spots that are accessible only on foot.

Tramping is highly organised in New Zealand and the whole country is criss-crossed with tracks, some of which are internationally famous and attract hikers from around the world. These are known as the Great Walks. The more popular Walks are well signposted (look for 'W' signs) and maintained and often radiate from city suburbs. The more demanding tracks may not be signposted but are marked on tramping maps. Some of the longer tracks are legendary, including the South Island's Abel Tasman (three to four days), Greenstone (two to three days), Heaphy (four to five days), Hollyford (five to six days), Kepler (four to five days), Milford (four days) and Routeburn (usually a three-day tramp through rainforests, mountains and alpine passes), and the North Island's Whirinaki Track (three to four days). Some tracks, such as the Abel Tasman, are accessible all year round, while others (such as the Routeburn) are at higher altitudes and may be impassable in winter.

As well as the well-known Walks, there are numerous less-popular tracks, which are just as enjoyable and often as spectacular. The Department of Conservation (DOC) provides information and advice about tracks, and also operates visitor centres and publishes numerous useful pamphlets. Each of the roughly 50 national, forest and marine parks has its own DOC headquarters, where you can obtain information about local tracks.

When tramping independently, you need to carry your own food and equipment (take plenty of warm clothing even in summer). Accommodation can be found in DOC huts (there are over 950) situated along tracks, which may be free or require a modest fee, and where bunks, cooking facilities and clean water are provided. There's no charge for children under 11, while older children with a 'youth ticket' are charged half-price. DOC also sells an annual huts pass, although this isn't valid for huts on the Great Walks. Accommodation in DOC huts is basic and is provided on a first-come, first-served basis. Some independent trampers prefer to take tents, which can usually be pitched near huts but cannot usually be pitched alongside tracks.

You must book to walk the Great Walks and obtain a Great Walks Pass (sold at DOC offices and national park offices), even when walking independently. The Abel Tasman, Milford and Routeburn Tracks have a separate booking system and passes can be obtained by email from DOC.

October to April is unofficially regarded as the tramping season and the most popular routes can be congested in January and February, although it's relatively easy to find a quieter, lesser known track. You should avoid tramping in winter, particularly in the South Island, where weather conditions can be severe on high-altitude walks and some paths are closed due to the danger of avalanches.

Gambling

Gambling has long been a passion in New Zealand, where gamblers wage over $2bn a year on all forms of betting. As a result of a ban on trackside betting (see box), gambling in New Zealand was until the '80s mainly restricted to lotteries and off-course gambling on horse racing, and both were government-regulated; from 1932, the Art Union lotteries were run by Hammond and McArthur under government regulation, and the Golden Kiwi lottery was introduced in 1962. Betting on horses was taken over in 1951 by the state-run Totalisator Agency Board (known as the TAB or tote), the world's first national off-course betting agency.

> **Gambling increased dramatically in popularity in the '80s.**

Lotto (a weekly lottery based on a draw of numbers) began in 1987 and by the early years of the 21st century was regularly played by nearly 70 per cent of the population – around 400,000 Kiwis watch the televised draw on Saturday nights. In 1988, electronic gaming machines (one-armed bandits, called 'pokie machines' or 'pokies') became legal for chartered clubs, hotels, Returned and Services Associations (RSA – the ex-service organisation) and sports clubs.

In 1989, the government approved the introduction of casinos, and by 2003 six had been built, one each in Auckland, Christchurch, Dunedin and Hamilton, and two in Queenstown.

These developments caused a reduction in the amount spent on horse race betting, to which the TAB responded by offering gambling on other sports. Nevertheless, whereas in 1987, horse racing had been the dominant betting force, accounting for over 85 per cent of the total spent on gambling, by the turn of the millennium gaming machines were in the lead, with 35 per cent, followed by casinos (26 per cent) and Lotteries Commission games (Lotto, Instant Kiwi and Daily Keno, with 21 per cent), while racing and betting on sports such as cricket and rugby, attracted a mere 18 per cent.

The popularity of gambling in New Zealand has certainly had negative social consequences: there are a lot of gambling addicts – a condition which is now recognised as a serious illness, requiring treatment – but the industry has also increased employment and tourism and made a contribution to the economy.

Horse Racing

Despite the huge fall in the amount wagered on horse racing, it still has a central place in Kiwi culture, with some 800 race meetings a year, attended by over a million people. There are three racing codes: thoroughbred racing, harness racing (trotting) and greyhound racing – all controlled by the New Zealand Racing Board.

New Zealand breeds racehorses which are prized throughout the racing world and a source of national pride. Over a century ago, the New Zealand horse *Carbine* set an

> New Zealand's first race meeting was held in 1835, in the Bay of Islands, but indulgence in horse racing and betting raised the hackles of the Protestant church, which campaigned against them. From the latter part of the 19th century, restrictions were introduced and in 1910 bookmakers were banned from race meetings.

unbeaten weight-carrying record in the Melbourne Cup (one of the world's most famous horse races), and the country's reputation for producing fine horses has continued ever since, including champions such as *Balmerino*, *Bonecrusher*, *Ethereal*, *Horlicks*, *Phar Lap*, *Cardigan Bay* and *Sunline*. New Zealand-bred horses have played a significant part in Australian racing history and have a great record in the Melbourne Cup. They've also enjoyed success at Aintree in England (where the legendary Grand National race is run), in the Japan Cup and in Dubai.

Social Clubs

There are many social clubs and organisations in New Zealand, including Anglo-New Zealand Clubs, Business Clubs, International

Men's and Women's Clubs, Rotary Clubs and Returned and Servicemen's Association (RSA) clubs. Expatriates from many countries have their own clubs in major cities, a list of which is often maintained by embassies and consulates in New Zealand. The Country Women's Institutes of New Zealand and the Women's Division Federation Farmers (WDFF) play an important part in the social life of women in rural areas, where there are few formal social facilities. All towns have a YWCA and YMCA, many of which organise extensive social programmes. In keeping with the country's sporting heritage, there are a range of sports clubs in most towns, the most common of which are rugby, soccer, cricket, lawn bowls, hockey and netball.

Many clubs organise activities such as art, bridge, chess, music, outings, sports, and theatre and cinema trips. Joining a local club is one of the best ways to meet people and make friends, to integrate into your local community and New Zealand society in general.

THE ARTS

Culture (in the restricted sense of the term) isn't one of the words generally associated with New Zealand, and it's true that in many parts of the country cultural events can be rather thin on the ground. However, New Zealand's cities have a lively arts and cultural scene, even if Kiwis are sometimes accused of paying too much attention to anything British rather than developing a home-grown culture.

'High' culture such as classical music, opera and theatre is popular in New Zealand's major cities, but is seen as the preserve of better-educated, wealthier Kiwis. That said, the free 'Opera in the Park' and 'Symphony under the Stars' events held in Auckland in summer are popular with all sections of society. Festivals directed towards learning and workshops in the arts are popular in New Zealand, reflecting the Kiwi passion for learning to do things themselves.

New Zealand doesn't tend to make heroes of its artists and writers, as it does with its sports stars. A notable exception from the world of the arts is opera singer Dame Kiri Te Kanewa, a national icon of the first order.

Literature

New Zealand isn't noted for its literary giants but the country has produced a number of notable writers. Katherine Mansfield and Frank Sargeson are among New Zealand's most famous writers. Indeed, such has been their influence that it's sometimes argued they've inhibited the country's other writers. However, others have also enjoyed success, including the writer of

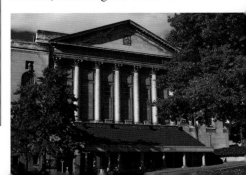

detective yarns, Ngaio Marsh, and Keri Hulme, who won the prestigious Booker Prize.

Katherine Mansfield is New Zealand's most famous writer, and is closely associated with D. H. Lawrence and her friend (and sometime rival) Virginia Woolf. She lived most of her adult life in England and, latterly, the south of France and Switzerland, where she went for the sake of her health, before dying of tuberculosis at the age of just 34. Mansfield is particularly known for her short stories, which were noted for their use of the 'stream of consciousness' technique, and which share with Chekhov's tales an attention to the details of human behaviour. Sargeson is also best known for his short stories, though much less famous outside New Zealand than Mansfield.

Less 'literary' than Mansfield and Sargeson, Ngaio Marsh enjoyed considerable success – particularly her 32 detective novels about Roderick Alleyn, a very English police inspector. She was also a theatre director, and divided her time between England and New Zealand. Most of her stories are set in Europe (mainly in English theatres and country houses) but four have New Zealand settings, with Alleyn on holiday or secondment to the New Zealand police. Some critics have suggested that her novels' English country settings allowed her to avoid the more difficult task of establishing a New Zealand novel tradition. In any case, her books have literary merit, showing greater depth of characterisation and more humour than is common in the genre.

Film

New Zealand has long been a popular location with international filmmakers, who are drawn by its abundance of spectacular scenery and low labour costs (especially compared with Hollywood). The Indian film industry, for example, has made or partly made at least 100 films in New Zealand. Kiwis also make their own films and some have enjoyed international acclaim, notably *Heavenly Creatures*, *Once Were Warriors* and *The Piano*, all of which are serious, sometimes intense productions.

> **The Lord of the Rings film trilogy grossed US$2,916,544,743 worldwide – give or take a few dollars.**

But by far and away the most successful Kiwi films have been the adaptations of J. R. R. Tolkien's *Lord of the Rings* trilogy, directed by the Kiwi Peter Jackson. The first film, *The Fellowship of the Ring*

(released in December 2001), won four Oscars, the second, *The Two Towers* (December 2002), won two, and the third, *Return of the King* (December 2003), won an astonishing 11. As well as generating enormous publicity for New Zealand (whose scenery was spectacularly showcased), the trilogy created employment for a large number of Kiwis: over 2,000 worked as crew and over 15,000 as extras. Extensive marketing campaigns have capitalised on the exposure from the trilogy, and NZ Post has even issued commemorative stamps.

New Zealand has produced several actors of note, including Sam Neill, Kerry Fox and Russell Crowe (who was born in New Zealand but raised in Australia, where he stills lives), and hosts several popular annual film festivals, including the International Film Festival in Auckland and the 'Incredible Film Festival', showing B movies and *avant garde* films.

Going to the cinema and watching films on video and DVD is popular in New Zealand. Most towns have a cinema, and major cities boast multi-screen centres; Auckland has an IMAX screen at the Force Entertainment Centre.

Film Classification	
Classification	Audience
G	general viewing
PG	parental guidance recommended for young children (aged under 13)
R16	restricted to those aged 16 or over
R18	restricted to those aged 18 or over

Films are graded by censors according to a unique classification system (see box for the main categories).

Note that only R16 and R18 films are restricted by law to the relevant audience. The censors frequently add a descriptive tag to their rating, such as 'violent content' or 'explicit sexual content,' which gives additional guidance and makes it easier for parents to decide which films their children shouldn't see – and allows children to determine which films they **must** see at any cost.

Children aged from 3 to 15 must show ID cards when buying tickets, which are discounted. There are also concessions for senior citizens and the disabled.

Theatre, Opera & Ballet

New Zealand has several resident professional theatre companies in the main cities and a number of repertory theatre groups throughout the country, even in smaller towns. Among New Zealand's best known playwrights are Bruce Mason, Joe Musaphia, Greg McGee and

Roger Hall, whose play *Middle Aged Spread* was a major success in London's West End. Wellington is particularly known for its passion for theatre, and hosts the renowned International Festival of Arts biennially (in even numbered years). Auckland, Christchurch and Dunedin also have active theatre scenes.

The New Zealand Opera Company dates back to 1954 and the National Opera was established in 1979, although New Zealand's Opera companies are better known outside the country than within thanks to their overseas tours.

> The city of Auckland runs an 'Opera in the Park' season annually in January.

The New Zealand Ballet was founded in 1953 and the National School of Ballet (now part of the New Zealand School of Dance) was established in 1968. Like its counterparts in opera, the New Zealand Ballet has an excellent repertoire of 19th century and more modern works, and performs regularly in New Zealand and abroad.

Music

When people think about music and New Zealand, the name that most readily comes to mind is Kiri Te Kanewa, the country's biggest international music star. Dame Kiri Te Kanewa, to give her full title, is a part-Maori opera singer who has become a national icon and is probably most internationally famous (at least in the UK) for singing at the wedding of Prince Charles and Lady Diana Spencer. But the Kiwi classical music scene is more than just Dame Kiri.

Other prominent New Zealand musicians include organist Gillian Weir and pianists Michael Houston and Maurice Till. New Zealand's Symphony Orchestra regularly tours the country and undertakes overseas tours, particularly to Australia and Japan. Most major cities also have their own symphony and concert orchestras. And New Zealand is noted for its metropolitan brass bands (a local tradition), which frequently take part in international competitions and have been world champions on several occasions.

There are few well known New Zealand rock and pop bands, Crowded House (see below) being one of the few to attain international fame; most groups leave for Europe as soon as they achieve some success. Internationally known rock and pop stars do, however, tour New Zealand on a regular basis, mainly in November and December (tickets for top acts cost at least $50). There are rock, folk and jazz clubs in most cities, although these tend to be quieter and less cosmopolitan than those found in Europe and North America.

Neil Finn is New Zealand's most prominent and successful rock-pop musician, a member of the country's two best-known bands, Split Enz and Crowded House. Split Enz were formed by Neil Finn's elder brother, Tim, and Neil joined in the mid-'70s.

> The standard of museums and art galleries is generally high (many have 'living' or interactive displays), and admission is usually free – except for collections housed in historic buildings, where a small charge is made (the New Zealand Historic Places Trust maintains 43 sites around the country).

They were the first New Zealand band to achieve international success, especially with the song *I Got You*, and had unusual, eclectic influences: art rock, pop, punk, rock, swing and vaudeville (i.e. just about everything).

When they disbanded, Neil Finn formed Crowded House (named after the rented accommodation they shared while recording in Los Angeles), which included his brother Tim for a while; they enjoyed huge worldwide success, notably with the songs *Don't Dream It's Over* (which reached number two in the US chart in 1987) and *Weather With You* (a UK top ten hit in 1992). The group broke up in 1996 and Neil Finn went solo, as well as collaborating again with his brother.

Museums

The large number of museums in New Zealand – over 300, which is a lot in a country with just over 4m people – surely puts to the sword the idea that Kiwis are interested only in dangerous sports, beer and sheep worrying; even in small towns you're likely to find a museum where you can learn something about the local history and culture.

Most exhibits in New Zealand museums and galleries are from recent history, although you can enjoy ancient treasures and old masters (the few that the Yanks don't own, that is) at art galleries in the major cities. However, there's a strong preference for contemporary works and many of the exhibits are by present-day Maori and *Pākehā* artists.

Among the most famous museums and galleries in New Zealand are the Auckland Art Gallery, the Auckland Museum (in the Domain), the New Zealand Maritime Museum (also in Auckland), the Te Papa or Museum of New Zealand in Wellington (which has excellent displays of Pacific and Maori cultures as well as exhibits about New Zealand history and European settlement), the Canterbury Museum and the Robert McDougall Art Gallery in Christchurch, which is one of the few galleries to exhibit European masters.

9.

RETAIL THERAPY

New Zealand isn't renowned for the excitement or variety of its shopping, and acquisitiveness isn't hardwired into the national psyche. This is probably yet another legacy of the pioneer days, when many Kiwis were largely self-sufficient, shopping only for items they couldn't grow or make themselves. Indeed, this tendency is present today, particularly in rural areas, where many people still prefer to grow and make whatever they can. But times have changed and New Zealand's shopping is more interesting and varied than it used to be, and most cities now have a good selection of international chain stores and specialist shops.

> Consumer spending accounts for around 60 per cent of New Zealand's economy.

Those from the UK will recognise several names on the New Zealand high street, although it's important to note that these retailers don't usually sell the same products as their British equivalents. For example, Woolworths is a major supermarket chain and Boots is purely a chemist, so you shouldn't expect to buy music and household goods there as you can in the UK. Australians will also find some of their favourite stores in New Zealand, many of which are operated on a franchise basis.

Although New Zealand shoppers complain endlessly about increasing prices, they get a better deal than they did in the past, thanks to the recent removal or reduction of punitive taxes on imported goods (such as electrical equipment) and increased competition. Competition has additionally forced retailers to give increased thought to the quality of goods and services they offer and their presentation, which in the past was at best uninspired and at worst poor.

Debit or credit (EFTPOS) cards are the preferred method of payment in most shops and they can even be used to pay court fines. Credit cards (e.g. Visa and MasterCard) are widely accepted, even in out-of-the-way places, although convenience stores may not accept them. New Zealanders also have a passion for store charge cards. On the other hand, many shops are reluctant to accept cheques, as there are no cheque guarantee cards in New Zealand. If you're paying by cheque, you also need some form of identification, for example a credit card or driving licence.

Goods and services tax (GST) at 12.5 per cent is levied on almost everything you buy in New Zealand. You can assume that tax is included in the price unless there's an indication to the contrary. Usually, tax-exclusive prices are displayed only in outlets that attract mainly tradesmen and business customers, e.g. a hardware store that serves local farmers.

OPENING HOURS

The standard store opening hours in New Zealand are 8.30 or 9am until 5pm, Mondays to Fridays, and 8.30 or 9am to noon on Saturdays. Shops don't always open on Saturday afternoons, although those in tourist areas often do (and on Sundays).

Most shops open until 8.30 or 9pm one day a week (usually Thursday or Friday). Limited Sunday opening is permitted but as some shops remain closed while others open, planning a Sunday shopping trip can be an uncertain business. As in other countries, supermarkets tend to buck the trend and in cities many stay open until late every day. The traditional New Zealand 'dairy' (see below) operates an open-all-hours policy, remaining open from when the proprietor gets up until he's too tired to continue (usually until 9 or 10pm). All shops are closed on Christmas Day, Good Friday and Easter Sunday.

The churches and trade unions fought long and hard against the introduction of Saturday and Sunday trading, arguing that if people were made to work on Saturdays it would destroy family life and have all sorts of other dire consequences. Although convenience and commercial interest prevailed – helped by the demands of the country's growing tourist industry – there are still limited weekend shopping times in many places.

Queuing

Kiwis are like the British when it comes to the sometimes thorny matter of queuing. It's important to form and maintain orderly queues wherever you are in New Zealand – in the bank, at a bus stop, at a supermarket checkout, anywhere. It's regarded as bad manners to indulge in the sort of queue ignoring or jumping which is common in Mediterranean countries, as it goes against the entrenched Kiwi idea of fair play. You have been warned.

TYPES OF SHOP

As in most developed countries, many modern shopping centres – sometimes called 'mega-centres' – have been built outside towns, with the result that shops have moved out of town centres and left them run-down and neglected.

Thankfully, there are still plenty of smaller shops in most city suburbs and towns. Most famously, there are the 'dairies' (see below), the Kiwi name for the country's many convenience stores that are found in most communities and which sell a wide range of foodstuffs and basic goods. Increasingly, however, petrol (gas) station shops perform the same function – and are particularly handy in the evenings and on Saturday afternoons and Sundays, when most other shops are closed. Other typical shops in most town centres include a baker, butcher, chemist (pharmacy), greengrocer (fruit and vegetables), and a grocer or general store.

Many Kiwis frequent out-of-town shopping centres, which are more than simply places to shop, as most contain a variety of bars, cafes, cinemas and restaurants, and visiting them has become a popular leisure activity – despite Kiwis' professed love of the great outdoors.

Colville, Coromandel

Dairies

The dairy is a great New Zealand tradition. It isn't just a dairy – in fact in most cases it isn't a dairy at all (few New Zealanders can remember when dairies made butter and cheese), and a more accurate description nowadays would be a convenience store or mini-market.

The dairy was once the mainstay of New Zealand shopping, where everyone did most of their daily shopping. Nowadays, with the proliferation of supermarkets and shopping centres, most tend to be patronised only for the odd items that have been forgotten at the supermarket or in 'emergencies', and many are suffering from declining trade and look rather run down. However, the traditional dairy soldiers on, and is the one place (apart from petrol stations) where you can be sure of buying essentials on Sundays when everywhere else is closed. Dairies are also a focal point for the local community and an excellent source of information, advice and local gossip.

Dairies sell a 'little bit of everything', particularly tinned and packet foods, and in some you can buy fresh fruit, vegetables and meat (often local produce). There's usually a display of confectionery (lollies), a variety of soft drinks (but generally no alcohol) and an impressive range of ice cream, which is of excellent quality and consumed enthusiastically in New Zealand. A dairy is also often the best place to buy snacks (at any time

Dairies are noted for their friendly service (they're usually owner-operated) and if there's anything you particularly want, the proprietor will usually obtain it for you. Prices in dairies are inevitably higher than in supermarkets.

of day) and usually offers a choice of sandwiches and pies, although they may be limited to mince or bacon and egg. In country areas you may also find hardware and clothing, although you shouldn't expect much choice.

Supermarkets

A notable local feature of New Zealand supermarkets is that friendliness is still the rule rather than the exception and many Kiwi checkout staff will greet you with a smile – which will come as a shock to foreigners used to surly indifference.

There's a huge variety of supermarkets in New Zealand and it's wise to do some local research when moving to a new area. Some supermarkets, such as Pak 'N' Save, operate on a pile-'em-high-and-sell-'em-cheap basis, which means you can expect warehouse-style decor (i.e. none), little choice, budget brands and minimal service, but rock-bottom prices. New World is a slightly more upmarket supermarket and has recently refurbished its stores, with the emphasis on fresh food and delicatessen counters. The Australian retail giant Woolworths has almost 90 stores throughout New Zealand, which include Woolworths, Woolworths Quickstop and Micro stores.

Several supermarkets offer attractive surroundings, a wide choice of household brands, separate bakery and delicatessen counters, and packing and 'load-your-car' services, but their prices are correspondingly higher. The better quality supermarkets offer some popular brands from the US and Europe, although shipping costs make these expensive and there's usually a New Zealand equivalent that's just as good.

Note that supermarkets sell wine and beer, but don't sell any other alcohol, which you must buy from hotel (pub) bottle shops or specialist liquor stores (see **Alcohol** below).

> Many supermarkets are located out of town, so you may need a car to get there, although a few supermarkets in cities offer free shuttle buses for car-less customers.

Chain & Department Stores

New Zealand has its fair share of chain and department stores. New Zealand-owned Warehouse is the country's largest chain store and its slogan, 'where everyone gets a bargain', indicates that American-style retailing has arrived in New Zealand. Warehouse's enormous red outlets are found throughout the country and have been blamed for the closure of increasing numbers of New Zealand's smaller urban shops. Farmers is New Zealand's most famous department store; it doesn't have anything to do with farming but sells most general goods, generally of medium quality and at competitive prices (ideal for the thrifty Kiwi). It was also New Zealand's first mail-order retailer.

Swedish Rounding

Most stores use 'Swedish rounding' for cash purchases, whereby prices are rounded to the nearest tenth of a dollar: prices ending with 5, 6, 7, 8 and 9 cents are rounded up, and prices ending with 1, 2, 3 and 4 cents are rounded down. This procedure doesn't apply to electronic payments (by EFTPOS, debit and credit cards) and cheque payments.

In smart suburbs in major cities, many shops that used to sell everyday goods (such as food) have been taken over by outlets selling arts and crafts, gifts, stationery, and Maori and Polynesian artefacts and reproductions. Although interesting for visitors, these are of little use to residents, who often need to visit shopping centres and supermarkets for the essentials, which is particularly true in many shopping arcades in Auckland and Wellington.

FOOD

You shouldn't worry that you'll have to survive on a diet of lamb/mutton, fish and chips and pies in New Zealand. Kiwis are much more adventurous and cosmopolitan in their eating than they used to be and as a result the country now has a wealth of specialist food shops and supermarket counters.

One of the pleasures of life in New Zealand is the wide range of fresh food that's available at reasonable prices. New Zealand is a major food producer (and exporter), particularly of meat, dairy produce and fruit, and although the choice may not be as wide as in some other countries, the quality is excellent.

On the other hand, the availability of many foods, particularly fruit and vegetables, tends to be seasonal, as most shops sell only what's available from local farmers; when out-of-season produce is available (e.g. strawberries in mid-winter), it's expensive. Imported produce is limited by the government's concern not to introduce alien pests and diseases.

Meat

Meat is usually good value in New Zealand, as it's one of the country's major industries, and most families can afford to serve meat at every meal (not that this is necessarily a good thing). There are over 40m sheep in New Zealand and the country exports around $2bn worth of lamb annually. Not surprisingly, lamb is good value and all joints are inexpensive and readily available.

There's also a range of lamb products such as burgers, pates, pies and sausages (known as snarlers). Hogget is one-year-old lamb, i.e. it actually is a lamb and not mutton sold as lamb as in many other countries. If you have the freezer space, you may wish to consider buying a whole lamb (jointed or not), which can cost as little as $100.

> Food in New Zealand is measured in metric quantities, though older shop assistants are familiar with the former Imperial system of ounces and pounds.

Poultry, pork and beef are also common, although less popular than lamb; New Zealanders particularly like their steak, which is excellent quality and sometimes served garnished with oysters in restaurants, when it's known as a 'carpet bagger'. Venison is an increasingly popular meat in New Zealand and is available from many butchers and supermarkets (the country has become a major exporter of venison in recent years).

You can buy meat from a supermarket or a local butcher, where it may be fresher and locally produced – the grazing lamb you passed on your way to work in the morning could be riding home in your car in the evening!

Metric/Imperial Conversion

Weight

Imperial	Metric	Metric	Imperial
1 UK pint	0.57 litre	1 litre	1.75 UK pints
1 US pint	0.47 litre	1 litre	2.13 US pints
1 UK gallon	4.54 litres	1 litre	0.22 UK gallon
1 US gallon	3.78 litres	1 litre	0.26 US gallon

Capacity

Imperial	Metric	Metric	Imperial
1 UK pint	0.57 litre	1 litre	1.75 UK pints
1 US pint	0.47 litre	1 litre	2.13 US pints
1 UK gallon	4.54 litres	1 litre	0.22 UK gallon
1 US gallon	3.78 litres	1 litre	0.26 US gallon

Note: An American 'cup' = around 250ml or 0.25 litre.

Green-lipped mussel

Seafood

A wide range of seafood is available in New Zealand. If you want 'international' species such as cod and haddock, you can find them, but there's also a huge variety of local fish such as snapper and grouper. Popular seafood includes green-lipped mussels, Pacific oysters, scallops, smoked eel, pipi and tuatua (types of shellfish), paua (abalone), toheroa (local clams) and shark (sometimes known as flake or lemon fish).

New Zealand whitebait isn't the same as whitebait in other countries but is a tiny, thread-like, transparent fish with a subtle flavour.

Generally, seafood isn't as good value as meat; much of New Zealand's catch goes for export and the country's wholesalers need to buy fish from South America to satisfy local demand. It's illegal to deal in trout commercially, so if you enjoy trout you usually need to catch it yourself. This isn't difficult, as the country's rivers, lakes and streams are teeming with rainbow and European trout. The same applies to oysters, which are frequently found in New Zealand's clear coastal waters and can be harvested freely.

Dairy Produce

Dairy products are plentiful and cheap in New Zealand – so much so that hotels and motels often leave a free bottle of milk in rooms – and are one of the country's major exports. The quality of dairy produce is high and there's plenty of variety; it's possible to buy a wide range of New Zealand versions of soft cheeses such as Brie and Camembert, as well as many imported cheeses.

ALCOHOL

New Zealand used to have some of the world's more bizarre licensing laws, which dated back to the UK's oppressive legislation introduced during the First World War, when workers were kept as far away from alcohol as possible lest their performance in the munitions factories was affected – with possibly disastrous consequences. New Zealand's laws have been reformed in recent years, however, and it's now possible to buy alcohol on any day of the week in a variety of outlets, provided you're aged over 18.

Pubs (known as hotels) usually have a 'bottle sales counter' or a separate 'bottle shop' (equivalent to an American liquor store or a British off-licence) on the premises, although these have limited opening hours, relatively high prices and a poor selection compared with similar establishments in other countries.

Bottle shops usually have a good choice of beer, but the selection of wines and spirits is usually limited. Spirits must be purchased at dedicated bottle shops such as Liquor King (💻 www.liquorking.co.nz), Liquorland (💻 www.liquorland.co.nz) and Super Liquor (💻 www.superliquor.co.nz), all of whom offer online orders and home deliveries.

> When buying alcohol, if you look younger than 25 you may be asked to prove your age, even though the legal age for buying alcohol is 18.

Supermarkets have entered the alcohol sector in recent years but are currently permitted to sell only wine and beer (of which they stock a wide variety at competitive prices).

They're easily the cheapest place to buy wine unless you buy direct from vineyards (known as wineries), which are allowed to sell their produce direct to the public and can be a good source of inexpensive wine (although don't expect any bargains – prices are pretty much the same as in bottle shops and may be higher). Dairies and grocery shops can also obtain a licence to sell wine, although few do. Most wine sold in New Zealand is locally made or Australian; although European and North and South American wines are available, they aren't popular and are too expensive for most people.

Wine is sold in 75cl bottles and boxes and barrels (casks) of varying capacities. Beer is sold in bottles and cans (330ml or 440ml, usually in trays of 24 – known in typically poetic Kiwi fashion as a 'two dozen lot'), with bottled beer being the more popular. You can also buy a flagon containing 2.25 litres, which is sometimes still known as a 'half g' (half a gallon) because it's equivalent to four pints.

New Zealanders aren't generally huge spirit drinkers, mainly because spirits aren't as widely available as beer and wine and are expensive. However, if you miss your favourite tipple, most major international brands can be found, including American, Canadian and Scotch whisky and bourbon, as well as local gin (such as 42 Below) and vodka (which is relatively good value).

CLOTHES

New Zealanders aren't noted for their fashion-consciousness ('New Zealand fashion' is an oxymoron, particularly for men), although a wide range of clothing, both locally made and imported, is available.

As in any country, prices vary considerably with quality and retailer, although clothes in

Continental to UK/US Size Comparison

Women's Clothes

Continental	34	36	38	40	42	44	46	48	50	52
UK		8	10	12	14	16	18	20	22	24	26
US		6	8	10	12	14	16	18	20	22	24

Men's Shirts

Continental	36	37	38	39	40	41	42	43	44	46
UK/US	14	14	15	15	16	16	17	17	18	-

Shoes (Women's and Men's)

Continental	35	36	37	37	38	39	40	41	42	42	43	44
UK		2	3	3	4	4	5	6	7	7	8	9	9
US		4	5	5	6	6	7	8	9	9	10	10	11

New Zealand are generally more expensive than in Europe and North America. The cheapest clothing is available from chain stores, such as K-Mart or Farmers, where you'll find uninspiring designs but plenty of choice, while department stores stock better quality clothes at higher prices. Millers Fashion Club – which, like many New Zealand retailers, originated in Australia – is a leading chain of women's clothing stores, while Glassons, Max and Jean Jones are also popular nationwide chains.

'Factory outlet' shops are a growing influence in the clothing industry and include Dressmart in Auckland, which offers good value and unparalleled choice. At the other end of the scale, the main cities have an increasing number of trendy boutiques and 'designer' stores, where you'll find high-profile brands from leading American, Australian and European designers (e.g. Barbour, Driza-Bone and Timberland) – with correspondingly high prices. There are also several up-and-coming local designers, including Chrissie Potter and Amanda Nicolle.

Unless you're a fashion 'victim' or move in the trendiest circles, it isn't usually worth buying designer clothing in New Zealand, where most people aren't susceptible to label snobbery. Casual clothing

is acceptable for most situations, and country or farm clothing is considered fashionable – even by those who never go near a farm, let alone work on one.

Cotton clothes are the cheapest and most popular, as they're cool in summer and warm in winter, particularly when worn in layers. Canterbury is famous for its rugby shirts, which can be worn for any occasion. Despite the ready availability of wool, woollen garments can be expensive, although anything in sheepskin is a bargain (you never know, it might come back into fashion one day). Hand-knitted garments are popular, and Swanndri is a well known brand of woollen shirts and jackets, which have become something of a classic and are affectionately known as 'swannis'. Shoes tend to be expensive, even though the country manufactures a million pairs annually.

BUYING SECOND-HAND

There's a lively second-hand market in New Zealand for almost everything, from antiques to cars, computers to photographic equipment – it appeals to Kiwi practicality, thriftiness and the pioneer ethos of recycling things until they fall to pieces. As a result there are often bargains to be found, particularly if you're quick off the mark. Many towns have a second -hand or junk store and charity shops (e.g. Salvation Army) selling new and second-hand articles, where most of your money goes to help those in need. In cities you can even

buy goods which have been rescued from the city dump, which are displayed in a warehouse at the site.

The classified advertisements in local newspapers are another good source of bargains, particularly for furniture and large household appliances, although if you're looking for items such as boats, cameras or motorcycles, you may be better off looking through the small ads. in specialist magazines. Shopping centre and newsagent bulletin boards and company notice boards may also prove fruitful.

Another place to pick up a bargain is at an auction, although it helps to have specialist knowledge about what you're planning to buy, as you'll be competing with experts. Auctions are held in New Zealand throughout the year for everything from antiques and paintings to cars and property.

There are antique shops and centres in most towns, and antique street markets and fairs are common in the major cities, where you can pick up interesting early New Zealand artefacts – but you must get there early to beat the dealers to the best buys. Car boot (trunk) and garage (yard) sales, where people sell their surplus belongings at bargain prices, are gaining popularity in New Zealand. Sales may be advertised in local newspapers and through signs on local roads (they're usually held at weekends).

HOME SHOPPING

Home shopping by mail, phone or via the internet is popular in New Zealand, particularly in rural areas. In addition to dedicated mail-order companies, major department stores produce mail-order catalogues. TV shopping is also increasingly popular and there are a number of 24-hour shopping channels in New Zealand.

Internet shopping has exploded in Australia in recent years and now accounts for an increasing percentage of purchases. All prices on websites selling to domestic buyers must include GST. GST and duty must also be paid on imported goods, although no GST is payable if the total amount owing is less than $50.

Trade Me

New Zealand's most successful website is Trade Me (🖳 www.trademe.co.nz) – the country's equivalent of Ebay – which was sold to John Fairfax in 2006 for $700m.

RECEIPTS & GUARANTEES

When shopping in New Zealand, you should always insist on a receipt and keep it until you've left the shop or reached home. This isn't just in case you need to return to exchange goods, which may be impossible without the receipt, but also to verify that you've paid if an automatic alarm goes off as you're leaving the shop, or any other questions arise. If you're paying in cash, you should check receipts immediately (particularly in supermarkets), because if you're overcharged it's often impossible to obtain redress later.

You need your receipt to return an item for repair or replacement (usually to the place of purchase) during the warranty period. It's wise to keep receipts and records of major purchases made while you're resident in New Zealand, particularly if you're staying for a short period only. This may save you time and money when you leave the country and are required to declare your belongings in your new country of residence.

If you buy something which is faulty, damaged or doesn't work or measure up to the manufacturer's or vendor's claims, you can return it and obtain a replacement or your money back (unless you bought it at auction). Note that extended warranties or money-back guarantees don't affect your statutory rights as a purchaser, although the legal status of a warranty may be unclear.

Some shops offer an exchange of goods or a money-back guarantee for any reason, which isn't required by law. However, this is usually only for a limited period and goods must be returned unused and as new. Some shops attempt to restrict your rights to a credit note or to replacement goods when an item is faulty or unfit for use, which is illegal. Signs such as 'no refunds given', 'no responsibility for loss or damage', 'goods left for repair at your own risk' and 'all care but no

responsibility taken' are meaningless and unlawful.

All goods must be of 'merchantable' (reasonable) quality and fit for the purpose for which they were sold, and it's illegal for sellers to include a clause in the conditions of sale that exempts them from liability for defects, product faults and lack of care.

Consumer protection laws are monitored and enforced in New Zealand by the Ministry of Consumer Affairs (🖳 www.consumer-ministry.govt.nz), which has local offices throughout the country. You can also obtain advice and assistance from a local Citizens' Advice Bureau (🖳 www.cab.org.nz).

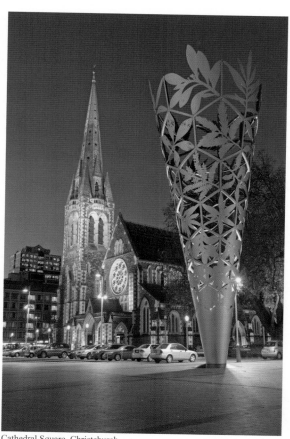

Cathedral Square, Christchurch

10.
ODDS & ENDS

A country's culture is influenced by various factors and reflected in myriad ways. Among the principal influences are its climate, geography and religion, which are considered here along with various cultural manifestations, including crime, the flag and anthem, government, pets, tipping and toilets.

> 'New Zealand is not a small country but a large village.'
>
> Peter Jackson (New Zealand film director)

CLIMATE

New Zealand doesn't always enjoy the dry, sunny, warm weather that the holiday brochures and tourist authorities like to project. It's situated in the Roaring Forties, between latitude 40°S and 50°S, so called because of its prevailing westerly winds due to the Coriolis effect as a result of the earth's rotation. The west coast of the south island takes the brunt of this weather and gets 500cm (200in) of rain a year. As a result, it's densely forested and much less populated than the east coast.

New Zealand's climate often exhibits the clichéd 'four seasons in one day' and this probably goes some way to accounting for the flexibility of the average New Zealander, as no one knows what the elements are going to throw at them when they wake up in the morning. Winter can be chilly, grey, wet and windy, particularly in the south island. Even the north of the north island can be cloudy and damp for weeks on end; Auckland has twice as much rain as London – though it also enjoys twice as much sunshine (you can even grow hibiscus in your garden).

Earthquakes

It's sometimes forgotten that New Zealand is in what's known as 'an active geological region', which is a euphemism for a scary place with earthquakes, tsunamis and volcanoes. The country sits on the Pacific 'rim of fire', where (like California) the Pacific plate is subducting, i.e. going under the Tasman tectonic plate. Every so often the plates judder and slip slightly, which releases the tension. New Zealand experiences hundreds of earthquakes each year, although only some are noticeable – and only in certain areas – most feel like the vibration from a heavy truck passing.

The biggest earthquake in living memory was in 1931 in Napier and Hastings (Hawke's Bay), which registered 7.8 on the Richter scale and razed Napier to the ground. The country suffers a very large earthquake every few hundred years and these can cause tsunamis. The last big one was in the 15th century, generating waves of over 10m (33ft), which destroyed many coastal Maori settlements, therefore a major earthquake is long overdue. The threat of tsunamis is particularly acute in the Bay of Plenty and eastern Coromandel. In view of this geological time bomb, the laid-back temperament of New Zealanders is all the more remarkable. (The same phenomenon occurs in California, where the lifestyle and climate is so pleasant that no one wants to leave.)

> 'There's a real purity in New Zealand that doesn't exist in the States. It's not an easy thing to find in our world any more. It's a unique place because it is so far away from the rest of the world. There is a sense of isolation and also of being protected.'
>
> Elijah Wood (American actor)

CRIME

The crime rate in New Zealand is increasing but it's still much lower than in most countries. This is especially true in rural areas, where you can generally leave your car and house unlocked, and honesty boxes are used for selling fruit and vegetables. Most Kiwis are law-abiding, and crime and corruption are rare, probably because of the highly developed Kiwi sense of fair play. Burglary and theft are the country's most common crimes, notably theft from cars in the cities. Most cities are safe to walk around at night, but it's advisable to check whether there are any no-go areas or late-night venues that are to be avoided. The most worrying crime trend in New Zealand is the growing number of violent attacks and rapes, usually against Asians and Pacific Islanders, which are racially motivated. There's also an alarming increase in drug-related crime.

New Zealand has a favourable climate for the cultivation of cannabis (also known as dope, marijuana, weed, etc.), which is enthusiastically grown in many parts of the country – particularly in Northland, which has some of the country's warmest year-round weather. The recreational smoking of cannabis is common, but New Zealand has a much less serious hard drug problem than the US and Europe due to its strict border controls, which are aimed at keeping agricultural diseases and pests out of the country but also effectively discourage drug smuggling.

New Zealand has a taste for 'restorative' justice, whereby an offender meets his victims under controlled conditions in order that he can acknowledge and face up to his crime (and its consequences) and make redress to the victims.

> Australia's flag is similar to New Zealand's, with white stars instead of red – you're strongly advised not to confuse the two.

FLAG & NATIONAL ANTHEM

Flag

New Zealand's flag consists of the union flag (Union Jack) in the top left quarter and four red stars with white borders, representing the constellation of Cruz (the Southern Cross), in the right half on a dark blue background. It's twice as long as it is wide (the same as the Union Flag).

The first flag of New Zealand, which became known as the flag of the United Tribes of New Zealand, was adopted in 1834. It was seen as a symbol of the independence declared by Maori chiefs (although it was replaced by the Union Flag after the signing of the Treaty of Waitangi in 1840) and is still flown on the flag pole at Waitangi on Waitangi Day (February 6th).

As in Australia, a number of alternative flags have been proposed for the country, one of which has a silver fern on a black background (similar to the Canadian maple leaf flag). In 2003, a trust was formed

with the aim of bringing about a non-binding referendum on the subject, which requires 10 per cent of electors signing a petition which is then presented to parliament. The petition was launched in 2005 but failed to attract sufficient signatures.

Anthem

New Zealand is a curiosity because it has two national anthems, *God Save the Queen* (which is also the British national anthem) and *God Defend New Zealand*. The two have equal status, although the latter is in more common use. On official occasions only the first verse of *God Defend New Zealand* is sung.

The words of God Defend New Zealand (see box) were written as a poem in the 1870s by Thomas Bracken; a competition was held to compose music for the words (for a prize of ten guineas) won by John Joseph Woods. The song became increasingly popular during the late 19th and early 20th centuries, and in 1940, the New Zealand government purchased the copyright and made it New Zealand's national hymn for that year's centennial celebrations. In 1977, it became the country's second national anthem (with the permission of Queen Elizabeth II). There are at least two Maori versions of the English words (see box)

God Defend New Zealand (Thomas Bracken)

English	Maori
God of nations at thy feet,	E Ihoa Atua,
In the bonds of love we meet,	O nga Iwi matoura
Hear our voices, we entreat,	Ata whaka rongona;
God defend our free land.	Me aroha noa
Guard Pacific's triple star,	Kia hua ko te pai;
From the shafts of strife and war,	Kia tau to atawhai;
Make her praises heard afar,	Manaakitia mai
God defend New Zealand.	Aotearoa.
Men of every creed and race,	Ona mano tangata
Gather here before thy face,	Kiri Whero, kiri ma,
Asking thee to bless this place,	Iwi Maori Pakeha,
God defend our free land.	Repeke katoa,
From dissension, envy, hate,	Nei ka tono ko nga he
And corruption guard our state,	Mau e whakaahu ke,
Make our country good and great,	Kia ora marire
God defend New Zealand.	Aotearoa
Peace, not war, shall be our boast,	Tona mana kia tu
But, should foes assail our coast,	Tona kaha kia u;
Make us then a mighty host,	Tona rongo hei paku
God defend our free land.	Ki te ao katoa
Lord of battles in thy might,	Aua rawa nga whawhai
Put our enemies to flight,	Nga tutu a tata mai;
Let our cause be just and right,	Kia tupu nui ai
God defend New Zealand.	Aotearoa
Let our love for thee increase,	Waiha tona takiwa
May thy blessings never cease,	Ko te ao marama;
Give us plenty, give us peace,	Kia whiti tona ra
God defend our free land.	Taiawhio noa.
From dishonour and from shame,	Ko te hae me te ngangau
Guard our country's spotless name,	Meinga kia kore kau;
Crown her with immortal fame,	Waiho i te rongo mau
God defend New Zealand.	Aotearoa
May our mountains ever be,	Tona pai me toitu
Freedom's ramparts on the sea,	Tika rawa, ponu pu;
Make us faithful unto thee,	Tona noho, tana tu;
God defend our free land.	Iwi no Ihoa.
Guide her in the nation's van,	Kaua mona whakama;
Preaching love and truth to man,	Kia hau te ingoa;
Working out thy glorious plan,	Kia tu hei tauira;
God defend New Zealand.	Aotearoa.

Rotorua

GEOGRAPHY

New Zealand lies in the South Pacific Ocean, south-east of Australia, and comprises two main islands, called the North Island and the South Island (they were named in the 19th century by the British, who obviously exercised a great deal of effort and imagination in christening them), plus numerous smaller islands (of which Stewart and Chatham are the most important). Associated with New Zealand are Ross Dependency (in Antarctica) and Niue, Tokelau and the Cook Islands (in the Pacific Ocean). The capital of the country is Wellington, although Auckland is the largest city. Contrary to popular belief (and to the eternal relief of most New Zealanders), New Zealand isn't just off the coast of Australia, but some 2,000km (1,250mi) away across the Tasman Sea. New Zealand covers an area of 270,534km^2 (104,461mi^2), which makes it comparable in size to the UK.

New Zealand is a mountainous country, some 60 per cent of which is between 200m (655ft) and 1,000m (3,280ft) above sea level, with over 220 mountains above 2,000m (6,550ft). The principal mountain ranges in the North Island extend along the eastern side, where the north central region has three active volcanic peaks: Mount Ruapehu (2,797m/9,176ft), the highest point on the island, Mount Ngauruhoe (2,291m/7,516ft) and Mount Tongariro (1,968m/6,456ft). Mount Taranaki (2,518m/8,261ft), a solitary extinct volcanic cone, is situated near the western extremity of the island.

> New Zealand is situated the same distance eastwards from Australia as London is from Moscow.

The North Island has numerous rivers, most of which rise in the eastern and central mountains, including the Waikato River (435km/270mi), the longest river in New Zealand. It flows north out of Lake Taupo (606km^2/233mi^2), the country's largest lake (where mineral springs are also found), into the Tasman Sea in the west.

The North Island has an irregular coastline, particularly on its northern extremity, the Auckland Peninsula, where it's just 10km/6mi wide.

The South Island has a more regular coastline than the North Island and in the south-west is characterised by deep fiords. The chief mountain range of the South Island is the Southern Alps, a massive range extending from the south-west to the north-east for almost the entire length of the island (17 peaks in the range are over 3,000m/9,842ft high). Mount Cook (3,754m/12,316ft) is the highest point in New Zealand and rises from the centre of the range, which also contains a number of glaciers. Most of the rivers of the South Island, including the Clutha River (338km/210mi long), the longest river on the island, rise in the Southern Alps. The largest lake is Lake Te Anau (342km^2/132mi^2) in the southern part of the Southern Alps. The Canterbury plains in the east and the Southland plains in the extreme south are the only extensive flat areas on the South Island.

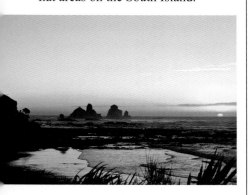

The islands of New Zealand emerged in the Tertiary period and contain a complete series of marine sedimentary rocks, some of which date from the early Paleozoic era. Much of the topography of New Zealand has resulted from warping and block faulting, although volcanic action has also played a part in its formation, particularly the North Island, where it continues to this day. Geysers and mineral hot springs occur in the volcanic area, particularly around Rotorua.

> 'If the people of New Zealand want to be part of our world, I believe they should hop off their islands and push 'em closer.'
>
> Lewis Black (American comedian)

GOVERNMENT

New Zealand is a parliamentary democracy with a constitutional monarchy. Under the New Zealand Royal Titles Act of 1953, Queen Elizabeth II is the Queen of New Zealand and is represented as head of state by a Governor-General. The political system is modelled on the UK's, although there's no upper house, which was abolished in 1950. New Zealand doesn't have a Bill of Rights or a written constitution and one set of laws governs the whole country; there's no state or province system, as in Australia, Canada or the US.

Political Parties

Politics in New Zealand has traditionally been dominated by two parties: the National Party, which favours right-wing social policies and a market-orientated approach to the economy, and the Labour Party. The Labour Party traditionally favoured left-of-centre policies, including comprehensive social welfare spending, but during the '80s 'borrowed' what were previously thought to be National Party policies, including economic reform and financial market deregulation. Other parties which currently have a voice include the Maori Party, New Zealand First

New Zealand has no formal, written constitution; the constitutional framework consists of a mixture of various documents (including certain acts of the United Kingdom and New Zealand Parliaments), the Treaty of Waitangi (see chapter 2) and constitutional conventions.

(a National Party splinter group), ACT (a free market liberal party), the Greens and United Future. In July 2005, the Labour Party was the largest party and currently forms a coalition government with the Progressive Party. Most elections attract a string of independents and minority parties, together with what can best be described as 'loony' parties (such as Legalise Cannabis and Natural Law).

Voting & Elections

New Zealand changed (in 1993) to a system of proportional representation (PR) from the first-past-the-post (FPP) system previously used. The kind of PR used in New Zealand is known as the Mixed Member Proportional (MMP) system, which is designed to ensure that each party's share of seats in parliament corresponds to its share of the vote. Voters have two votes: a 'party vote' for the party of their choice and a vote for their preferred candidate. Parties are allocated seats in proportion to the number of party votes they receive, and then candidates are allocated to those seats according to the votes they polled individually (don't worry if you find this baffling – Kiwis do also).

The House of Representatives consists of 120 MPs, one representing each of the 62 electoral districts and 51 who are allocated according to the number of votes each party receives. The final seven seats are reserved for candidates from Maori electoral districts. Some politicians have recently proposed that the number of MPs be reduced to save money (a sensible idea, which would no doubt prove popular in most countries!).

New Zealand's new system of MMP, while generally recognised as an improvement over FPP, has caused something of an upheaval in the political system and allowed smaller parties to be represented in parliament for the first time, although no party can obtain a seat in parliament unless it obtains at least 5 per cent of the total vote. It has also created a situation where it's impossible for a single party to obtain an overall majority and thus two or more parties are forced to co-operate in a coalition to form a government. Some politicians have argued for a return to FPP, although this is unlikely to happen.

Parliamentary elections are held every three years, although the government can call an early election (which it rarely does, preferring to allow each parliament to run its course). Although many New Zealanders are apathetic about politics on a daily basis, they're usually keen to exercise their right to vote and the turnout in elections is rarely less than 80 per cent. Additionally, the New Zealand government doesn't hesitate to call referenda on subjects considered of great importance to the country.

Recent referenda have included proportional representation (which was accepted by a small majority) and changes to the national superannuation system, which was rejected by a small percentage.

MILITARY SERVICE

There's no conscription (draft) in New Zealand, where members of the armed forces are volunteers. The minimum age for enlistment has recently been raised to 17 in line with United Nations guidelines on

the enlistment of minors. The New Zealand Army, Royal New Zealand Air Force (RNZAF) and Royal New Zealand Navy (RNZN) are separate services under the control of the Ministry of Defence. The army numbers around 4,400 regular personnel, the air force around 2,700 and the navy around 2,000. In addition there's a part-time reserve force called the Territorial Army (or 'Terries'), which trains in the evenings and at weekends and can be called up to assist the regular forces in an emergency. Members of the armed forces can expect to be posted to a new base every two to three years, a practice which may be changed, as it's believed to be largely responsible for the high number of service personnel who resign after their initial term. In a bid to make military life more attractive, the navy has recently (among other steps) introduced maternity uniform, which allows women to continue military service during a pregnancy!

In line with the government's 'e-solutions' policy, the defence

> New Zealand is a signatory to a number of defence treaties, including the Five Power Defence Agreement with Australia, Malaysia, Singapore and the UK, and the ANZUS alliance with Australia and the USA.

ministry has introduced an 'e-recruiting' strategy, thought to be in the world's first in the armed forces. Prospective recruits can now sign up online and it's hoped that this method may encourage more people to enlist. The size of New Zealand's military forces reflects the small size of the country, and there has been discussion about whether the navy, and some other elements of the armed forces, are viable on such a small scale, and whether they should be merged with the Australian armed services.

For its part, Australia periodically takes its smaller neighbour to task for spending, what it considers, to be too little on defence. (Australia spends around 2 per cent of its GDP on defending not only Australia, but also the surrounding region.)

> New Zealand is a signatory to a number of defence treaties, including the **Five Power Defence Agreement** with Australia, Malaysia, Singapore and the UK, and the **ANZUS** alliance with Australia and the USA.

New Zealand contributed forces to the western alliance during the Gulf War, contributes to peacekeeping duties around the world and has a particularly strong presence in East Timor, Mozambique and Sierra Leone, where New Zealand troops are in charge of de-mining operations. New Zealand operates a strict anti-nuclear defence policy and doesn't allow visits by foreign military forces carrying nuclear weapons, e.g. warships, which

has caused friction between New Zealand and the USA.

PETS

New Zealanders are enthusiastic animal lovers and many people keep dogs and cats. However, pets have received a 'bad press' in recent years, as they're believed to be responsible for the decimation of New Zealand's wildlife. Cats and dogs aren't indigenous to New Zealand, and flightless birds such as the kiwi had few natural predators until the first European settlers landed their pets on the country's shores. If you plan to take a pet to New Zealand, it's important to check the latest regulations, which are complex. Given the distance (unless you're travelling from Australia) and container regulations, it's advisable to entrust the transportation of pets to a specialist shipping company.

New Zealand has strict regulations regarding the import of animals in order to prevent animal diseases

Don't let your dog roam free in country areas, where it may pose a threat to wildlife.

entering the country, and pets and other animals cannot be imported without authorisation from customs. You must obtain an import permit, which is available from the Executive Co-ordinator, Biosecurity New Zealand, PO Box 2526, Wellington (☎ 04-470 2754, 🖥 www.biosecurity.govt.nz). If your pet needs to undergo a period of quarantine, the import permit will be approved only if it's accompanied by a letter from a MAF-approved quarantine establishment (there are only three), confirming that your cat or dog has a reserved place. You require a 'zoo-sanitary certificate' and a health certificate from a veterinary surgeon in your home country, and your pet will need to undergo a period of quarantine after its arrival in New Zealand (except as described below). All animals must be vaccinated against

rabies and must have had a rabies neutralising antibody tritation test no less than six months before going into quarantine. A repeat test must be done within 30 days of the start of quarantine.

Cats and dogs imported from Australia, Hawaii, Norway, Singapore, Sweden and the UK, aren't required to be quarantined, provided they're microchipped, are older than 16 weeks, and have been resident in the exporting country for a minimum of six months before travel. The cost of transporting a cat or small dog from Europe or the USA, including all necessary paperwork, is likely to be at least $750 (but can be much more), with quarantine accommodation costing from around $50 per day.

For further information contact the Ministry of Agriculture and Forestry, PO Box 2526, Wellington (☎ 04-474 4100, 🖥 www.maf.govt.nz), a New Zealand diplomatic mission or NZ Customs (freephone 0800-428 786 or 09-300 5399 from abroad).

NUCLEAR-FREE POLICY

New Zealand is a defiantly nuclear-free country. Anti-nuclear sentiment grew in the '70s and '80s, mainly due to French nuclear testing in the Pacific at Moruroa atoll, and concern about nuclear reactors and warheads on US vessels calling at New Zealand ports. David Lange's Labour government introduced legislation banning such visits in 1985, and in 1987, New Zealand passed legislation (the New Zealand Nuclear Free Zone, Disarmament and Arms Control Act) making

the country a nuclear-free zone. Recent years have seen some calls to revoke this anti-nuclear legislation, but Kiwi public opinion remains strongly in favour of New Zealand's nuclear-free status.

> 'It is the test of a good religion whether you can joke about it.'
>
> G. K. Chesterton (British writer)

RELIGION

The majority of New Zealanders are Christians – at least nominally – the largest denominations (in order of number of adherents) being Anglican, Roman Catholic and Presbyterian. Immigration in recent years has brought Buddhists, Hindus and Muslims to the country – around 50,000 of each – and New Zealand also has a sizeable Jewish population. Maori (who tend to be more religious than *Pâkehâ*) have two main religions that mix Christian and traditional beliefs: *Ringatu*, which dates from the 19th century, and *Ratana*, from the 20th century. Some Maori are Jehovah's Witnesses or Mormons, and Methodism is popular in some Pacific Island communities – it's said that religious faith often depends on which missionary got there first.

Judging by the number of churches in New Zealand, you'd think it was a very religious country – some kind of South Pacific Bible Belt. However, the country's large number of churches gives a false impression, as most date back to a time when Christianity was central to everyday

life. Today, New Zealand is a secular society, and state schools don't provide religious instruction unless they're former church schools now funded by the state. Christianity retains some significance in Kiwi society, but much less than it once did, and congregations have been in decline for many years. New Zealand's parliament begins its day with a Christian prayer, and Christian values and principles still have influence, although adherence to them doesn't often stretch to attending church.

TIME DIFFERENCE

New Zealand lies within a single time zone. Summer daylight saving time – an advance of one hour – is observed between the first Sunday

> New Zealand was one of the first countries in the world to officially adopt a nationally observed standard time, New Zealand Mean Time, which was adopted on 2nd November 1868 and set at 11 hours 30 minutes ahead of Greenwich Mean Time.

in October and the third Sunday in March. New Zealand hasn't taken to the 24-hour clock system, and times in most timetables are shown according to the 12-hour clock system, where times are marked either 'am' or 'pm', or are printed in light type to indicate before noon and heavy type to indicate after noon. If in doubt, it's better to ask than to arrive 12 hours late (or early) for your flight or bus!

Bear in mind that there's a substantial time difference between New Zealand and Europe (and to a lesser extent the USA) and you should check the local time abroad before making international telephone calls. For example, when calling western Europe, you need to phone either first thing in the morning or last thing at night (the difference between New Zealand and the UK is 12 hours). The time difference between Wellington at noon in January and some major international cities is shown below:

TIPPING

Tipping isn't a general custom in New Zealand (Americans please note!), although you may wish to leave a tip when you've had exceptional service or have received good value. New Zealanders almost never tip and, in fact, some people regard it as patronising or even insulting and refuse tips. Neither is it customary to round up amounts (e.g. taxi fares) to the nearest dollar or so, although most people won't complain if you do. Service charges aren't added to bills in hotels and restaurants, and you won't be expected to add a tip.

TOILETS

Public toilets in New Zealand are generally clean and are commonly found in bus and railway stations, council and tourist offices, department stores, parks and shopping centres. The most sanitary toilets are found in airports, car parks, galleries, hotels, large stores, museums, petrol stations, popular beaches, public and private offices, and restaurants. Hotel (i.e. pub) and bar toilets vary from no-go areas to spotless. New Zealanders don't use euphemisms like bathroom, powder room or restroom as Americans do, and the toilet is more likely to be referred to as the 'loo', which is considered quite a polite term, or the

Time Differences						
WELL'TON	**SYDNEY**	**LONDON**	**CAPE TOWN**	**TOKYO**	**LA**	**NEW YORK**
noon	10am	midnight	2am	9am	4pm	7pm (the previous day)

'dunny'. Public toilets are usually free (when they aren't, you may be required to pay a few cents to gain access to a cubicle) and don't normally have an attendant.

Some toilets have nappy (diaper) changing facilities and facilities for nursing mothers, and an increasing number also have special facilities for the disabled.

Toilets are usually marked with the familiar international male and female symbols (so you won't need to distinguish between male and female kiwis), whereas disabled toilets are usually used by both sexes and indicated by the international wheelchair sign. Toilets for the disabled may be locked to keep out 'unauthorised' users, in which case there will be a notice nearby explaining where the key can be obtained.

APPENDICES

APPENDIX A: USEFUL ADDRESSES

In New Zealand

Listed below are the contact details for the embassies and high commissions of the main English-speaking countries in Wellington. A full list of embassies and consulates in New Zealand is available from the website of the New Zealand Ministry of Foreign Affairs and Trade (🖥 www.mfat.govt.nz/Embassies/2-Foreign-Embassies/index.php).

Australia: Australian Embassy, 72–76 Hobson Street, Thorndon, Wellington (☎ 4-473 6411, 🖥 www.australia.org.nz).

Canada: Canadian Embassy, 125 The Terrace, Wellington (☎ 4-473 9577, 🖥 http://geo.international.gc.ca/asia/newzealand).

Ireland: Consulate General of Ireland, 7 Citigroup Building, 23 Customs Street East, Auckland (☎ 9-977 2252, 🖥 www.ireland.co.nz).

South Africa: South African Embassy, Rhodes Place, State Circle, Yarralumla, Canberra, ACT, Australia (which is also responsible for New Zealand, ☎ +61-2-6273 2424, 🖥 www.sahc.org.au).

UK: British Embassy, 44 Hill Street, Thorndon, Wellington (☎ 4-924 2888, 🖥 www.britain.org.nz).

USA: American Embassy, 29 Fitzherbert Terrace, Thorndon, Wellington (☎ 4-462 6000, 🖥 http://wellington.usembassy.gov).

Abroad

Listed below are the contact details for New Zealand embassies and high commissions in the main English-speaking countries. A full list is available at 🖥 www.mfat.govt.nz/Embassies/1-NZ-Embassies/index.php.

Australia: New Zealand High Commission, Commonwealth Avenue, Canberra, ACT 2600, Australia (☎ +61-2-6270 4211, 🖥 www.nzembassy.com/australia).

Canada: New Zealand High Commission, Metropolitan House (suite 727), 99 Bank Street, Ottawa, Ontario K1P 6L2, Canada (☎ +1-613-238 5991, 🖳 www.nzembassy.com/canada).

Ireland: New Zealand High Commission, New Zealand House, Second Floor, 80 Haymarket, London SW1Y 4TQ, United Kingdom (which is also responsible for Ireland, ☎ +44-20-7930 8422, 🖳 www.nzembassy.com/uk).

South Africa: New Zealand High Commission, Block C (2nd floor), Hatfield Gardens, 1110 Arcadia Street, Hatfield, Pretoria 0083, South Africa (☎ +27-12-342 8256-9, 🖳 www.nzembassy.com/southafrica).

United Kingdom: New Zealand High Commission, New Zealand House, Second Floor, 80 Haymarket, London SW1Y 4TQ, UK (☎ +44-020-7930 8422, 🖳 www.nzembassy.com/uk).

USA: New Zealand Embassy, 37 Observatory Circle NW, Washington, DC 20008, USA (☎ +1-202-328 4800, 🖳 www.nzembassy.com/usa).

> The business hours of embassies vary and they close on their own country's national holidays as well as on New Zealand public holidays. Always telephone to confirm opening hours before visiting.

APPENDIX B: FURTHER READING

A selection of books about New Zealand is listed below; the publication title is followed by the name of the author(s) and the publisher's name in brackets.

Culture

Cultural Atlas of Australia, New Zealand and the South Pacific, Gordon Johnson (Facts on File)

Cultural Questions: New Zealand Identity in a Transitional Age, Ruth Brown (Kapako)

A Destiny Apart: New Zealand's Search for a National Identity, Kenneth Sinclair (Allen & Unwin)

Food & Wine

Celebrating New Zealand Wine, Joelle Thomson & Andrew Charles Coffey (New Holland)

Edmonds Illustrated Cookbook, Edmonds (Hachette Livre NZ)

Harvest: Naturally Good New Zealand Food, Penny Oliver & Ian Batchelor (New Holland)

New Taste New Zealand, Lauraine Jacobs & Stephen Robinson (Ten Speed Press)

Pocket Guide to the Wines of New Zealand, Michael Cooper (Mitchell Beazley)

Rough Guide to Auckland Restaurants, Mark Graham (Rough Guides)

Simply New Zealand: A Culinary Journey, Ian Baker (New Holland)

Wine Atlas of New Zealand, Michael Cooper (Hodder Moa Beckett)

History

The New Zealand Wars, James Belich (Penguin)

History of New Zealand, George William Rusden (Elibron Classics)

A History of New Zealand, Keith Sinclair (Pelican)

New Zealand and the Second World War: The People, the Battles and the Legacy, Ian McGibbon (Hodder Moa Beckett)

New Zealand's Top 100 History-makers, Joseph Romanos (Trio Books)

Oxford Illustrated History of New Zealand, Keith Sinclair (Oxford University Press)

The Penguin History of New Zealand, Michael King (Penguin)

Language

A Concise Dictionary of New Zealand Sign Language, Graeme Kennedy (Bridget Williams)

A Dictionary of Maori Words in New Zealand English, John Macalister (Oxford University Press)

Dictionary of New Zealand English, H. W. Oarsman (Oxford University Press)

The Godzone Dictionary, Max Cryer (Exisle)

Languages of New Zealand, Alan Bell & others (Victoria University Press)

New Zealand English: Its Origins and Evolution (Cambridge University Press)

New Zealand Ways of Speaking English, Allan Bell & Janet Holmes (Multilingual Matters)

A Personal Kiwi-Yankee Dictionary, Louis S. Leland Jr

The Reed Dictionary of New Zealand Slang, D. McGill (Reed NZ)

Sign Language Interpreting: Theory and Practice in Australia and New Zealand, Jemina Napier (Federation Press)

Living & Working

Buying a Home in New Zealand, David Hampshire (Survival Books)

Living and Working in New Zealand, edited by David Hampshire (Survival Books)

Retiring to Australia and New Zealand, Deborah Penrith & Alison Ripley (Vacation Work)

Maori New Zealand

The Rough Guide to Maori New Zealand (Rough Guides)

Exploring Maori Values, John Patterson (Dunmore Press)

Maori Art and Culture ed. D. C. Starzecka (British Museum Press)

Maori Legends, Alistair Campbell (Viking Sevenseas)

Maori Myths and Tribal legends, Antony Alpers (Longman)

Te Marae: a Guide to Customs and Protocol, Hiwi Tauroa (Reed Books)

People

Being Pakeha: An Encounter with New Zealand and the Maori Renaissance, Michael King (Hodder & Stoughton)

The Governors: New Zealand's Governors and Governors-General, Gavin McLean (Otago University Press)

A Land of Two Halves: An Accidental Tour of New Zealand, Joe Bennett (Scribner)

A Man's Country? The Image of the Pakeha Male, Jock Phillips (Penguin)

My Home Now: Migrants and Refugees to New Zealand Tell Their Stories, Gail Thomas et al (Cape Catley)

Visitor Guides

25 Ultimate Experiences New Zealand, Mark Ellingham (Rough Guides)

Australia and New Zealand on a Shoestring (Lonely Planet)

Blue Guide New Zealand (A & C Black)

Eyewitness Travel Guide New Zealand (Dorling Kindersley)

Frommer's New Zealand from $50 a Day, Elizabeth Hanson & Richard Adams (Macmillan)

Insight Guide New Zealand, Craig Dowling (APA Publications)

Kiwi Tracks: New Zealand Journey, Andrew Stevenson (Lonely Planet)

Let's Go New Zealand (Macmillan)

Lonely Planet New Zealand, Carolyn Bain & others (Lonely Planet)

Maverick Guide to New Zealand, Robert W. Bone (Pelican)

Rough Guide to New Zealand, Laura Harper & others (The Rough Guides)

Fiction

All the Nice Girls, Barbara Anderson (Vintage)

The Bone People, Keri Hulme (Picador)

The Collected Stories of Katherine Mansfield, Katherine Mansfield (Penguin)

Dogside Story, Patricia Grace (Talanoa)

Fifty Ways of Saying Fabulous, Graeme Aitken (Headline)

The God Boy, Ian Cross (Penguin)

The Miserables, Damien Wilkins (Faber)

Once Were Warriors, Alan Duff (Virago/Random House)

Potiki, Patricia Grace (Penguin)

The Stories of Frank Sargeson, Frank Sargeson (Penguin)

Strangers and Journeys, Maurice Shadbolt (Hodder/Atheneum)

Miscellaneous

AA Road Atlas New Zealand (Automobile Association)

Back Country New Zealand (Hodder)

Beach Houses of Australia and New Zealand 2, Stephen Crafti (Images Publishing)

Facts New Zealand, Nicky Chapman (David Bateman)

Landscapes of New Zealand, Warren Jacobs & Jill Worrall (New Holland

New Zealand: A Natural History, Tui De Roy & Mark Jones (Firefly)

The Penguin Natural World of New Zealand, Gerald Hutching (Penguin)

Politics in New Zealand, Richard Mulgan (Auckland UP)

Sanctuary: New Zealand's Spectacular Nature Reserves, Eric Dorfman (Penguin Putnam)

Tramping in New Zealand, Jim DuFresne (Lonely Planet)

Truth About New Zealand, A. N. Field (Veritas)

Whale Watching in Australian and New Zealand Waters, Peter Gill & Cecilia Burke (New Holland)

APPENDIX C: USEFUL WEBSITES

This appendix contains a list of useful websites for anyone wishing to learn more about New Zealand and New Zealanders.

Government

Arts Council of New Zealand (💻 www.creativenz.govt.nz). Provides information about the world of the arts, arts funding and the work of the Arts Council.

Immigration New Zealand (💻 www.immigration.govt.nz). Information about New Zealand's culture, history and lifestyle, plus extensive information about entry requirements and the skills sought.

Inland Revenue (💻 www.ird.govt.nz). Everything you need to know about taxation in New Zealand, whether you're a resident, non-resident or visitor.

Ministry for Culture & Heritage (💻 www.mch.govt.nz).

Ministry of Education (💻 www.minedu.govt.nz).

Ministry of Health (💻 www.moh.govt.nz). Extensive information about everything health-related, including an informative a–z of health topics.

Ministry of Women's Affairs (💻 www.mwa.govt.nz). Information and statistics about the lot of women in equal-opportunity New Zealand, and about the Ministry's work, including its Action Plan for New Zealand Women.

New Zealand Elections (💻 www.elections.org.nz). New Zealand electoral system explained in detail.

New Zealand Government (💻 www.govt.nz). In addition to extensive information about government organisations and services, this website also contains useful information and news about various aspects of visiting and living in New Zealand.

New Zealand Trade and Enterprise (💻 www.nzte.govt.nz). Advice and information for those contemplating doing business in or with New Zealand.

Statistics New Zealand (💻 www.stats.govt.nz). Facts and figures about many aspects of life in New Zealand.

Te Ara (🖥 www.teara.govt.nz) The encyclopaedia of New Zealand (*te ara* is 'the pathway' in Maori).

Maori

Maori (🖥 www.maori.org.nz). Dubs itself the 'main Maori site on the net', with information and features about Maori customs, genealogy, language, performing arts and more.

Maori News (🖥 http://maorinews.com). Maori news, views, commentary and writings.

Maori Television (🖥 www.maoritelevision.com). The website of the television channel devoted to Maori culture and life.

Maori UK (🖥 www.maori.org.uk). Providers of Maori language & culture courses in London, UK.

Media

The New Zealand Herald (🖥 www.nzherald.co.nz). New Zealand's largest newspaper online. As well as coverage of business, news and sport, there are articles about culture, employment, entertainment, lifestyle, motoring, property, technology and travel.

NZ On Air (🖥 www.nzonair.govt.nz). Promotes and fosters the development of New Zealand's culture on the airwaves by funding locally-made television programmes, public radio networks and access to radio.

Online Newspapers (🖥 www.onlinenewspapers.com/nz.htm). Links to the websites of all New Zealand's major newspapers.

Otago Daily Times (🖥 www.odt.co.nz). A good summary of regional, national and international news and sport.

Television New Zealand (🖥 http://tvnz.co.nz). The public TV service that operates TV One and TV2.

Migrants

Auckland Regional Migrant Services (🖥 www.arms-mrc.org.nz). A non-profit organisation which helps migrants and refugees to settle in the Auckland region.

Citizens Advice Bureau (🖥 www.cab.org.nz)

Emigrate NZ (🖥 www.emigratenz.org). New Zealand immigration guide.

The Emigration Group (🖥 www.jobfastrack.co.nz/tegindex.php). The leading consultants regarding New Zealand emigration.

Human Resource Institute of New Zealand (🖥 www.hrinz.org.nz). Information about all aspects of human resources and employment in New Zealand.

Job Fast Track (🖥 www.jobfastrack.co.nz/jobindex.php). Find a job in New Zealand.

Kiwi Ora (🖥 www.kiwi-ora.com). Information to help new immigrants settle in New Zealand.

Real Estate Institute (🖥 www.realestate.co.nz). Peruse a wealth of properties and check prices online.

Miscellaneous

Enzed (🖥 www.enzed.com). Information from websites in New Zealand and the rest of the world.

Film New Zealand (🖥 www.filmnz.com). A website that covers all aspects of New Zealand's burgeoning film industry, including plenty of information for those considering making a film there, including data about film crews, locations, permits, tax and transport. There's also a feature about the making of the *Lord of the Rings* trilogy.

Geography New Zealand (🖥 www.nzgeography.com). New Zealand's online geographical resource.

Met Service (🖥 www.metservice.co.nz/default/index.php). New Zealand's National Meteorological Service.

NZ English to US English Dictionary (🖥 http://nz.com/NZ/Culture/NZDic.html). A useful resource for Americans bewildered by Kiwis' sometimes unusual way with the English language.

New Zealand in History (🖥 http://history-nz.org). This website describes itself as 'a brief overview of prehistoric, colonial and modern periods.'

New Zealand Museums Online (🖥 www.nzmuseums.co.nz). This website allows you to take a tour of New Zealand's museums, by area, collection or name.

New Zealand Post (🖥 www.nzpost.co.nz). Everything you need to know about the country's postal services.

New Zealand Rugby World (🖥 www.nzrugbyworld.com). Everything you could want to know about the latest happenings in the world of New Zealand rugby.

New Zealand Wine and Grape Industry (🖥 www.nzwine.com). Information about the country's wine exports, events, production statistics, regions and styles.

NZ History (🖥 www.nzhistory.net.nz). New Zealand's history online.

Sport and Recreation New Zealand (🖥 www.sparc.org.nz). Information about all aspects of sport in New Zealand, and becoming active and healthy.

Trade me (🖥 www.trademe.co.nz). Online auction site – New Zealand's answer to Ebay.

Wikipedia New Zealand (🖥 http://en.wikipedia.org/wiki/New_Zealand). Comprehensive information about all aspects of New Zealand.

Travel & Tourism

Air New Zealand (🖥 www.airnewzealand.co.nz). Book a flight online.

Backpacker Board (🖥 www.backpackerboard.co.nz). Travel guide for backpackers in New Zealand.

Destination New Zealand (🖥 www.destination-nz.com). Information about accommodation, activities, facts and figures, tours and transport, plus commercial information, maps and a newsletter.

The New Zealand Guide Book (🖥 www.nz.com). Information about places in New Zealand, facts and figures, food, history, language and natural history.

New Zealand Tourism (🖥 www.tourism.net.nz). A wealth of information about accommodation, attractions, culture, history, key facts, travel, weather and more.

Tourism New Zealand (🖥 www.newzealand.com). The official New Zealand tourist website; as well as the usual tourist information, there are some informative feature articles about various aspects of New Zealand's culture, history and lifestyle.

APPENDIX D: GLOSSARY

New Zealand English

Some of the words and phrases in this glossary are Kiwi inventions, while others are borrowed from or shared with the British and Australians.

A

A & P Show (Agricultural & Pastoral): an event usually lasting three or four days at which farmers display their produce and compete for prizes
Afghan: popular crunchy chocolate biscuit
arvo & sarvo: short for 'afternoon' and 'this afternoon' respectively

B

bach: a holiday home, usually small and basic – pronounced 'batch'
beaut: great, splendid or terrific
big bikkies: lots of money
bite your bum: go away, get lost
bludge: to sponge off others or the state, e.g. a 'dole bludger' is a recipient of unemployment benefit
boohai: to go wrong or an out of the way location, i.e. 'up the boohai'
box of birds or box of budgies: in a good mood or very good
brekkie: breakfast
bro: brother, gang member; may jokingly denote all Maori people
buggerlugs: a version of 'mate', i.e. "how're you, buggerlugs?" – not an insult
bugger: blast, curse it or damn; only mildly rude
bun fight: a party or social gathering with food
bush: dense areas of native plants
bust a gut: to try very hard to do something
buzzy bee: a wooden bee toy with wheels, which makes a clacking noise when pulled by its string
BYO: bring your own (wine or beer), often seen posted outside restaurants

C

capsicum: pepper (vegetable)
cardie or cardy: short for 'cardigan', i.e. a v-neck jumper with buttons up the front
carked it: died
cervena: farmed deer
chilly bin: cooler or cool bag
chippie or chippy: carpenter; somewhere selling fish and chips
chocolate fish: chocolate covered marshmallow fish (yuk) or praise for a job well done, i.e. 'good job, mate, you deserve a chocolate fish'
choice: very good or a good idea
chook: chicken
chrissy: short for 'Christmas'

chunder: to vomit

cockie, cocky or cow-cocky: farmer

college: high school rather than university

couldn't see the road to the dunny if it had red flags on it: a drunk or very stupid person

courgette: zucchini

crib: holiday home (see 'bach' above), mainly used in Otago and Southland

crook: sick or unwell

cuz: cousin

D

dag: humorous person or situation

dags: dried dirt and faeces which stick to the wool around a sheep's bottom

dairy: corner shop or convenience store selling all kinds of goods and often open for long hours

The Ditch: Tasman Sea

dreaded lurgy: cold or flu, sometimes a venereal disease

dunny: bathroom, lavatory or toilet

dux: top student in the final year of high school

E

eh: a speech particle added to the end of a statement to intensify, seek agreement, or transform into an interrogative

electric jug: a metal, ceramic or heavy plastic jug used to boil water (also called a hot water jug)

electric puha: slang term for marijuana

Erewhon: fictional name, an anagram of 'nowhere', inspird by the high country sheep farm in Canterbury called Mesopotamia Station

eskimo pie: small block of ice cream coated in chocolate (choc-ice)

eyes out: going at full tilt, as fast or strongly a possible

FG

flash: very good or impressive

flatting: sharing a flat (apartment)

g'day: universal Kiwi greeting

get off the grass: stop messing me around, no way

give your ferret a run: have sex

going bush: become reclusive or go off by oneself

good on ya: congratulations or well done

greasies: fish and chips

gumboots or gummies: rubber boots, Wellington boots

H

half-pie: half-heartedly

hang back: be reluctant

hard yakka: hard, usually physical, work

hissy fit: throw a tantrum, usually when you don't get your own way

home 'n hosed: complete something safely and/or successfully

hoon: yob, young adult with a fast car and loud stereo

hosing down: raining heavily

hottie: hot water bottle

IJKL

ice block: popsicle, ice lolly
jandal: thonged sandals, flip-flops
Kiwi (capital K): native of New Zealand
kiwi (small k): small, endangered, flightless bird
ladies a plate: when ordering, a dish of food to share
L & P: Lemon & Paeroa, a lemonade-like drink
lemon, lime and bitters: popular soft drink

MN

Maori: New Zealand's indigenous people
mate: friend, but commonly also used with strangers
metal road: gravel-surfaced country road
mountain oysters: lamb's testicles
nana: grandmother
nandy: grandfather

O

OE: Overseas Experience, a young Kiwi's mandatory trip abroad
off your face: totally drunk
onya: short for 'good on yer', i.e. well done

P

pack a sad: be in an unhappy state
Pakeha: non-Maori New Zealander, invariably of European origin

pav: pavlova, the national dessert
pie-cart: converted caravan from which food is sold, at road-sides and events, e.g. funfairs and sporting events
pike out: to give up when encountering difficulties or obstacles
pikelet: small pancake, often spread with cream and jam
piker: somebody who gives in easily (see pike out above)
pinky bar: chocolate-covered marshmallow
puckeroo: something that's broken or doesn't work properly

R

rack off: clear off, go away
rark up: tell somebody off severely
rattle your dags: hurry up, get a move on!
rellies: relatives, i.e. your family members
root: have sex
rooted: feel very tired

S

sarnie: sandwich
savs and pavs: saveloys and pavlova; traditional Kiwi party food
scarfie: university student (i.e. one who wears a scarf), particularly used for students at universities on the South Island
scull: to drink beer quickly
shark and tatties: fish and chips

she'll be right: no problem, everything will be fine
shippie: prostitute who serves those working on the ships which dock at New Zealand's ports
shout: turn, as in when buying drinks
sickie: day taken off work because of sickness (allegedly), as in 'to throw a sickie'
skiting: boasting, showing off
smoko: break from work, from the days when most people would take the opportunity to smoke during work breaks
spit the dummy: throw a tantrum
strewth: general expression of surprise or frustration
stubby: small bottle of beer
suck the kumara: die
sunnies: sunglasses
sweet-as: cool or impressive

T

ta: thanks
tata: goodbye
tea: evening meal, dinner
Tiki tour: scenic tour, going 'the pretty way'
tramping: hiking (rather than vagrancy)
togs: bathing costume, swimsuit
trots: diarrhoea

UVW

up shit creek in leaky gumboots: in big trouble
ute: utility vehicle, small pick-up truck

Vegemite: savoury yeast spread, New Zealand's equivalent of Marmite
Waikikamukau: mythical hick town (pronounced 'why kick a moo cow')
whinge: complain
wop-wops: out of the way, the ends of the earth

YZ

yack: natter
you ain't wrong: correct, that's right
you make a better door than a window: said to anybody blocking your view
you think you're a flowerpot because you've got a hole in your bum: you love yourself
zambuck: St John Ambulance officer

Common Maori Words

ae: yes
ao: cloud
Aotearoa: Land of the Long White Cloud, the Maori name for New Zealand, widely used by all Kiwis
atua: gods, spirits
awa: river/valley
e hoa: friendly form of address, indicating friend.
e noho ra: goodbye (from the person going)
haere mai: welcome, come in
haere ra: goodbye (from the person staying)
haka: posture dance
hakari: feasts
hangi: feast cooked in an earthen oven
hau: wind
hapu: sub-tribe of an *iwi*
Hawaiki: mythical ancient homeland of the Maori people
heke: descend
hine: daughter, girl
hongi: formal greeting, consisting of pressing noses
hui: tribal gathering, meeting
ika: fish
iti: small
iwi: people, tribe
ka pai: thank you
kai: food
kainga: village
kaore: no
kapa haka: war dance done for display
karakia: chants, prayer
karanga: welcoming call or chant

kaumatua: Maori elder, respected member of tribe
kauri: huge forest tree
kawa: behaviour protocols
kea: alpine parrot
kete: woven basket
kia ora: hello
kiwi: flightless bird
koha: gift, present
korero: stories
koru: spiral, used in Maori carving (inspired by the unfurling fern frond)
kumara: sweet potato
mana: authority, prestige, esteem
manga: river, stream
manu: bird
manuhiri: guest or visitor
manuka: shrubby plant and the source of honey and oils
Maori: originally meant ordinary or usual; now refers to the Maori people and langauge
Maoritanga: Maori culture and customs
marae: tribal meeting area, often consisting of several buildings
mata: headland
maunga: mountain
mere: fighting club made of greenstone
miti: speeches
moana: sea or lake
moko: traditional facial tattoos
motu: island
muri: end
nga: the (plural)

ngai, Ngati: clan, people or tribe
noa: non-sacred
nui: large, great
o: the place of
one: beach, sand, mud
ora: healthy, safe
pa: fortified settlement
Pakeha: non-Maori, white man
pakehi: swampland
papa: flat, broad slab
paua: abalone
pipi: cockle
po: night
pohutukawa: large coastal tree with red flowers
poi: ball used by women in dances
ponga: tree fern
pounamu: greenstone or jade
powhiri: sung welcome
puke: hill
puna: spring
ra: the sun
rangi: the sky, heavens
roa: long
rohe: tribal area
roto: lake
rua: two
runga: top
taiaha: long fighting club
tahu: light
tamariki: children
tane: man, male
tangata: people
Tangata whenua: indigenous Maori, people of the land
tangi: funeral, lamentation
taniwha: demon or spirit

taonga: treasures, prized possessions
tapu: sacred, taboo
te: the (singular)
te Ika a Maui: The fish of Maui, the North Island
te reo Maori: the Maori language
te Wai Pounamu: South Island
tena koe: hello (to one person)
tena Koutou: hello (to several people)
tiki: a greenstone or wooden figure worn around the neck
tukutuku: wall panels in marae
tupuna: ancestors
utu: revenge, paying ones dues
wai: water
wahine: woman, female
waiata: songs
wairua: spirit
waka: canoe
waka taua: war canoe
wero: challenge
whakapapa: family tree, ancestry
whanau: extended family
whare: house
whare kai: eating house
whare manuhiri: house for visitors
whare puni: family sleeping house
whare runanga: meeting house
whare paku: toilet
whare runanga: meeting house
whare taonga: museum
whakairo: carved house
whenua: country or land

INDEX

A

Accommodation 61
   Buying A Home 63
   Holiday Homes 62
   Rented Property 62
A Change Of Culture 13
New Zealand Is Different 13
Alcohol 181
A New Life 22
Appearance & Dress 143
Attitudes To Foreigners 43

B

Banking 81
   Bank Charges 81
   Cheques 81
   Credit & Charge Cards 82
   Opening An Account 82
   Opening Hours 82
Black Economy 121
Body Language 109
Breaking The Ice 85
Bureaucracy 60
   Civil Servants 60
Business Etiquette 122
Buying Or Hiring A Car 64
   Buying A Car 65
   Car Hire 64
Buying Second-hand 184

C

Cafes, Pubs & Restaurants 150
   Cafes 150
   Maori Cuisine 154
   Restaurants 152

Climate 189
   Earthquakes 189
Clothes 182
Confrontation 98
Cost Of Living 83
Crime 190
Culture Shock 14
      Reducing The Effects 18
      Stages Of Culture Shock 15

D

Dealing With The Police 98
Drinking 156
   Pubs 157
   Wine 157
Driving 127
   Car Inspection 133
   Kiwi Drivers 132
   Motorcycles 133
   Petrol Stations 134
   Roads 127
   Rules Of The Road 128

E

Eating 143
   Conversation 150
   Formal & Informal Dining 146
   Meals 144
   Table Manners 148
Education 72
   Private Schools 73
   Universities 73
Emergency Services 66

F

Families 21
Finding A Job 116
    Government Employment Service 117
    Qualifications 116
    Registration 116
    Salary 117
Food 179
    Dairy Produce 181
    Meat 179
    Seafood 181
Foreign Languages 109
Friends & Neighbours 44
    Relationship With Australia 45
    Relationship With Britain 44
    Relationship With The Usa 47

G

Geography 193
Getting Started 59
Government 194
    Political Parties 194
    Voting & Elections 195

H

Health Services 66
    Doctors 68
    Emergency Treatment 68
    Hospitals 69
    Medicines 68
    State Healthcare 67
Home Shopping 185

I

Icons 48
    Icons – Flora & Fauna 56

Icons – People 48
Icons – Physical 50
Icons – Symbols 52
Immigration 59
    Residence Permits 60
Insurance 69
    Accident Compensation 70
    Car Insurance 71
    Earthquake Insurance 71
    House Insurance 70
Invitations 92
    Extending Invitations 94
    Receiving Invitations 92

M

Manners & Greetings 105
Maori 37, 105
    Culture 40
    Education 108
    Land Rights 40
    Maori Influence On English 106
    Official Use 107
    Politics 39
    Pronunciation 106
    Social Justice 39
    The Haka 42
Meeting Maori & Pacific Islanders 97
Meeting People 90
    Paying 92
Military Service 196

N

Neighbours 85
    Community Regulations 85
New Zealand English 101
    Differences From Australian English 104

Differences From British English 103
Regional Accents 104
Nuclear-free Policy 198

O

Odds & Ends 189
On The Move 127
Opening Hours 176

P

Pets 197
Popular Culture 159
Diy & Gardening 159
Gambling 167
Social Clubs 168
Sport 160
Tramping 165
Public Transport 134
Ferries 139
Local Buses 136
Long-distance Buses 137
Taxis 139
Trains 134
Trams & Trolleybuses 136

QR

Receipts & Guarantees 185
Religion 199
Retail Therapy 175

S

Self-employment 120
Finance 121
Government Help 121
Restrictions 120

Sexual Attitudes 86
Abuse Of Women 89
Homosexuals 89
Men 87
Women 88
Stages Of Culture Shock 15
Starting A Business 119
Business Entities 119
Legislation 120
Staying Informed 76
Books 80
Internet 78
Post 80
Press 79
Radio 78

T

Taboos 95
Taxes 83
The Arts 169
Film 170
Literature 169
Museums 173
Music 172
Theatre, Opera & Ballet 171
The Class System 43
The Flag & Anthem 191
Anthem 191
Flag 191
The Language Barrier 101
The New Zealanders At Play 143
The New Zealanders At Work 113
The People 29
Family Life 36
Pioneering Spirit 32
Rural Life 36
Self-image 29
Sense Of Equality 32
Sense Of Humour 35

The Kiwi Character 30
Time Difference 199
Timeline 26
Tipping 200
Toilets 200
Topics Of Conversation 96
Types Of Shop 176
    Chain & Department Stores 178
    Dairies 177
    Supermarkets 178

U

Utilities 74
    Electricity 74
    Gas 75
    Telephone 75
    Water & Sewerage 76

W

When To Avoid Doing Business 124
    Other Holidays 124
Who Are The New Zealanders? 25
Work Ethic 113
Working Women 114
Work Visas & Permits 115

Survival Books

Essential reading for anyone planning to live, work, retire or buy a home abroad

Survival Books was established in 1987 and by the mid-'90s was the leading publisher of books for people planning to live, work, buy property or retire abroad.

From the outset, our philosophy has been to provide the most comprehensive and up-to-date information available. Our titles routinely contain up to twice as much information as other books and are updated frequently. All our books contain colour photographs and some are printed in two colours or full colour throughout. They also contain original cartoons, illustrations and maps.

Survival Books are written by people with first-hand experience of the countries and the people they describe, and therefore provide invaluable insights that cannot be obtained from official publications or websites, and information that is more reliable and objective than that provided by the majority of unofficial sites.

Survival Books are designed to be easy – and interesting – to read. They contain a comprehensive list of contents and index, and extensive appendices, including useful addresses, further reading, useful websites and glossaries to help you obtain additional information as well as metric conversion tables and other useful reference material.

Our primary goal is to provide you with the essential information necessary for a trouble-free life or property purchase and to save you time, trouble and money.

We believe our books are the best – they are certainly the best-selling. But don't take our word for it – read what reviewers and readers have said about Survival Books at the front of this book.

Buying a Home Series

Buying a home abroad is not only a major financial transaction but also a potentially life-changing experience; it's therefore essential to get it right. Our Buying a Home guides are required reading for anyone planning to purchase property abroad and are packed with vital information to guide you through the property jungle and help you avoid disasters that can turn a dream home into a nightmare.

The purpose of our Buying a Home guides is to enable you to choose the most favourable location and the most appropriate property for your requirements, and to reduce your risk of making an expensive mistake by making informed decisions and calculated judgements rather than uneducated and hopeful guesses. Most importantly, they will help you save money and will repay your investment many times over.

Buying a Home guides are the most comprehensive and up-to-date source of information available about buying property abroad – whether you're seeking a detached house or an apartment, a holiday or a permanent home (or an investment property), these books will prove invaluable.

For a full list of our current titles, visit our website at
www.survivalbooks.net

Living and Working Series

Our Living and Working guides are essential reading for anyone planning to spend a period abroad – whether it's an extended holiday or permanent migration – and are packed with priceless information designed to help you avoid costly mistakes and save both time and money.

Living and Working guides are the most comprehensive and up-to-date source of practical information available about everyday life abroad. They aren't, however, simply a catalogue of dry facts and figures, but are written in a highly readable style – entertaining, practical and occasionally humorous.

Our aim is to provide you with the comprehensive practical information necessary for a trouble-free life. You may have visited a country as a tourist, but living and working there is a different matter altogether; adjusting to a new environment and culture and making a home in any foreign country can be a traumatic and stressful experience. You need to adapt to new customs and traditions, discover the local way of doing things (such as finding a home, paying bills and obtaining insurance) and learn all over again how to overcome the everyday obstacles of life.

All these subjects and many, many more are covered in depth in our Living and Working guides – don't leave home without them.

The Survival Handbooks!

Culture Wise Series

Our *Culture Wise* series of guides is essential reading for anyone who wants to understand how a country really 'works'. Whether you're planning to stay for a few days or a lifetime, these guides will help you quickly find your feet and settle into your new surroundings.

Culture Wise guides:
• Reduce the anxiety factor in adapting to a foreign culture
• Explain how to behave in everyday situations in order to avoid cultural and social gaffes
• Help you get along with your neighbours, make friends and establish lasting business relationships
• Enhance your understanding of a country and its people.

People often underestimate the extent of cultural isolation they can face abroad, particularly in a country with a different language. At first glance, many countries seem an 'easy' option, often with millions of visitors from all corners of the globe and well-established expatriate communities. But, sooner or later, newcomers find that most countries are indeed 'foreign' – and many come unstuck as a result.

Culture Wise guides will enable you to quickly adapt to the local way of life and feel at home, and – just as importantly – avoid the worst effects of culture shock.

The essential guides to Culture, Customs & Business Etiquette

Other Survival Books

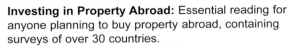

Investing in Property Abroad: Essential reading for anyone planning to buy property abroad, containing surveys of over 30 countries.

The Best Places to Buy a Home in France/Spain: Unique guides to where to buy property in France and Spain, containing detailed regional profiles and market reports.

Buying, Selling and Letting Property: The best source of information about buying, selling and letting property in the UK.

Earning Money From Your Home: Income from property in France and Spain, including short- and long-term letting.

Foreigners in France/Spain: Triumphs & Disasters: Real-life experiences of people who have emigrated to France and Spain, recounted in their own words.

Making a Living: Comprehensive guides to self-employment and starting a business in France and Spain.

Renovating & Maintaining Your French Home: The ultimate guide to renovating and maintaining your dream home in France.

Retiring in France/Spain: Everything a prospective retiree needs to know about the two most popular international retirement destinations.

Running Gîtes and B&Bs in France: An essential book for anyone planning to invest in a gîte or bed & breakfast business in France.

Rural Living in France: An invaluable book for anyone seeking the 'good life', containing a wealth of practical information about all aspects of French country life.

Shooting Caterpillars in Spain: The hilarious and compelling story of two innocents abroad in the depths of Andalusia in the late '80s.

Wild Thyme in Ibiza: A fragrant account of how a three-month visit to the enchanted island of Ibiza in the mid-'60s turned into a 20-year sojourn.

For a full list of our current titles, visit our website at
www.survivalbooks.net

 **Photo Credits**

167 (© Akrytova Tetiana), 168 (© Neil Roy Johnson), 171 (© James Steidl), 174 (© Quayside), 178 (© Gina Smith), 183 (© Pavel Kapish), 187 (© Holger Mette), 188 (© Troy Casswell), 193 (© Joe Goodson), 196 (© EML), 197 (© Maciej Bogacz), 198 (© John Bell), 201 (© Andy Heywood), 202 (© Craig Hill) and 220 (© Ximagination)

www.123rf.com:
pages 10 (© Paulus Rusyanto), 17 (© Paulus Rusyanto), 34 (© Ron Sumner), 64 (© photos.com), 67 (© Ablestock Premium), 86 (© 123rf), 88 (© Geo Martinez), 92 (© Harris Shiffman), 93 (© Carsten Reisinger), 94 (© Serghei Starus), 99 (© Gina Smith), 100 (© Andrew Carr), 131 (© Maxim Kulemza), 141 (© Alex Hinds), 144 (© Zlatko Kostic), 145 (© Mark Huls), 147 (© Yang Yu), 149 (© Jaroslaw Grudzinski), 150 (© Maxim Pimenov), 154 (© Andres Rodriguez), 155 (© Monika Adamczyk), 160 (© Alison Bowden), 170 (© Ana Blazic), 173 (© Feng Yu), 176 (© Andres Rodriguez), 181 (© Oleksandr Staroseltsev), 185 (© Feng Yu), 186 (© Boguslaw Mazur), 190 (© photos. com), 191 (© Gino Santa Maria) and 200 (© Juan Manuel Ordonez)

www.survivalbooks.net:
pages 27, 37, 38, 41, 42, 47, 50, 61, 63, 66, 70, 76, 77, 96, 97, 106, 110, 129, 134, 137, 138, 156, 157, 158, 159, 177, 179 and 199 (© survival books)

Peter Farmer:
pages 22, 75, 80, 163, 169, 182, 184 and 195 (© Peter Farmer)

www.bigstockphotos.com:
pages 19 (© mike866), 48 (© unknown), 58 (© unknown), 194 (© unknown) and 220 (© SCPhotog).

Others:
pages 39, 78, 136 and 140 (© Grania Rogers); pages 30, 40, 84, 166 (Tourism New Zealand); and 44 (© www. britainonview.com)